KNOWLEDGE AND THE
FLOW OF INFORMATION

A Bradford Book

The MIT Press
Cambridge, Massachusetts

Knowledge

&

the Flow of Information

Fred I. Dretske

Second printing, 1982
First MIT Press edition, 1981

Library of Congress Catalog Card Number 81-21633
MIT ISBN 0-262-04063-8
Printed in the United States of America

Library of Congress Cataloging in Publication Data
appear on the last printed page of this book.

Acknowledgments

A first draft of a book (I am no longer sure it was this book) was completed in 1975-76. I am grateful to the National Endowment for the Humanities for its generous help in launching the project. I wish also to thank the Graduate School of the University of Wisconsin for its support.

After returning to teaching I inflicted the results of my research on a group of patient graduate students. To the participants of this seminar go my thanks for their skepticism and endurance. I am especially indebted to Gary Hatfield, David Ring, Fred Adams, Steve Kimbrough and Judy Callan for their dissatisfactions.

Several of my colleagues were kind enough to read chapters and register dissent. They are, collectively, responsible for at least some of the delay between first and final drafts. My warm appreciation to Berent Enc, Elliott Sober, and Dennis Stampe.

I am still a naive student of psychology and computer science, but I wish to thank William Epstein of the Psychology Department and Leonard Uhr of the Computer Science Department at Wisconsin for their special efforts to repair my ignorance. I hope no one blames them for my creative distortions of empirical fact.

Aside from the above, there are those who said and wrote things over the past few years that left a lasting impression on me while I struggled with this material. In some cases I can no longer remember exactly what they said—only that they changed the way I thought about a problem in some fundamental way. They may wish to disown responsibility, but I am grateful, nonetheless, for what I consider the salutary influence of Jerry Fodor, Daniel Dennett, Kenneth Sayre, Raymond Martin, Gerald Doppelt, Kent Machina and Charles Marks.

Finally, my appreciation to those alert, tenacious critics in philosophy departments at which I read portions of the manuscript. Revisions were often in progress before I left town.

Preface

In the beginning there was information. The word came later. The transition was achieved by the development of organisms with the capacity for selectively exploiting this information in order to survive and perpetuate their kind.

It is common to think of information as a much later arrival on the evolutionary scene, as something that depends on the interpretive efforts—and, hence, prior existence—of intelligent life. According to this view, something only *becomes* information when it is assigned a significance, interpreted as a sign, by some cognitive agent. Beauty is in the eye of the beholder, and information is in the head of the receiver. To speak of information as *out there*, independent of its actual or potential use by some interpreter, and antedating the historical appearance of all intelligent life, is bad metaphysics. Information is an artifact, a way of describing the significance *for some agent* of intrinsically meaningless events. We *invest* stimuli with meaning, and apart from such investment, they are informationally barren.

This is one way of thinking about information. It rests on a confusion, the confusion of *information* with *meaning.* Once this distinction is clearly understood, one is free to think about information (though not meaning) as an objective commodity, something whose generation, transmission, and reception do not require or in any way presuppose interpretive processes. One is therefore given a framework for understanding how meaning can evolve, how genuine cognitive systems—those with the resources for interpreting signals, holding beliefs, and acquiring knowledge—can develop out of lower-order, purely physical, information-processing mechanisms. The higher-level accomplishments associated with intelligent life can then be seen as manifestations of progressively more efficient ways of handling and coding information. Meaning, and the constellation of mental attitudes that exhibit it, are manufactured products. The raw material is information.

This, in very sweeping terms, is the thesis of the present work. It sounds ambitious. *Too* ambitious—something only a philosopher, ignorant of how little is really known about these matters, would seriously propose. Let me qualify it, therefore, by saying that what I have described is the object for which I am reaching, not, perhaps, the object I have succeeded in grasping. Readers will have to judge for themselves how far short of the goal I have fallen.

One is accustomed to hearing cognitive psychologists and computer scientists, not philosophers, talk about information. Scientifically speaking, or so it would appear from the last thirty years, the cognitive exploits of a person, planarian, or computer are to be understood in terms of complex information-handling processes. Philosophers, on the other hand, still seem disposed to think about knowledge, perception, memory, and intelligence with a completely different set of analytical tools: evidence, reasons, justification, belief, certainty, and inference. There is, consequently, a serious communication problem. Philosophers articulate theories of knowledge that, from the point of view of the cognitive sciences, appear to be irrelevant to the best available models of perception, learning, and recognition. And philosophers (with some notable exceptions) tend to ignore, disparage, or dismiss the scientist's computer programs, flow charts, and feedback loops as so much empirical chaff to his conceptual wheat. Without a common vocabulary with which to address the issues, this kind of isolation is inevitable. The result, I think, is an impoverishment of both.

This, indeed, is one of the reasons I have selected the concept of information as the central idea around which to organize this philosophical study. If contact is to be made between philosophy and the wealth of relevant material in the cognitive sciences, then some bridges must be built, if only terminological bridges, between philosophical treatments of knowledge, belief, and perception and those scientific disciplines concerned with the same dimensions of our mental life.

It is, of course, fashionable to talk about information. Magazine advertisements remind us that we live in an Age of Information. I am therefore sensitive to the charge that I have merely adopted a faddish terminological form in which to stuff less stylish philosophical substance. In a sense, I plead guilty to this charge. I *have* adopted, for philosophical purposes, a way of talking that has become prevalent in the cognitive sciences during the last few decades. This, though, is not *all* I have tried to do. I have also tried to put this way of talking on a philosophically respectable footing in order to illuminate some obscure areas in epistemology and the philosophy of mind.

It is much easier to talk about information than it is to say what it is you are talking about. A surprising number of books, and this includes textbooks, have the word *information* in their title without bothering to include it in their index. It has come to be an all-purpose word, one with the suggestive power to fulfill a variety of descriptive tasks. Its use in telecommunications and computer technology gives it a tough, brittle, technical sound, and yet it remains spongy, plastic, and amorphous enough to be serviceable in cognitive and semantic studies. In thinking about information, one tends to think of something objective and quantifiable—the electrical pulses surging down a copper wire, for example—and, at the same time, of something more abstract, of the *news* or *message* that these pulses carry—something not so clearly objective and quantifiable. For many purposes this is a useful ambiguity. It allows one to speak, for example, of information being picked up, processed, and passed along to the higher cognitive centers where it is used to control an organism's response to its surroundings. One is given a picture of cells communicating with one another in something like the way you and I communicate with one another. An organism's cognitive efforts begin to sound like community projects undertaken by loquacious neurons. Such pictures are nourished by a convenient ambiguity in the terms used to describe such processes.

For philosophical purposes something better is needed. It is not that philosophy is so much more precise, exact, or demanding than its scientific cousins. Quite the contrary. In most respects it operates with far fewer constraints on its theoretical flights. This book is a case in point. Nonetheless, the problems that define the study of philosophy are uniquely sensitive to conceptual issues. Getting straight about what one means is an essential first step. Words are the tools of philosophers, and if they are not sharp, they only disfigure the material.

Therefore, I launch this study by examining, in Part I, the notion of information. I begin by looking at some of the fundamental ideas of communication theory. This is a useful way to begin, *not* because this theory (in its standard interpretation and application) tells us what information is. It does not. It does not even try. Rather, I begin here because the underlying structure of this theory, when suitably supplemented, can be adapted to formulate a genuinely *semantic* theory of information, a theory of information that can be used in cognitive and semantic studies. If, in accordance with communication theory, we conceive of information as an objective commodity, as something defined in terms of the network of lawful relationships holding between distinct events and structures, one can, or so I argue, develop a plausible, and theoretically powerful, analysis of a signal's informational *content*.

Part II is an attempt to apply this idea of information to questions in the theory of knowledge. Knowledge is identified with information-caused belief. A discussion of skepticism follows. The skeptical challenge is given a slightly novel twist by casting the dispute in terms of different criteria for distinguishing between the information we receive over a channel and the channel over which we receive this information. Finally, in Chapter 6, I attempt to distinguish sensory processes on the one hand and cognitive processes on the other, between *seeing* a duck and *recognizing* it as a duck, in terms of the different way information about the duck is coded. Sensory processes are analog in nature; cognitive processes are digital.

The final part of this book, Part III, is devoted to an analysis of belief, concepts, and meaning (insofar as this is understood to be a property of our psychological states). Frankly, I am the most apprehensive about these three chapters. There is so much relevant material about which I am ignorant—some of the work in developmental psychology, for instance—that I am prepared to see portions of this analysis condemned as factually inadequate. Given studies A, B, and C, that just is not, or could not be, the way things actually happen. Nevertheless, if the details are wrong, the general framework, I would argue, must be right. If physical systems are capable of developing concepts, with the consequent capacity for holding beliefs, both true and false beliefs—if such systems are capable of representing, and misrepresenting, the condition of their surroundings—then the internal structures that qualify as beliefs or representations must develop in something like the way I describe. I see no other way for meaning, the sort of content we ascribe to internal states when we attribute knowledge and belief, to evolve. But this, I admit, may be because I do not see very well.

The entire project can be viewed as an exercise in naturalism—or, if you prefer, materialistic metaphysics. Can you bake a mental cake using only physical yeast and flour? The argument is that you can. Given the sort of information described in Part I, something that most reflective materialists should be willing to give, we have all the ingredients necessary for understanding the nature and function of our cognitive attitudes, all that is necessary for understanding how purely physical systems could occupy states having a content (meaning) characteristic of knowledge and belief. This, of course, does not show that human beings are nothing but complex physical systems, that the mind is really material, but it does show that for purposes of understanding one facet of our mental life, that having to do with our cognitive capabilities, it is not necessary to think of them as anything else.

Fred I. Dretske

University of Wisconsin
1979

Contents

(continued)

PART I
INFORMATION

Chapter 1
Communication Theory

The mathematical theory of information, or communication theory,[1] provides a measure for how much information is to be associated with a given state of affairs and, in turn, a measure for how much of this information is transmitted to, and thus available at, other points. The theory is purely quantitative. It deals with *amounts of information*—not, except indirectly and by implication, with the information that comes in those amounts.

So much would seem to be apparent from the very name of the theory. It purports to be a theory *of* information, and its mathematical expression suggests that it is concerned with this commodity in its quantitative aspect. Yet, this is controversial. Some authorities would deny that communication theory tells us *anything* about information. This is not to say that the theory is useless. It is only to say that its usefulness resides, not in what it tells us about information or amounts of information, but in what it tells us about a related, but nevertheless quite different, quantity. According to this view, the theory has simply been misnamed.

There is some merit to this charge. If the theory has not been misnamed, it has certainly been misused and misused in a way that seems to be encouraged by its name. Since this essay is an attempt to develop an information-based theory of knowledge, it is essential to be clear about what this theory tells us (if anything) about *information*. For this purpose I shall, in this chapter, give an elementary exposition of some of the theory's basic ideas. In later chapters we shall take up the question of whether what this theory tells us can be incorporated into a genuine theory *of information* as this is understood in cognitive and semantic studies. An affirmative answer to this question will then set the stage for the development of a genuine semantic theory of information and an application of this theory to epistemological topics and some problems in the philosophy of mind.

AMOUNT OF INFORMATION GENERATED

There are eight employees and one of them must perform some unpleasant task. Their employer has left the nasty business of selecting the unfortunate individual up to the group itself, asking only to be informed of the outcome once the decision is made. The group devises some procedure that it deems fair (drawing straws, flipping a coin), and Herman is selected. The name "Herman" is written on a memo and sent to the boss.

Information theory identifies the amount of information associated with, or generated by, the occurrence of an event (or the realization of a state of affairs) with the reduction in uncertainty, the elimination of possibilities, represented by that event or state of affairs. Initially there were eight candidates for the task. These eight possibilities were then reduced to one. Herman is the nominee. In a certain intuitive sense of "uncertainty" there is no longer any uncertainty as to who will do the job. The choice has been made. When an ensemble of possibilities is reduced in this way, the amount of information associated with the result is a function of how many possibilities were eliminated in reaching that result.

To measure the amount of information associated with Herman's selection, or the fact that Herman is the nominee, one could proceed in a number of different ways. One could say that the amount of information embodied in this result was 8, since the uncertainty, the number of possibilities, has been reduced by a factor of 8. Or one could say that since 7 possibilities have been eliminated, the amount of information is 7. Although these are possible measures for the amount of information generated by Herman's selection, there are reasons for choosing a different way of assigning numbers to this quantity. Imagine that the group agreed to make their selection by flipping a coin. In order to accomplish this, they divided themselves into two groups of four and flipped the coin to determine the group from which a further selection would be made. Once this was decided by the first flip, they subdivided the unlucky group of four into two smaller groups, each consisting of two individuals. A second flip of the coin determined from which of these two groups the final selection would be made. A third toss of the coin settled the matter between the two remaining contestants, and Herman was the unhappy survivor. If we treat tosses of the coin as the number of decisions or choices that are made in reducing the competitors from eight to one, we get the number 3. This is the number of *binary decisions*, choices between two competing (and equally probable) alternatives, that must be made in reducing eight alternatives to one. According to information theory, *this* is the proper (or, at least, convenient[2]) measure of the amount of information contained in the reduction of eight possibilities to one. Since a binary decision can be represented by a binary digit (0 or 1), we can represent Herman's selection by a sequence of three binary digits. It takes three *binary digits* (bits), one binary digit (0 or 1) for each flip of the coin (letting 1 = heads, 0 = tails), to completely specify the reduction of eight possibilities to one. The amount of information associated with the fact that Herman was selected is 3 bits.

Another way to think about the amount of information embodied in the narrowing of eight possibilities to one is to think about the eight employees as being partitioned into various natural classes of four persons each. Suppose, for example, that four of the employees are men, four women. Four of them (two men and two women) are tall, the other four short; and, finally, four of them (a tall and a short male and a tall and a short female) are new employees and the other four old employees. If we assign a binary digit to each of these classes, letting 1 stand for the class of males, 0 for the females, 1 for the class of tall people, 0 for the short, 1 for the new employees and 0 for the old, then a sequence of *three binary digits* suffices to uniquely specify one of the employees. Letting the first digit in the sequence stand for the sex of the employee, the second for the height, and the third for length of employment, Herman can be specified with the sequence 101 since

Herman is a male (1), short (0), and a new (1) employee. Using this code, the memo could have contained the symbols 101 instead of the name Herman. The same information would have been conveyed.

The decision procedure adopted by the group, the method of flipping a coin and eliminating half the survivors with each toss, is merely a way of artificially partitioning the group so that three binary decisions suffice to narrow the possibilities to one. According to this way of measuring information, the note with "Herman" scrawled on it contains 3 bits of information. If there had been four employees instead of eight, the same note would have carried only *2 bits* of information, since it would have taken only two coin tosses to narrow the competitors from four to one. And if there had been sixteen employees, the note would have carried *4 bits* of information. Every time we double the number of employees, we add one bit of information, since each doubling of the number of individuals (or possibilities) requires *one* additional toss of the coin to effect the same reduction.

It is important to notice that we are talking about *amounts* of information. There are three bits of information associated with the selection of Herman, but there would also be three bits of information generated by the selection of any of the other seven employees. If Margaret had been selected, for example, the *quantitative* result would have been the same: three bits. As long as eight possibilities have been reduced to one, no matter what that one is, the amount of information associated with the result is the same. And, since the mathematical theory of information deals exclusively with the quantitative aspects of these situations, exclusively with amounts of information, the result, from the point of view of this theory, would be the same whether Margaret or Herman was the nominee. In both cases the result of the selection procedure, and the note to the boss, would contain exactly the *same* amount of information. This theory does not provide a way of distinguishing between what we intuitively take to be the difference between the information that *Herman* was selected and the information that *Margaret* was selected. This latter is a difference in the informational *content* of a state of affairs (or message), a difference that the quantitative theory ignores. We will return to this important point in the following chapter.

There is a general formula for computing the amount of information generated by the reduction of n possibilities (all equally likely) to 1. If s (the *source*) is some mechanism or process the result of which is the reduction of n equally likely possibilities to 1, and we write $I(s)$ to denote the amount of information associated with, or generated by, s, then

(1.1) $I(s) = \log n$

where log is the logarithm to the base 2. The logarithm to the base 2 of n is simply the power to which 2 must be raised to get n. So, for instance, $\log 4 = 2$ because $2^2 = 4$; $\log 8 = 3$ because $2^3 = 8$; and $\log 16 = 4$ because $2^4 = 16$. Numbers that are not integral multiples of 2 also have logarithms, of course, but special tables (or a pocket calculator) would have to be used to find the value of the function in these cases. If there were 10 employees, for instance, the amount of information associated with the selection of Herman would be approximately 3.3 bits, since $\log 10 = 3.3$.

This last point deserves special comment, since it forces one to distinguish between two quite different things: (1) the amount of information (in bits) generated by a given state of affairs, and (2) the number of binary digits, the number of binary symbols (such as 0 and 1), that are used to represent, code, or describe that state of affairs. In our example these numbers were the same. The selection of Herman generated 3 bits of information, and we used 3 binary digits (101) to describe the results of that selection. One way to express this is to say that we *encoded* 3 bits of information in 3 binary digits. But what if there had been *ten* employees and the message was to be encoded in binary symbols (instead of the name Herman)? As one can see from the above formula, the amount of information now generated by Herman's selection is 3.3 bits. How can this information be encoded in binary digits? We cannot use *fractions* of a symbol. We cannot use 3/10 of the symbol 1 or 0 to carry this additional piece of information. We must, of course, use *four* symbols (at least) to represent or describe a state of affairs that has a measure of 3.3 bits. At least four binary digits will be required to encode less than four bits of information. This is mildly inefficient, but it is the best we can do if we insist on using a binary code to communicate fractional amounts of information. Information theorists would say that this encoding of the information is somewhat *redundant*, since we are using a code (a sequence of four binary digits) capable of carrying four bits of information to carry only 3.3 bits. As we shall see, redundancy has its uses, but since the transmission of symbols costs money, an attempt is made to minimize this quantity in telecommunications.

If our eight employees chose to communicate with their employer in code, using binary digits instead of names, they could have chosen a less efficient code. As it turns out, they were operating at peak efficiency since their message, 101, carried three bits of information. But if they had partitioned themselves differently, letting the first digit stand for eye color (two of them had blue eyes, six had brown eyes), the second digit for hair color (three of them were blondes, five were brunettes), and so on, it is conceivable that they would have required four or more symbols to communicate the information that Herman had been selected. Their message might have been 10010, which, interpreted, means a brown-eyed brunette over six feet tall, married, and wearing glasses. This is a way of specifying Herman, but it is an inefficient way of doing so. In informational terms, the message has a degree of redundancy; five binary digits are being used to carry only three bits of information. Assuming that no other employee has a name beginning with the letters "Her . . .," the *six* letters "Herman" are also redundant in specifying who was selected. Three letters, or possibly even one letter, would have sufficed.

It is important to keep this distinction in mind. The amount of information associated with a state of affairs has to do, simply, with the extent to which that state of affairs constitutes a reduction in the number of possibilities. If the possibilities have been reduced from 8 to 1, as they were in our original example, then the amount of information $I(s)$ associated with this result is 3 bits. We may choose to describe this reduction of possibilities in a variety of ways—some efficient, some inefficient. Given the right code, I can describe what happened (Herman was selected) with three binary symbols: 101. But other codes may require four, twenty, or a thousand symbols to express the *same* three bits of information.

I shall refer to the quantity $I(s)$ as the average amount of information generated at the source s. In the technical literature this quantity is also referred to as the *entropy* of the source, and I shall occasionally use this terminology when it is convenient. It should be noticed, however, that *any* situation may be regarded as a *source* of information. If there is a process at r which consists in the reduction of alternatives, regardless of whether the outcome of this process depends on what occurred at s, then $I(r)$ is a measure of the entropy of the source r. If the events occurring at s and r are interdependent, then there will be an interdependence between $I(s)$ and $I(r)$. Nevertheless, $I(s)$ and $I(r)$ remain distinct (though interdependent) quantities.

Formula (1.1) gives us a way of calculating the amount of information only if each of the n alternatives at s is *equally likely*. If the alternatives are not equally likely, then we cannot use (1.1) to calculate the entropy of s. Suppose, for example, that we are flipping a coin that is strongly biased toward heads; the probability of getting heads on any given flip of the coin is .9. The outcome of one flip of this coin does not represent 1 bit of information as it did in the case of a fair coin. With a fair coin the likelihood of heads is equal to the likelihood of tails (=.5). Hence, applying formula (1.1), we find that the outcome of one flip of the coin represents 1 bit of information: log 2 = 1. With a biased coin, however, the amount of information is less. Intuitively, one can see why this should be so. One can anticipate the news about the biased coin. Although one will occasionally be wrong, most of the time (90 percent of the time) one will be right in predicting heads. It is a bit like listening to the weather forecast during the monsoon season (probability of rain on any given day = .9) and listening to the forecast during the normal season (when, say, the probability of rain = .5). In both cases *some* information is conveyed by a forecast (whether it be "rain" or "sunny") but the forecasts during the monsoon period will, on the average, be less informative. Everyone will be expecting rain anyway, and most of the time they will be right without the help of the official forecast. During the monsoon season the official forecast eliminates less "uncertainty" (on the average) and therefore embodies less information.

If we have a range of possibilities $s_1, s_2, \ldots, s_n$, not all of which are equally likely, and we write the probability of s_i's occurrence as $p(s_i)$, then the amount of information generated by the occurrence of s_i is

(1.2) $I(s_i) = \log 1/p(s_i)$
                                             $= -\log p(s_i)$ (since $\log 1/x = -\log x$)

This is sometimes called the *surprisal* of the particular event (s_i) that occurs.[3] In our coin example (probability of heads = .9), the amount of information associated with the appearance of a head is .15 bits ($\log 1/.9 = .15$), and the information generated by the appearance of a tail is 3.33 bits ($\log 1/.1 = 3.33$).

When the probability of each alternative possibility is the same, as it was in our original example, the surprisal of each outcome is the same. Since the probability of Herman's being selected was .125, the amount of information associated with his selection = $\log 1/.125 = \log 8 = 3$. Hence, formula (1.2) gives the same answer as (1.1) when the probabilities are equal.[4]

Communication theory, however, is not directly concerned with the amount of information associated with the occurrence of a *specific* event or signal. It deals with *sources* rather than with particular messages. "If different messages contain different amounts of information, then it is reasonable to talk about the average amount of information per message we can expect to get from the source—the average for all the different messages the source may select."[5] When we toss our biased coin, for example, it will sometimes turn up heads (generating only .15 bits of information) and sometimes turn up tails (generating 3.32 bits of information). Given the bias of the coin, heads will turn up much more frequently. Hence, if we are interested in tosses of the coin as a source of information, we will be interested in the average amount of information that many tosses of the coin can be expected to yield. We can expect to get 3.32 bits one-tenth of the time and .15 bits nine-tenths of the time. *On the average*, then, we will get something more than .15 bits but something substantially less than 3.32 bits. The formula for computing the average amount of information $I(s)$ associated with a given source (capable of yielding different individual states, each with its own surprisal) is

(1.3) $I(s) = \Sigma p(s_i) \cdot I(s_i)$

That is, we take the surprisal value of all the specific individual possibilities for that source $I(s_i)$ and weight them according to the probability of their occurrence $p(s_i)$. The sum is the average

amount of information generated by that source, the entropy of
s. In our coin-tossing case, the surprisal of heads = .15, and the
probability of heads occurring is .9. The surprisal of tails = 3.32,
and the probability of tails occurring is .1. Hence, in accordance
with (1.3), we calculate the average amount of information
generated by coin tosses as

$$I(s) = p(s_1) \cdot I(s_1) + p(s_2) \cdot I(s_2)$$
$$= .9\,(.15) \qquad + .1\,(3.32)$$
$$= .467 \text{ bits}$$

In most applications of information theory it is formula (1.3) that
is important. As Bar-Hillel notes, communication engineers have
no use for the surprisal value of a particular state of affairs; they
use the formula for calculating the surprisal value, (1.2), only as
a "stepping stone" in the calculation of the average information
generated by a source.[6] This preoccupation with averages is
perfectly understandable. What the engineer wants is a concept
that characterizes the whole statistical nature of the information
source. He is not concerned with individual messages. A communication system must face the problem of handling any message
that the source can produce. "If it is not possible or practicable
to design a system that can handle everything perfectly, then
the system should be designed to handle well the jobs it is most
likely to be asked to do. . . . This sort of consideration leads at
once to the necessity of characterizing the statistical nature of
the whole ensemble of messages which a given kind of source
can and will produce."[7] The concept of *entropy* or *average
information*, as used in communication theory, does just this.

The reader will recall that in flipping an honest coin (where
the probability of heads = the probability of tails = .5), the surprisal value of both heads and tails was 1 bit. Since the probability of their respective occurrence was equal, the average
amount of information associated with the process of flipping
an honest coin was

$$I(s) \quad = .5\,(1) + .5\,(1)$$
$$= 1 \text{ bit}$$

What this tells us is that, *on the average*, less information is generated by flipping a biased coin than is generated by flipping an
honest coin. This result is obtained because the type of event

(heads) that generates the *least* information in the biased coin occurs *most* frequently, and the average is correspondingly reduced.

Although, generally speaking, the greatest *average information* is obtained when the possibilities are equally likely, the greatest *surprisal values* are to be obtained when the possibilities are not equally likely. Although we can average more information with an honest coin than with a biased coin, the *individual tosses* of the biased coin have the potential for contributing 3.3 bits of information (when the coin lands tails) to the average, a quantity of information far in excess of what the individual tosses of the honest coin can contribute (1 bit).

As $p(s_i)$ approaches 1, the amount of information associated with the occurrence of s_i goes to 0. In the limiting case, when the probability of a condition or state of affairs is unity $[p(s_i) = 1]$, *no information* is associated with, or generated by, the occurrence of s_i. This is merely another way of saying that no information is generated by the occurrence of events for which there are no possible alternatives (the probability of all alternatives = 0). If we suppose (in accordance with the theory of relativity) that no signal *can* travel faster than the speed of light, then a signal's traveling at a speed less than (or equal to) the speed of light generates zero information. And if (as some philosophers suppose) individuals have some of their properties *essentially*, then the possession of these properties by these individuals generates zero information. If water is necessarily H_2O, no information is associated with its *being* H_2O. And although information is presumably generated by some object's being a cube (there are other possible shapes it might have been), no additional information is associated with this cube's having six faces (since it is not possible for a cube to have anything other than six faces).

These limiting cases are not merely of idle, theoretical interest. Their existence is of considerable importance to the epistemological applications of information theory, and we will return to them again in later chapters.

AMOUNT OF INFORMATION TRANSMITTED

Up to this point we have been talking about the amount of

information associated with a given state of affairs and the average amount of information generated by a source. In our example the source in question was the process by means of which Herman was selected. On the average this source will generate 3 bits of information. Furthermore, each of the particular results of that process (e.g., Herman's selection) has a surprisal value of 3 bits. That is how much information they contribute to the average. $I(s)$ is the average amount of information associated with s, the process occurring in the room where the employees are assembled. $I(s_7)$ is the amount of information associated with one (the seventh) particular outcome of that process: the amount of information associated with Herman's selection on that particular day in that particular room.

Think, now, about the events transpiring in the employer's office a few moments after Herman has been selected, and think of them quite independently of what occurred earlier at s. Let r stand for the general situation in the employer's office and r_i for the various possible instantiations of r. The employer receives a memo with the name "Herman" (or the symbols "101") written on it. Ignoring complications for the moment, there were originally eight different messages that the boss *might* have received. The memo could have had any one of eight different names on it (or any one of the eight different triads of 0s and 1s). Once the memo arrives with the name "Herman" on it (call this possibility r_7), the "uncertainty" vanishes. The possibilities have been narrowed to one. Assuming that the eight different messages are equally likely, we can use formula (1.1) to compute the *average* amount of information associated with the employer's receipt of such a memo: $I(r)$ = 3 bits. The amount of information associated with the *particular* message that was actually received (bearing the name "Herman") is also 3 bits. That is, $I(r_7) = 3$. The surprisal value of the message actually received (r_7) is the same as the surprisal value of any of the other messages he might have received. Hence, for any value of i, $I(r) = I(r_i)$.

If this description of the information associated with the events occurring in the employer's office seems like a trivial restatement of something already described, the reader should bear in mind that we are talking about two quite different situations. s_7 refers to a state of affairs that obtains in the room where the employees are assembled. It refers to *Herman's selection*. r_7, on the other hand, refers to *the name "Herman" appearing on the memo delivered to the boss*. $I(s_7)$ and $I(r_7)$ both equal 3 bits, but the fact that they are equal is not a trivial truth because $s_7 \neq r_7$. Similarly, though $I(s) = I(r)$, their numerical equality is a contingent fact, since source (s) and receiver (r) are physically distinct situations.

The fact that $I(r) = I(s)$ is not, of course, accidental. The reduction of possibilities at r is correlated with the reduction of possibilities at s by means of the employees' determination to make their note to the boss an accurate indication of what transpired in their selection process. Things could be different. Imagine that the employees are all solicitous about Shirley's delicate health. They agree to name Herman on their note to the boss if, by chance, Shirley should be the nominee according to their selection process. In this case, $I(s)$ would still be 3 bits since any one of the eight employees, including Shirley, could be selected by their coin-flipping decision procedure, and all are equally likely to be chosen. Nonetheless, given their intention to protect Shirley, there are really only 7 names that could appear on the note to their employer. Hence (unknown to the boss), the reduction in possibilities at r is actually a reduction from 7 to 1. The appearance of the name "Herman" on the memo has a surprisal value of *less* than 3 bits, since it is twice as likely that Herman's name will appear there as anyone else's. In this case $I(r_7) = \log 1/p(r_7) = \log 1/.25 = 4 = 2$ bits. The surprisal value of anyone else's name appearing on the memo remains 3 bits. Hence, the average information associated with a name appearing on the memo (under these circumstances) must be calculated in accordance with (1.3).

$$I(r) = \Sigma p(r_i) \cdot I(r_i)$$
$$= .125\,(3) + .125\,(3) + .125\,(3) + .125\,(3) + .125\,(3) +$$
$$.125\,(3) + .25\,(2)$$
$$= 2.75 \text{ bits}$$

Any situation may be taken, in isolation, as a generator of information. Once something happens, we can take what did happen as a reduction of what *could* have happened to what *did* happen and obtain an appropriate measure of the amount of information associated with the result. This is the way we are now treating the events in the employer's office. A sheet of paper arrives with the name "Herman" on it. In our original example, this piece of paper could have had any one of eight different names on it. Hence, $I(r)$ = 3 bits of information. But we can also look upon these events in the employer's office, the situation designated by r, not as a *generator* of information, but as a *receiver* of information, and specifically, as a receiver of information about s. We are talking about the same situation r, but we are asking a different question about it. How much of $I(r)$ is information about s? Of the information generated at s, $I(s)$, how much of it arrives at r?

We are now asking about the informational value of situation r, but we are *not* asking about $I(r)$. We are asking how much of $I(r)$ is information received from or about s. I shall use the symbol $I_s(r)$ to designate this new quantity. The r in parentheses indicates that we are asking about the amount of information associated with r, but the subscript s is meant to signify that we are asking about that portion of $I(r)$ that is information received *from s*.

A few examples should clarify this distinction. In our original case $I(r_7)$ was 3 bits; this is how much information was associated with the name "Herman" appearing on the memo. But, in a sense, this 3 bits of information *originated* in the room where the employees were assembled. It originated there in the sense that Herman's selection by the employees *determined* which name was to appear on the memo. The reduction in possibilities at s, the reduction that makes $I(s_7)$ = 3 bits, simultaneously reduces the possibilities at r from 8 to 1, thereby making $I(r_7)$ = 3 bits. Given the circumstances,[8] the 3 bits of information associated with "Herman" appearing on the memo (r_7) do not constitute any *further* reduction in possibilities beyond that associated with Herman's being selected (s_7). In this sense, then, $I(r_7)$ is just *old* information, information about what happened at s. Hence, $I_s(r) = I(s)$ = 3 bits.

Change the example slightly. The employees scrawl the name "Herman" on the memo and give it to a new, careless messenger. On his way to the employer's office the messenger loses the memo. He knows the message contained the name of one of the employees, but he does not remember which one. Rather than return for a new note, he writes the name "Herman" on a sheet of paper and delivers it. Things turn out as they did in the first case; Herman is assigned the task and no one is the wiser about the messenger's carelessness or irresponsibility. Nonetheless, there are significant differences between the two situations in terms of the information transmitted from s to r. In this second case $I(s)$ is still 3 bits. $I(r)$ is also 3 bits, since (we may suppose) the messenger selected the name "Herman" at random; he could have put (and was equally likely to have put) any one of eight different names on the note. But $I_s(r) = 0$. No information is transmitted from s to r. The reduction of possibilities at r, the reduction that makes $I(r) = 3$ bits, is quite *independent* of the reduction which occurred at s and makes $I(s) = 3$ bits. Another way of expressing this is to say that there is no information at r about s. $I_s(r)$ is a measure of the information *in* situation r *about* situation s. Since there are 3 bits of information available at r but none of it is information from s, $I(r) = 3$ bits, but $I_s(r) = 0$. Technically speaking, the information available at r is *noise* (noise = a measure of the information, or reduction in possibilities, at r that is independent of what happened at s).[9]

$I_s(r)$ is a measure of the amount of dependency between s and r. There is a reduction in possibilities at r, and $I_s(r)$ is a measure of how much of this reduction is to be accounted for by the events that occurred at s, how much of the reduction at r (information at r) is *old information* (information generated at s).

The relationships among the three quantities we have been discussing can be diagramed as in Figure 1.1.[10]

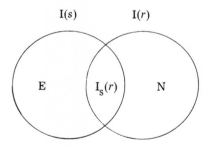

Figure 1.1

$I_s(r)$ is that part of the $I(s)$ circle that is included in the $I(r)$ circle. In our original example *all* of $I(s)$ was included in $I(r)$; the message to the employer contained *all* the information generated at s pertaining to the outcome of the selection process. Furthermore, the message contained no additional information of relevance to this example. Hence, $I(s) = I(r) = I_s(r) = 3$ bits, and this situation could be represented by Figure 1.2.

I(s)   I(r)

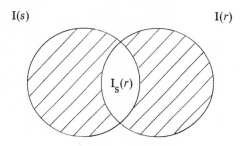

Figure 1.2

The crosshatched areas are devoid of information. All the information in the $I(s)$ circle is contained in the $I(r)$ circle. There is perfect communication between s and r. Our modified example, the situation where the messenger loses the note sent to the boss and composes a new one, would be diagramed as in Figure 1.3.

I(s)   I(r)

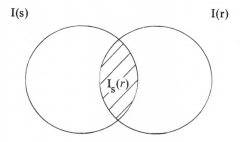

Figure 1.3

There is no flow of information between s and r. None of the information generated at s, $I(s)$, is contained in the information associated with r, $I(r)$.

Figures 1.2 and 1.3 represent the extreme cases, perfect communication and zero communication. There are, of course, degrees. We have had one example of this. When the employees refused to name Shirley in their note to the boss, despite her nomination by their selection procedure, $I(s)$ was 3 bits but $I(r)$ and I_s (r) were less than 3 bits. The appropriate diagram is given in Figure 1.4.

I(s)   I(r)

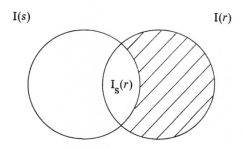

Figure 1.4

In this situation some of the information generated at s is lost; not all of it arrives at r. The information that Herman was selected by the employees' decision procedure is not communicated; the note containing the name "Herman" carries only the information that *either* Herman or Shirley was selected.[11] Since this information is lost, there is some part of the $I(s)$ circle that contains information (is not crosshatched) but which is not included in the $I(r)$ circle. It should be understood that these diagrams represent the situation as it exists with respect to the *average* value of these quantities.

These diagrams, I hope, give the reader a *rough*, intuitive feel for the relationships among $I(s)$, $I(r)$, and $I_s(r)$. I have not yet indicated how $I_s(r)$ is to be measured. It is fairly clear from the diagrams that $I_s(r)$ cannot be greater than $I(s)$ or $I(r)$. The information received at r from s cannot be greater than the total amount of information generated at s, nor can it be greater than the total amount of information available at r. Aside from these limits, however, nothing has been said about how to compute $I_s(r)$. Communication theory provides us with several formulas for computing this quantity. Since I am not interested in the precise, quantitative application for these formulas—only in the underlying principles they illustrate—I will introduce them by way of two other formulas that the reader may find more suggestive.[12] The information transmitted from s to r is the total amount of information available at r, $I(r)$, minus a quantity that is called *noise* (that half-moon portion of the $I(r)$ circle labeled N in Figure 1.1).

(1.4) $I_s(r) = I(r)$ - noise

An alternative way of calculating this quantity, and this should be evident from inspection of Figure 1.1, is

(1.5) $I_s(r) = I(s)$ - equivocation

where the equivocation is that part of the $I(s)$ circle labeled E. The equivocation is that information generated at s which is *not* transmitted to r. And the noise is that information available at r that is not received from s. One may think of the information generated at s as divided into two parts: (1) that portion that is transmitted to r [$I_s(r)$], and (2) that portion that is not transmitted (equivocation). Similarly, the total information available at r may be divided into two parts: (1) that part which represents the information received from s, $I_s(r)$, and (2) that residual portion whose source (if it has another source) is something other than s (noise). If one thinks of *all* the activities occurring in the room where the employees are assembled, not just the results of their selection of a candidate, then there is a great deal of information generated in this room (e.g., where Herman is standing when the coin is flipped for the first time) that is not transmitted to the employer's office. This information represents equivocation, and the total amount of information generated at s, $I(s)$, equals this equivocation plus the information transmitted to r, $I_s(r)$—hence formula (1.5). Similarly, information is associated with the note to the employer that does not have its source in the outcome of the employees' selection procedure (or any other events transpiring at s). For instance, the message was placed in the middle of the employer's desk; it could have been placed in any one of a number of different positions on the desk. In the technical sense of information appropriate to information theory this is information, since it represents the reduction of possibilities. Nonetheless, it is not information received from s. It is *noise*. The *total* information available in the employer's office, $I(r)$, is the sum of this noise and the information received from s, $I_s(r)$. This, of course, is simply a restatement of formula (1.4).

There is seldom, if ever, noiseless communication. In this sense, Figure 1.2 is an idealization and so is our description of the original example. When the memo arrived in the employer's office with the name "Herman" on it, it was said that this constituted a reduction of eight possibilities to one. Any one of eight different names could have appeared on the memo. Hence, $I(r)$ was set equal to 3 bits. But, clearly, even if there are only eight different names that might appear on the memo, each name can appear there in a variety of different ways. It could be printed or in script; different-colored ink could be used; the name could be placed in the center of the paper or in one of the corners. If we include all these possibilities, then the actual inscription on the memo represents a reduction of a great many more possibilities than eight. $I(r)$ is much larger than 3 bits. Nevertheless, from the point of view of communication about *who* was selected, all this additional information at r is *noise*. However large $I(r)$ may be, $I_s(r)$ is still 3 bits. These other parameters give us a noisy signal, but the message still gets through.

An increase in the noise (in the technical sense of information available at the receiver that is independent of the information generated at the source) does not necessarily entail a reduction in the amount of information transmitted. As should be apparent from Figure 1.1 the $I(r)$ circle can grow much larger by increasing N (the noise), that area lying outside the $I(s)$ circle, without reducing $I_s(r)$. In actual concrete situations an increase in the noise (the ordinary snap-crackle-pop sort of noise) not only will increase N (the noise in the technical sense) but also will obscure part of the received signal, thereby reducing $I_s(r)$ *by increasing the equivocation*. In such cases N is increased by a movement of the $I(r)$ circle to the right, thus decreasing the area of overlap with the $I(s)$ circle. Noise is increased *at the expense* of $I_s(r)$. As long, however, as there is no increase in the equivocation [assuming $I(s)$ remains constant], the information transmitted remains the same no matter how great the noise becomes. For example, the radio report,

(a) There will be rain on Sunday (snap, crackle, pop, hiss)

has a good deal of noise, but the noise does not interfere with any part of the message being transmitted from the radio studio. In calculating $I(r)$, we would have to include these "pops" and "hisses" (they represent reductions in possibility *at r*), but since they do not increase the equivocation, the amount of transmitted information $I_s(r)$ remains what it would be without the static. Contrast (a) with (b):

(b) There will be rain on (snap)-nday (crackle, pop, hiss)

Here we have the same amount of noise, but the amount of transmitted information is reduced because the noise increases the equivocation. The equivocation is increased because part of the signal from the broadcasting studio is obscured, leaving an ambiguous (equivocal) message. Given the events occurring at *r*, the forecast could have been for either rain on *Sunday* or rain on *Monday*. The fact that the announcer said "Sunday" is information that is *lost*, and the amount of information lost is what is measured by the equivocation. If noise increases the amount of lost information, it reduces the amount of information transmitted; but if it leaves the equivocation unaffected, $I_s(r)$ remains the same.[13]

Up to this point we have relied heavily on an example that some will find objectionable. They will find it objectionable, or at least suspicious, because it involves a use of *language*. It may be felt that the informational analysis (so far as it has been given) derives a specious plausibility from its application to a situation in which there is something like *real information* being communicated by means of linguistic symbols (e.g., the word "Herman"). To appreciate the fact that the names, linguistically meaningful symbols, play no essential part in this example, or in the information-theoretic description of it, consider an analogous situation. There are eight mischievous boys and a missing cookie. Who took it? An inspection reveals crumbs on Junior's lips. From an information-theoretic standpoint this case is identical to the last. Any one of eight boys could have taken the cookie, and any one was as likely to take it as any other one. Hence, Junior's eating the cookie represents a reduction of eight possibilities to one. $I(s)$ = 3 bits. With some routine assumptions we may suppose that the crumbs on Junior's lips *carry* 3 bits of information about who ate the cookie; that is, $I_s(r)$ = 3 bits. Of course, the amount of information r carries about s may be less than 3 bits, but the same is true of our employee-employer example.

In this example, the location of the crumbs (*on* Junior's lips) plays the same informational role as did the inscription "Herman" in the preceding example. Nothing need be assumed about the *meaning* or *reference* of this name—any more than we need assume something about the meaning or reference of the crumbs on Junior's lips. From the point of view of communication theory, all that need be assumed (for information to be transmitted) is that the appearance of the inscription "Herman" on the memo to the boss *depends* in a certain way on the outcome of the employees' selection process. If these physical marks on paper (whatever their conventional meaning) depend on Herman's selection in the same way that the crumbs on Junior's lips depend on his having eaten the cookie, then these marks on paper carry information about the results of the selection process in the same way that the crumbs carry information about who ate the cookie. This, at least, is what communication theory tells us. The manner in which this theory applies to the transmission of information by linguistic means is the same as the way it applies to the transmission of information by any other means. This generality is one of its strengths.

Formula (1.4) tells us that the amount of information transmitted between s and r equals the amount of information available at r, $I(r)$, minus the noise. Formula (1.5) tells us that the amount of transmitted information can be computed by subtracting the equivocation from $I(s)$. Since we have a way of calculating $I(r)$ and $I(s)$ [formulas (1.1), (1.2), and (1.3)], all we need to determine $I_s(r)$ is some measure of the noise and the equivocation.

Once again, it is the *average value* of these quantities that is usually computed, since as we have seen, this is the quantity of chief interest in engineering applications. We shall, however, develop the formulas for *average noise* and *average equivocation* in terms of an *individual event's contribution to the average*, since it is the latter quantity that will figure most importantly in our later discussion.

The formulas for calculating the *noise* and the *equivocation* may appear rather complicated, but the basic idea is really quite simple. E and N are measures of the amount of *independence* between the events occurring at the source and at the receiver. If these events are *totally* independent (the way the order of cards in one well-shuffled deck of playing cards is independent of the order in an independently shuffled deck), then E and N will be maximum. Hence, $I_s(r)$ will be at a minimum. If, on the other hand, the events occurring at r are not independent of the events occurring at s (the way the behavior of a doorbell is not independent of the events occurring at the door button), then E and N will be commensurately reduced. If there is zero independence (maximum dependence), then E and N will be zero and the amount of transmitted information $I_s(r)$ will be optimal: $I_s(r) = I(s)$. The following formulas are merely ways of computing the amount of independence between the events (and possible events) occurring at s and r.

To use the familiar numbers of our original example, suppose there are eight possibilities at s and the seventh one (s_7) occurs (Herman is chosen). We shall write $P(r_i/s_7)$ for the conditional probability of r_i (the ith event at r) given s_7. For example, $P(r_7/s_7)$ is the conditional probability of Herman's name appearing on the memo given the fact that Herman was selected. If r_6 is taken to stand for Shirley's name appearing on the memo, then $P(r_6/s_7)$ is the conditional probability of Shirley's name appearing on the memo given that Herman was selected. We calculate s_7's contribution to the average noise with the formula[14]

(1.6) $$N(s_7) = -\Sigma P(r_i/s_7) \cdot \log P(r_i/s_7)$$

According to the terms of our original example, there were eight possibilities for r_i, eight different names that could appear on the memo. Hence, when we expand the summation in (1.6), we get eight terms:

$$N(s_7) = -[P(r_1/s_7) \cdot \log P(r_1/s_7) + \cdots + P(r_8/s_7) \cdot \log P(r_8/s_7)]$$

Furthermore, circumstances were originally conceived to be such that the memo would inevitably carry the name of the person selected by the employees: i.e., the conditional probability of r_7, given s_7, was 1, and the conditional probability of any other r_i (say r_1) was 0. The events occurring at r were not independent of the events occurring at s. This lack of independence is reflected in the terms of (1.6). Consider the first term in the expansion of $N(s_7)$:

$$P(r_1/s_7) \cdot \log P(r_1/s_7)$$

Since, as we have seen, the probability of r_1 (Donald's name appearing on the memo), given the fact that Herman was selected, is 0, this term must equal 0 since $P(r_1/s_7) = 0$. The same is true for every other term in the expansion except the seventh:

$$P(r_7/s_7) \cdot \log P(r_7/s_7)$$

The conditional probability of Herman's name appearing on the memo, given the fact that Herman was selected, is 1. Hence, this term reduces to

$$1 \cdot \log 1$$

and since the logarithm of 1 is 0, this term also equals 0. Hence, s_7's contribution to the average noise is 0. The same result would be obtained if we calculated the contribution of any other possible event at s (e.g., s_6, the selection of Shirley). Neither the event that actually occurred (s_7) nor any of the other events that might have occurred contribute anything to the average noise. Hence, the average noise will be zero. Therefore, in accordance with (1.4), we find that the amount of transmitted information $I_s(r)$ is optimal.

To calculate the average noise N, we merely sum up the individual contributions and weight them according to the probability of their occurrence:

(1.7) $N = p(s_1) \cdot N(s_1) + p(s_2) \cdot N(s_2) + \cdots + P(s_8) \cdot N(s_8)$

Since $N(s_i) = 0$ for every i in this example, $N = 0$.

The equivocation E is computed in a parallel fashion. We select the various events that might occur at r, $r_1, r_2, \ldots, r_8$, and calculate their individual contributions to the average equivocation:

(1.8) $E(r_7) = -\Sigma P(s_i/r_7) \cdot \log P(s_i/r_7)$

To obtain the average equivocation E, we sum up the individual contributions and weight them according to their respective probabilities of occurrence:

(1.9) $E = p(r_1)E(r_1) + \cdots + p(r_8)E(r_8)$

On any particular occasion, of course, only *one* of the r_i events will occur (e.g., *Herman's* name will appear on the memo). This event will have a certain equivocation associated with it, an amount of equivocation determined by (1.8). The equivocation associated with this particular event may be much more, or much less, than the average equivocation associated with the process as a whole (the kind of equivocation we would *average* if we repeated the whole process again and again). Recall, for example, the sort of situation described in our modified example, the situation in which the employees were solicitous of Shirley's health. If *either* Shirley or Herman was selected, the name "Herman" would appear on the memo to the boss. If anyone else was selected, their name would appear. Suppose Herman is selected and the name "Herman" appears on the note to the employer. Clearly, in this case, there is some equivocation. If we calculate the amount of equivocation contributed by this particular event in accordance with (1.8), we find two terms in the expansion that do not equal zero:

$$E(r_7) = -[P(s_6/r_7) \cdot \log P(s_6/r_7) + P(s_7 r_7) \cdot \log P(s_7/r_7)]$$

If we assume that the conditional probability of Herman's having been selected, given that his name appears on the memo, is .5 and the conditional probability of Shirley's having been selected, given that Herman's name appears on the memo, is .5, then

$$E(r_7) = -(.5 \log .5 + .5 \log .5) = 1 \text{ bit}$$

Hence, when Herman's name appears on the memo, this event has an equivocation of 1 bit associated with it. This equivocation arises from the fact that this event at r does not uniquely specify what happened at s. All Herman's name on the memo tells us (or *would* tell us if we knew enough about the circumstances of the case) is that *either* Herman or Shirley was selected. The event that occurs at r, r_7, reduces the possibilities at s from 8 to 2. Therefore, the amount of transmitted information is 2 bits, and this is found by subtracting the equivocation from the amount of information associated with the selection of Herman: i.e., $I_s(r_7) = I(s_7) - E(r_7) = 3 - 1 = 2$ bits. But the *average equivocation* is much less than 1 bit. When Donald's name appears on the memo, there is *no* equivocation, as an examination of (1.8) will reveal, and the same is true for the other six names. Hence, the average equivocation (given that the probability of Herman's name appearing on the memo = .25) is .25 bits,

$$E = 0 + 0 + 0 + 0 + 0 + 0 + .25(1) = .25 \text{ bits}$$

Therefore, the average amount of transmitted information $I_s(r)$ is 2.75 bits. The difference between the equivocation associated with a particular event and the average equivocation is important. For when we talk about what can be *known*, we will be concerned, not with averages, but with the amount of information transmitted by (hence, the equivocation associated with) *particular signals*. For example, in this situation it may be possible for the employer to know that Donald was selected when he receives a memo with the name "Donald" on it, but not possible to know that Herman was selected (even if he *was* selected) when he receives a memo with the name "Herman" on it. Things may turn out this way because, as we have just seen, a memo with the name "Donald" on it carries *more information* about who was selected than does a memo with the name "Herman" on it.

CAUSALITY AND INFORMATION

It may seem as though the transmission of information, as this has been described, is a process that depends on the causal interrelatedness of source and receiver. The way one gets a message from s to r is by initiating a sequence of events at s that culminates in a corresponding sequence at r. In abstract terms, the message is borne from s and r by a causal process which determines what happens at r in terms of what happens at s.

The flow of information may, and in most familiar instances obviously does, depend on underlying causal processes. Nevertheless, the informational relationships between s and r must be distinguished from the system of causal relationships existing between these points.

Consider the following, extremely simplified (and, by now,

familiar) situation. There is a variable at s that can assume any one of four different values: s_1, s_2, s_3, or s_4. There is also a variable at r that can assume four different values. Let us suppose that on a specific occasion the sequence of events in Figure 1.5 occurs.

Figure 1.5

The solid arrow between s_2 and r_2 is meant to indicate a causal connection. The s variable taking on the value of s_2 *causes* the r variable to assume the value r_2. This is the causal story. What is the information-theoretic story?

With the data so far supplied there is very little one can say about the amount of information transmitted from s to r. Assuming all values of the s variable to be equally likely, the information generated at s by the occurrence of s_2 is 2 bits. But how much of this information arrives at r? How much of the information generated by s_2 is carried by r_2? These are questions that cannot yet be answered. One cannot tell how much information has been transmitted because a crucial fact has been omitted from this causal story: viz., is there any *other* value of the variable s (besides s_2) that would have produced r_2? We have not yet been given the facts that are essential to the determination of the signal's *equivocation*.

In order to illustrate this, let us supplement our description of the actual situation (s_2 occurs and causes r_2) with a description of the relationship between the other possible values for the variables. Letting a broken line indicate a causal connection which does not actually obtain (because the events it relates do not occur), but a connection which *would* exist if the appropriate value of s occurred, assume that the system of causal connections is as indicated in Figure 1.6. In this hypothetical situation, s_2 not only causes r_2, it is the *only* value of s that will bring about r_2. Consulting the formula for equivocation, (1.8), one finds that the equivocation of the signal r_2 is zero. Hence,

Sending Station   *Receiving Station*

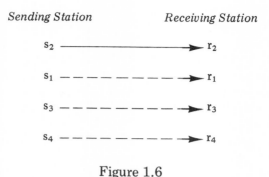

Figure 1.6

$I_s(r_2) = I(s_2)$; the amount of information the signal carries about the source is equal to the amount of information generated at the source by the occurrence of s_2.

Contrast this possible state of affairs with Figure 1.7. As before, the solid arrow represents the actual situation: s_2 occurs and brings about r_2. Broken arrows indicate causal connections that do not actually obtain (because the cause does not occur), but connections that would exist if the appropriate causal antecedent existed.

Sending Station   *Receiving Station*

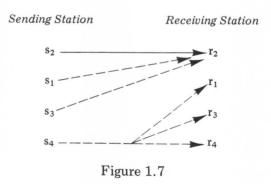

Figure 1.7

The broken arrow from s_4 splits into three branches, indicating that there is no uniform result associated with the occurrence of this event. Some of the time (34 percent) it results in r_1, some of the time in r_3 (33 percent), and some of the time in r_4 (33 percent). If one prefers *not* to speak of the same event type having different effects under identical circumstances, one can think of the branching arrow leading from s_4 as representing some random, noncausal relationship between s_4 and the events at r.

Since the events at s are equally likely, $I(s_2) = 2$ bits. In contrast to the previous situation, however, the occurrence of r_2 does not represent the arrival of 2 bits of information from s. A calculation of the equivocation associated with the signal r_2 in accordance with (1.8) reveals that the equivocation is now approximately 1.6 bits. Hence, r_2 carries only .4 bits of information about s.[15] Given what *actually* happens, and the causal relationships that *actually* obtain, this situation cannot be distinguished from the previous one. Nonetheless, in informational terms they are quite different. The causal story (Figure 1.5) does not tell us how much information is transmitted because it fails to tell us whether the causal sequence is embedded in a network of possibilities similar to that depicted in Figure 1.6 or Figure 1.7.

Interestingly enough, if s_4 should occur in the latter communication system, the event that occurs at r (either r_1, r_3, or r_4) would carry a full 2 bits of information about the source. Since the equivocation associated with the signal r_1 (also r_3 and r_4) is zero, this event (should it occur) will carry *all* the information associated with the occurrence of s_4.

This is a perfectly acceptable result from an informal standpoint. Intuitively, the signal r_2 does not "tell" one what (specifically) happened at s, while the signals r_1, r_3, and r_4 do. From an ordinary point of view, then, r_1 carries *more* information about what happened at s than does r_2.

Despite the loose causal connection between s_4 and r_1, and the tight causal connection between s_2 and r_2, r_1 carries more information about s than does r_2. On the average, the unpredictable signals will occur much less frequently than the predictable signal (r_2), but when they do occur, they carry a full charge of information.

What this reveals is that the transmission of information between two points does *not* depend on the presence of deterministic processes between transmitter and receiver. In every imagined instance, r_2 was brought about, produced, caused, and determined by s_2. In one imagined situation (Figure 1.6) this signal carried 2 bits of information about s; in another (Figure 1.7) it carried .4 bits. Conditions can be described in which it carries even less.

Without bothering to actually diagram it, imagine a person gazing at a particular playing card—say, the three of diamonds. Suppose he cannot see the face of the card. How much information is he receiving about the identity of the playing card (i.e., *which* card it is)? Well, since he cannot see the face of the card, and the backs all look the same, our ordinary judgment would be that he is receiving zero information about which card it is. There are 52 possibilities and the signal he is receiving does nothing to discriminate among these possibilities. Yet, by hypothesis, the sensory signal he is receiving has the *three of diamonds* as its causal antecedent; it is *this particular card* that is causally responsible for his sensory experience. But although it is this particular card that is determining the character of his sensory experience, any one of the other fifty-one cards would, from that angle and distance, have the very same kind of effect. This is what is meant by saying they all look the same from the back. Although there is a causal connection between the three of diamonds and the subject's sensory experience, the subject's sensory experience carries zero information about the identity of its causal antecedent. If s_3 denotes the (random) draw of the three of diamonds, then $I(s_3) = 5.7$ bits, but none of this information is embodied in the sensory effect of this event.

It may turn out, of course, that although the sensory message carries no information about *which* card it is, it does carry *some* information about the card—e.g., that *it is a playing card*. But even this may not be true. It all depends on whether something *other* than a playing card would have the very same (sensory) effect on him. If we suppose the subject so disoriented as to hallucinate playing cards when none are in front of him, then the sensory state produced in him by the three of diamonds does not even carry the information that there is a playing card in front of him. This is perfectly compatible with the supposition that it *is* the three of diamonds, this particular playing card, that is having an effect on the subject. After all, he is (by hypothesis) *seeing* the three of diamonds, albeit from the back, whatever else might have been happening if he were not seeing a playing card. The sensory state need not carry the information that the distal stimulus is a playing card, let alone the three of diamonds, despite the fact that it is a playing card, and in particular the three of diamonds, that is causing him to have the sensory experience.

An effect, therefore, may or may not embody information about its cause. It is this possibility that makes the idea of a perfect crime so fascinating. A's actions may result in B's death, but B's death may not bear witness to its cause. From an information-theoretic standpoint, the perfect crime is an illegal episode whose aftermath contains no information about the identity of the causally responsible agents. Equivocation is maximized.

Just as there may be little, if any, information contained in an effect about its cause, an event may carry information about events to which it stands in no regular causal relationship. The situation depicted in Figure 1.7 illustrates this. The occurrence of r_1 (or r_3 or r_4) contains a full 2 bits of information about the situation at s. Yet, the process by means of which this information is transmitted to r is not a causal process—at least not a deterministic one. We may suppose, for example, that at the point where the arrow from s_4 splits into three branches, there is a device which *randomly* yields r_1, r_3, or r_4. An electron is sent from s_4, scattered before reaching r (at the branching point), and unpredictably arrives in one of the three areas marked r_1, r_4, and r_3. This, we are told, is a nondeterministic process. If quantum theory is true, and there is reason to think it is true, then there is no way in principle of predicting where the electron is going to land. It will *sometimes* land in area r_1, but there is nothing that determines it to land there. Under identical circumstances it will, more often than not, land in one of the other two areas. Nevertheless, when the electron arrives at r_1, it carries 2 bits of information about the source.

Some people do not believe that there are indeterministic processes in nature. According to this view, the indeterminacy associated with quantum phenomena is a reflection of our theory's incompleteness. It is our *ignorance* that makes it appear that r_1 is undetermined by antecedent conditions, but when (or *if*) we achieve a better understanding of these matters (replacing quantum theory with some better approximation to the truth), it will be seen that r_1's occurrence is strictly determined—determined by what, in our present state of ignorance, may be called hidden variables.[16]

For our purposes it is not necessary to debate this point. The important fact is not whether universal determinism is true or not. This issue was raised only for the purpose of showing that, even *if* there are indeterministic processes in nature, this does *not* represent an obstacle to the transmission of information. As the above example illustrates, r_2 was determined by s_2, and yet it carried *less* information about the source than did the nondetermined r_1.

It may appear that I am confusing determinism with causality. It may be said, for example, that although s_4 does not *determine* what is going to happen at r, it nonetheless *causes* or *brings about* r_1 (or r_3 or r_4—whatever, in fact happens at r). Causality does not require determinism. Every event can have a cause without every event being determined, without every event being (in principle) predictable.

There is merit to this charge. In claiming that causality is not necessary to the flow of information, I have assumed that:

If C is the cause of E, then C is an essential part of some nomically sufficient condition for E.

This principle gives expression to a traditional idea, the idea that C cannot be the cause of E if (an event such as) C can occur, under relevantly similar circumstances, without (an event such as) E occurring. In other words, causality is a manifestation of a regular, lawlike, succession between events of type C and events of type E under relevantly similar conditions.[17] Since, in our hypothetical example, r_1's occurrence was assumed to be a chance affair, something that was not determined by s_4, there is no *regular succession* between events similar to s_4 and events similar to r_1. Sometimes r_1 occurs upon the occurrence of s_4, but at other times, under the same circumstances, r_1 does not occur (either r_3 or r_4 occurs). Hence, according to the above principle, s_4 is not the cause of r_1. Indeed, *nothing* causes r_1 to happen if (as assumed) there are no nomically sufficient conditions for its occurrence.

Whether one supposes that causality is necessary for the flow of information or not will depend, of course, on what one means by causality. If one accepts the above principle as constitutive of the concept of causality, then one will be forced to conclude that s_4 was not the cause (*nothing* was the cause) of r_1. If one rejects this analysis of causality, however, one may (depending on one's alternative analysis) consistently maintain that although nothing suffices for r_1, although this event is not determined, it was nonetheless brought about, or caused, by s_4.[18]

This is not the place to undertake an exhaustive analysis of causality.[19] For our purposes it will suffice to say something conditional in nature: viz., *if* one views the cause of an event as an essential part of some nomically sufficient condition for that event, then a causal relationship between A and B is *not* necessary for the transmission of information from A to B. The event B can contain the information that A occurred even if A and B are not, in this sense, causally related—even if, in this sense, there is no cause of B. Hereafter, when I speak of a causal relation between two events, I should be understood as meaning a relationship that qualifies under this traditional conception. What I say will not necessarily apply if causality is taken to be a relationship that does not require *regularity of succession* (of the event types under relevantly identical circumstances).

In light of these facts (and terminological decisions) the distinction between a causal relationship and an informational relationship should be clear. Questions about the flow of information are, for the most part, left unanswered by meticulous descriptions of the causal processes at work in the transmission of a signal. One can have full information without causality, and one can have no information with causality. And there is every shade of gray between these two extremes.

These facts must be appreciated if one is to understand the difference between an information-based theory of knowledge and a causal theory of knowledge. It is sometimes carelessly assumed, for example, because the reflection of light from an object *causes* certain events to occur on the periphery of our visual receptors, and these events (the proximal stimulus) in turn cause other events to occur in the central nervous system, ultimately yielding some response from the organism, that therefore the subject has, in some vague sense of "information," received information about the distal stimulus (the object from which the light was reflected). This simply does not follow. The subject may receive little or no information from such a stimulus. He may not receive the information that *there is* an object in front of him, let alone information about what object, or *what kind* of object, it is. Whether or not he has received this information is a question that cannot be settled by detailed descriptions of what actually occurs in a perceptual encounter.

The fact that a small moving bug on a light background causes a certain set of neurons to fire in the frog's brain and this, in turn, triggers a response on the part of the frog ("zapping" the bug with its tongue) does not mean that the neurons, or the frog, are receiving information to the effect that there is a bug nearby. They *may* be receiving this information, but the fact that the moving bug elicits a distinctive response (from both the cell and the frog) does not *itself* imply that any information is being transmitted in these interactions. To analyze this situation in informational terms, one needs to know more than what is *causing* the neurons to fire (or the frog to flick at the fly). One needs to know what else, if anything, produces this response. The boy who shouted "wolf" in response to a wolf invading his flock did *not* communicate the information that a wolf was present. The reason he did not is that his cry of "wolf" was also his way of responding to a variety of *other* situations—situations that did *not* involve the presence of a wolf. If the neural cells that "cry out" in response to a moving bug also react, in a relevantly similar way, to other sorts of stimuli, then they do not carry the information that there is a bug nearby. In this hypothetical case, although the firing of the neural cells would still be caused by a moving fly—and would, in turn, cause the frog's tongue to dart out—they would not carry the information that there was a fly to be caught. If the frog caught the fly, he would be lucky—the same way the boy who called "wolf" would be lucky if some hunter should patiently answer the boy's twentieth cry when, as it turns out, and for the first time, it was prompted by a real wolf.

This is merely a way of saying that, for information-theoretic purposes, one needs to know whether the causal situation is similar to that of Figure 1.6 or Figure 1.7. Knowing what caused the neural discharge is not enough; one must know something about the *possible* antecedents, causal or otherwise, of this event if one is to determine its informational measure. I do not mean to suggest by this example that the scientists who describe such experiments with frogs, and who refer to some of these neural cells as "bug detectors," are confused about the distinction between a causal and an informational relationship. Quite the contrary. It seems clear that certain neurons are labeled "bug detectors," not simply because a moving bug *causes* them to fire, but because, in the frog's natural habitat, *only* a moving bug (or relevantly equivalent stimulus) causes them to fire. It is this *informational* relationship to the stimulus that entitles the neural cell to be called a *detector* of bugs.[20]

This point is clearly made by W. R. A. Muntz in his discussion of color vision in frogs.[21] Certain cells in the dorsal thalamus of the frog are sensitive, not only to the presence or absence of light, but also to the color of this light. These cells respond much more strongly to blue light than to light of any other color. The question Muntz poses is whether this selective response is mere color dependence or true color vision. This distinction is illustrated by the human retinal cells called rods. These cells, responsible for vision in faint light, respond most strongly to blue-green light. In this sense they are color-dependent. "The rods, however, are not capable of color vision, because they cannot distinguish between a low-intensity blue-green and, say, a high-intensity yellow."[22] Although Muntz does not put the point in informational-theoretic terms, this is the same distinction we have just discussed—the distinction between a causal relationship and a genuine informational relationship. Although blue-green light will *cause* the rods to fire at a certain rate, yellow light of sufficiently high intensity will cause them to fire at the *same* rate. Hence the firing rate does not carry the information even when the stimulus *is* blue-green light because there is a positive equivocation associated with this signal. Since the neural discharge of these rods is equivocal with respect to the color (wavelength) of the stimulus, it does not contain the information that the stimulus is blue-green (rather than, say, yellow). The rods carry information, but not information about the *color* or the incoming light. Instead, they carry information about the *relative intensity in the blue-green portion of the spectrum* of the stimulus. Since a soft blue-green and an intense yellow are the same in this respect, the cell cannot distinguish between them. Although the cells are caused to fire by blue-green light, they are color-blind. They do not carry information about the color of the light that causes them to fire.

These examples illustrate the fact that a causal relationship between A and B does not *suffice* for the communication of information between A and B. But we have also suggested that a causal relationship between A and B was not necessary to the flow of information between these two points. Is this merely a theoretical possibility, or are there actual instances where this occurs? It is well known that the processes by means of which our visual receptors extract information from the incoming light are nondeterministic. For instance, photons impinge on the photosensitive pigment of the rods and cones of the retina. The absorption of these photons by the pigment, with the consequent transmission of an electrical pulse to the ganglion cells (a relatively peripheral set of cells mediating the transmission of the signal to the brain), is a quantum process. The arrival, say, of six photons at the surfaces of the highly sensitive rods (used in night vision) may result in no photon being absorbed. It may result in all six being absorbed. Or it may result in the absorption of some number between these two extremes. How many will be absorbed is, in principle, unpredictable. All that can be given is the various probabilities for n absorptions. It turns out that very few photons need be absorbed to generate an impulse from the ganglion cells with the consequent transmission of a signal to the brain and the occurrence of a visual experience (as of a "twinkle" of light). Let us suppose, for illustrative purposes, that the absorption of four photons will give rise to a sensation of light.[23] If we now arrange to have a light flash at very low intensity (delivering an average of only six photons per flash to the retina), we will have a situation very much like that depicted between s_4 and r_1 in Figure 1.7. Sometimes (when four or more quanta are absorbed) a sensation will occur (r_1). Sometimes (when fewer quanta are absorbed) no sensation will occur (either r_3 or r_4). When the subject will experience this "twinkle" of light is (according to quantum theory) unpredictable. It is not determined. Yet, this does not prevent the sensation of light from *carrying information* about the dimly lit test light. Assume that there is 1 bit of information associated with the test light: either the light is on or it is off, and it is equally likely to be either. Since there are only two possibilities, and they are equally likely, $I(s)$—

the amount of information generated by the light's being on—is 1 bit. If the light is so dim that a sensation occurs (four or more photons are absorbed) only 50 percent of the time the light flashes, the average information transmitted from the light to the perceiving subject is low. Nevertheless, if we assume that a sensation occurs only when the light is on, [24] then the sensation, *when* it occurs, carries a full bit of information. It contains the information that the light is on. It carries this information for the same reason that r_1 carried the information that s_4 occurred: viz., the equivocation of the signal is zero.

This is, perhaps, an extreme example of information being transmitted over an indeterministic channel. But although, it is an extreme case, it illustrates a common phenomenon in the communication and reception of information. Consider a doorbell circuit with a loose wire. Most of the time the doorbell does not work because the loose wire results in a broken circuit. Occasionally, however, stray factors cause the wire to make contact, and the circuit is completed. If we assume that the bell will not ring unless someone is pushing the button, it is fairly clear that a ringing bell signals someone's presence at the door. At least it contains the information that the doorbell button is being depressed, and it contains this information despite the fact that the bell usually does not ring when the button is being depressed. From the engineer's point of view the doorbell circuit represents a very unsatisfactory channel of communication (the *average* amount of information transmitted is very low). Nevertheless, as we have already seen, this does not prevent the system from occasionally transmitting as much information as can be communicated by a perfectly working doorbell system. Players with low batting averages sometimes get a hit. The only difference between this example and the last is that we are convinced that the "stray factors" mentioned above are not themselves truly indeterministic. What the previous example teaches us is that, even if they were, this would present no insurmountable obstacle to the communication of information.

When speaking of an information-bearing signal, one is usually speaking of some physical process that propagates from one place to another (light, electric current, sound waves, etc.) or a physical object, suitably inscribed, that is transported from here to there (letters, books, pictures, etc.). These are the material embodiments or realizations of the communication channel. From a theoretical point of view, however, the communication channel may be thought of as simply the set of dependency relations between s and r. If the statistical relations defining equivocation and noise between s and r are appropriate, then there is a channel between these two points, and information passes between them, even if there is no direct physical link joining s with r. Consider, for example, the situation depicted in Figure 1.8.

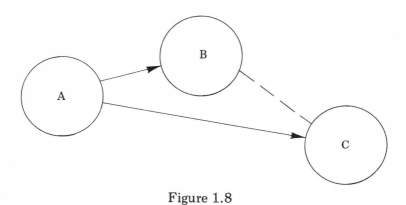

Figure 1.8

A is transmitting to both B and C via some physical channel (indicated by solid lines). B and C are isolated from one another in the sense that there is no physical signal passing directly between them. Though B and C are physically isolated from one another, there is nonetheless an informational link between them (indicated by the broken line). According to information theory, there is a channel between B and C. "Because of the common dependence of B and C on A, it will be possible to learn something about C by looking at B, and vice versa. In the sense of information theory, it is correct to say that a channel exists between B and C."[25]

For convenience let us call the channel between B and C a "ghost" channel. One can think of two television receivers tuned to the same program as being linked by a ghost channel. There is information at each of these receivers about the other. The correlation between the events occurring upon the screens of these two receivers is no accident. It is no coincidence that the commercial interrupts your program at the same time it interrupts mine. The information at B about C, $I_c(B)$, can equal the information generated at C, $I(C)$, despite the absence of a physical channel between them.

This is a further respect in which an informational link between B and C must be distinguished from a causal link. Nothing at B *causes* anything at C or vice versa; yet C contains information about B and B about C. If C is farther from the transmitter than B, the events occurring at C may occur later in time than those at B. This is irrelevant for the purposes of evaluating the informational relationship between B and C. Even though C occurs later, B carries information about what *will* happen at C (it receives it, so to speak, from A). This sounds strange only if the receipt of information is confused with causality. For, of course, no physical signal can travel backward in time carrying information from C to B.

Theories of knowledge that require some causal link between knower and known usually encounter some difficulty with our presumed knowledge of the future. For example, how can the occupants of B know anything about the events that will occur at C when these events have not yet happened (hence, cannot be the cause of anything now happening at B)? To handle this difficulty, special clauses are added to the causal theory of knowledge to permit such knowledge.[26] They are presented as explanations of what is meant by the required causal connection between the knowing subject and the state of affairs known to obtain. Their effect is to permit the occupants of B to know what *will happen* at C. Goldman, for example, arranges things so that even if there is no direct causal link, someone at B can know what will happen at C if the events at B and C have a common causal ancestor.[27] This is enough to satisfy the causal requirements of his theory. From the point of view of information theory, such embellishments are superfluous—epicyclic ways of trying to capture, in causal terminology, the idea of an informational link between two points. As we shall see, such embellishments are unnecessary. The only sense in which knowledge requires causality is the sense in which it requires information, and with this requirement there is no need to make out a special case for situations of this type.

Chapter 2
Communication and Information

Communication theory purports to tell us something about information, if not *what* it is, at least *how much* of it there is. In sketching the elements of this theory in the last chapter, we chose examples carefully to support this claim. Yet, this is controversial. It has been argued that the theory is more properly viewed as a theory of *signal transmission*, a theory about those physical events (signals) that, in some sense, carry information.[1] According to this view, signals are one thing, the information they carry, their semantic content, another. The mathematical theory of information may be an elegant device for codifying the statistical features of, and mutual dependencies between, those physical events on which communication depends, but information has to do, not with the vehicles we use to communicate, but with *what we communicate* by means of them. A genuine theory of information would be a theory about the *content* of our messages, not a theory about the form in which this content is embodied.

There is certainly a distinction between the message a signal bears and the signal bearing that message. Two knocks is the signal; that the coast is clear is the message. So much is clear. A distinction can also be drawn between the water a bucket holds and the bucket that holds the water. But, despite the difference, we can measure the bucket to find out how much water it contains. Why, then, can one not determine a signal's informational content, or at least how much information it contains, by taking the measure of the signal itself?

Shannon has said that the semantic aspects of communication are irrelevant to the engineering problem.[2] So they are. Nevertheless, as Warren Weaver notes in reacting to Shannon's remark: "But this does not mean that the engineering aspects are necessarily irrelevant to the semantic aspects".[3] It is this thread that I mean to pick up and develop in this chapter. Communication theory does not tell us what information is. It ignores questions having to do with the *content* of signals, what *specific information* they carry, in order to describe *how much* information they carry. In this sense Shannon is surely right: the semantic aspects are irrelevant to the engineering problems. Nevertheless, in telling us *how much* information a signal carries, communication theory imposes constraints on what information a signal *can* carry. These constraints, in turn, can be used to develop an account of what information a signal *does* carry. In this sense Weaver is surely right: communication theory is not irrelevant to a specification of a signal's information content. The measurement of a one-gallon bucket cannot tell you, specifically, what is in the bucket, but it can tell you something about what *can* be in the bucket. It can tell you, for example, that it cannot contain two gallons of lemonade. And if you know, on other grounds, that the bucket contains either two gallons of lemonade or one gallon of beer, the measurement will determine, quite unerringly, the contents of the bucket.

THE ORDINARY CONCEPT OF INFORMATION

What, then, are the "semantic aspects" of information, those aspects that communication theory fails to capture? Weaver warns the reader that in this theory the word "information" is used in a special sense that must not be confused with its ordinary usage. In particular, he says, *information* (as it is used in communication theory) should not be confused with *meaning*.[4] Other authors caution the reader not to confuse the sense of information appropriate to this theory with the *value* of the received information,[5] with *importance* or *truth*,[6] or with *knowledge*.[7] Most authorities would endorse Cherry's view that the theory is not concerned with the meaning or truth of messages; semantics lies outside the scope of the mathematical theory of information.[8]

These warnings are salutary when taken as an antidote to the excesses of some investigators. Norbert Wiener, for instance, deliberately treats as synonyms "amount of information" and "amount of meaning." He says, "The amount of meaning can be measured. It turns out that the less probable a message is, the more meaning it carries, which is entirely reasonable from the standpoint of common sense."[9] It takes only a moment's reflection to realize that this is *not* "entirely reasonable" from the standpoint of common sense. There is no simple equation between meaning (or amounts of meaning) and information (or amounts of information) as the latter is understood in the mathematical theory of information. The utterance "There is a gnu in my backyard" does not have *more meaning* than "There is a dog in my backyard" because the former is, statistically, less probable. It is not even clear that one can sensibly talk about "amounts of meaning" in this way, let alone identify them with the statistical rarity of the signs that are meaningful. To persist in this direction would lead one to the absurd view that among competent speakers of the language *gibberish* has more meaning than sensible discourse because it is much less frequent.

For my purposes, however, this talk of meaning is quite beside the point. The question is not whether communication theory provides one with an account of *meaning*, but whether it provides one with an account of *information*. Although information, as ordinarily understood, may be a semantic concept, this does not mean that we must assimilate it to the concept of *meaning*. For, on the face of it, there is no reason to think that every meaningful sign must carry information or, if it does, that the information it carries must be identical to its meaning.

Recently, for example, I was asked by an opponent at a duplicate bridge tournament what my partner's bid meant. My partner had bid "5 clubs" in response to my "4 no trump" (Blackwood convention). I replied that it *meant* that he had either 0 or 4 aces. This is the conventional meaning of that bid, and the meaning of all bids must be revealed to one's opponents. Puzzled, however, by our somewhat erratic bidding (and, doubtless, my incredulous stare at my partner), my opponent persisted: "I know what it means. What I want to know is what his bid told you, what information you got from it?" Now this, obviously, is a completely different question, one that (given the rules of duplicate bridge) I am not obliged to answer. For what information was conveyed (to me) by my partner's bid was *that he had no aces*. This information was communicated to me because I had three aces in my own hand; hence, he could not have all four aces. My opponent (having no aces in her own hand) did not get this piece of information. All she could tell (given my partner's bid) was *that he had either 0 or 4 aces*. To tell her what information had been communicated to me by my partner's bid was to reveal something about my *own* hand (viz., that I had at least one ace). Hence, though I was obliged to reveal what the bid *meant*, I was not obliged to reveal the information it conveyed.

In this case the information contained in a signal exceeds (in a sense) the conventional meaning of the signal. The same thing often happens with ordinary verbal communications. If I already know that someone lives in Wisconsin, but you do not, hearing him say he lives in Madison tells me where he lives but not you. A glance at the calendar tells you the date only if you already know the day of the week. What one learns, or can learn, from a signal (event, condition, or state of affairs), and hence the information carried by that signal, depends in part on what one already knows about the alternative possibilities.

On the other hand, an event or state of affairs that has no meaning in any conventional sense may carry substantial amounts of information. An experienced poker player can read the signs; he can tell, or be reasonably certain, when a bluff is in progress. His opponent's nervous mannerisms, excessively high bet, and forced appearance of confidence reveal, as surely as would a peek at his last card, that he did not fill his inside straight. In such a situation information is communicated, but the vehicle that carries the information (opponent's behavior and actions) has no meaning in the relevant conventional or semantic sense.[10]

Furthermore, even when the vehicle of communication is a meaningful sign or set of symbols, there need be no correspondence between the meaning of the symbols and the information conveyed. If I do *not* have a toothache, my saying that I have a toothache fails to carry the information that I have a toothache.

The words I utter, "I have a toothache," are meaningful. They mean that I have a toothache. Yet, regardless of what you happen to think, or come to believe, as a result of hearing me utter them, this is not the information they carry.

The information embodied in a signal (linguistic or otherwise) is only incidentally related to the meaning (if any) of that signal. Typically, of course, we communicate with one another, exchange information, by exploiting the conventional meaning of signs. We convey information by using signs that have a meaning corresponding to the information we wish to convey. But this practice should not lead one to confuse the meaning of a symbol with the information, or amount of information, carried by the symbol.

According to this usage, then, signals may *have* a meaning but they *carry* information. What information a signal carries is what it is capable of "telling" us, telling us *truly*, about another state of affairs. Roughly speaking, information is that commodity capable of yielding knowledge, and what information a signal carries is what we can learn from it. If everything I say to you is false, then I have given you no information. At least I have given you no information of the kind I purported to be giving. If you happen to know (on other grounds) that what I am saying is false, then you may nonetheless get information, information about *me* (I am lying), from what I say, but you will not get the information corresponding to the conventional meaning of what I say. When I say, "I have a toothache," what I say *means* that I have a toothache whether what I say is true or false. But when false, it fails to carry the information that I have a toothache because it is incapable of yielding the knowledge that I have a toothache. No one can *learn* that I have a toothache when I do not have one. This is why my partner's bid at the bridge table communicated to me, but not to our opponents, the information that he had no aces. Although the bid meant the same thing to all of us, the bid told me something it did not tell my opponent: viz., that he had no aces.

It is this sense, or use, of the term "information" that is operative in a wide variety of contexts. We say that a pamphlet contains information about how to probate a will. We say this because we believe that someone (suitably equipped) could *learn* something about probating a will by consulting the pamphlet. Information booths are not merely places where clerks are paid to utter meaningful sounds. What makes them *information* booths is that the clerks either *know*, or can quickly *find out*, about matters of interest to the average patron. One can *learn* something by making inquiries at such places.

When a scientist tells us that we can use the pupil of the eye as a source of information about another person's feeling or attitudes, that a thunder signature (sound) contains information about the lightning channel that produced it, that the dance of a honeybee contains information as to the whereabouts of the nectar, or that the light from a star carries information about the chemical constitution of that body, the scientist is clearly referring to information as something capable of yielding knowledge. A state of affairs contains information about X to just that extent to which a suitably placed observer could learn something about X by consulting it. This, I suggest, is the very same sense in which we speak of books, newspapers, and authorities as containing, or having, information about a particular topic, and I shall refer to it as the *nuclear* sense of the term "information."

In this sense of the term, *false* information and *mis*-information are not kinds of information—any more than decoy ducks and rubber ducks are kinds of ducks. And to speak of certain information as being reliable is to speak redundantly. I realize, of course, that we *do* speak, colloquially, of someone's information as being unreliable, about feeding false information to the spy, and about someone being misinformed in a way that suggests he *was* informed (just incorrectly). I have no wish to legislate about common usage. I am quite prepared to admit that there are uses of the term "information" that do no correspond with what I have called its nuclear sense. Nevertheless, if we consult a dictionary, we find information described most frequently in terms of "intelligence," "news," "instruction," and "knowledge." These terms are suggestive. They have a common nucleus. They all point in the same direction—the direction of truth. Information is what is capable of yielding knowledge, and since knowledge requires truth, information requires it also.

Whatever the vagaries of ordinary use, then, I think it fair to say that the nuclear concept described above is often the concept we mean to be expressing when we talk about information. Information is, after all, a valuable commodity. We spend billions on its collection, storage, and retrieval. People are tortured in attempts to extract it from them. Thousands of lives depend on whether the enemy has it. Given all the fuss, it would be surprising indeed if information had nothing to do with truth.

As we have seen, some authors have rejected the semantic relevance of communication theory and, as a consequence, the power of this theory to tell us anything important about information as commonly understood. They seem to have done so on the basis of the following kind of reasoning. Information is a semantic idea. Semantics is the study of meaning. Communication theory does not provide a satisfactory account of meaning. Hence communication theory does not provide a satisfactory account of information. The fallacy in this line of reasoning consists in the assumption that *meaning* is the *only* semantically relevant concept, that if a theory does not provide a satisfactory account of meaning, it does not provide a satisfactory account of *any* semantic concept.

I have not yet argued that communication theory does tell us something about information. This is a task for the remainder of this chapter. What I have tried to show in this brief section is that the ordinary, semantically relevant, sense of information (the nuclear concept described above) is something to be distinguished from the concept of *meaning*. Hence, I hope to have shown that the failure of information theory to tell us what meaning is should not be used to discredit it as a theory which tells us something about information. Whether the theory is capable of furnishing an adequate account of information, in the semantically relevant sense, is a question about whether it can provide an illuminating account of that commodity capable of yielding knowledge.

It should be understood at the outset, of course, that communication theory is not designed to tell us what the word "information" means. The theory is not a candidate for Webster's Dictionary. I have already tried to say, in a rough-and-ready way, what this term means. At least I have tried to isolate a "nuclear concept" that is, I believe, the concept we most commonly use the word to express. What is to be expected from information theory is what is to be expected from any scientific theory: a more or less complete, precise, and systematic description of those entities and processes underlying the phenomena of interest. Just as physics tells us what lightning is without telling us what "lightning" means (although the word may *come to mean* what the physicist tells us about the word's referent), so information theory should be able to tell us what information is without necessarily telling us what the word "information" means. We *already*, as fluent speakers of the language, know enough about what this word means to make the question, "What is it?" a significant, answerable, question. Information is a commodity that, given the right recipient, is capable of yielding knowledge. What we can learn, in terms of both content and amount, is limited by the information available. It is, moreover, a commodity that can be transmitted, received, exchanged, stored, lost, recovered, bought, and sold. In terms of what it can do, and what can be done to it, this is the sort of thing we are referring to when we talk about information. What we ask of information theory is that it tell us, exactly, what this thing is.

THE PROPER MEASURE OF INFORMATION

One of the most obvious respects in which communication theory is unprepared (I do not say *unequipped*) to deal with semantic issues is that meaning, truth, reference, and allied semantic notions apply to *particular* messages or acts of communication while the theory is preoccupied with *average* amounts of information (entropy). As Kenneth Sayre observes, "The difference between information theory and semantics in this respect is the difference between the study of the conditions for the communication of any message whatsoever and the study of the content of particular messages."[11]

Insofar as we are concerned with the informational *content* of a signal or message, the *what-it-is-we-can-learn* from that signal or message (in contrast to the *how-much-we-can-learn*), it does not make sense to speak of average information. If there is a way of measuring the amount of information associated with a particular message, then we can sensibly ask about the average amount of information associated with two or more messages. For instance, if Herman, while reading in the newspaper that his utility stock has declined, is told that his wife is waiting downstairs, we may suppose that there is some average to the amount of information he has received. But it surely makes no sense to ask about the average *content* of the two messages he received. Herman has learned two things: that his stock has declined and that his wife is waiting. There is no average to *what he has learned*, although there may be an average to *how* much he has learned. The content of a message is not a *quantity* that can be averaged. All we can average is the *amount* of content.

Hence, if information theory is to tell us anything about the informational content of signals, it must forsake its concern with averages and tell us something about the information contained in *particular* messages and signals. For it is only particular messages and signals that *have* a content.

Suppose that there are 64 possibilities at s and these are reduced to one, say s_2. We can think of the situation at s as consisting of a checkerboard on which a marker is to be randomly placed. Each of the 64 squares is assigned a number. The marker lands on square 2. Since 64 possibilities have been reduced to 1, there are 6 bits of information associated with this occurrence: $I(s_2) = 6$ bits. Suppose, moreover, that we desire to communicate this information to some distant receiver r. The only available channel for the transmission of this information is a channel that is severely restricted. All that can be transmitted is a binary digit (0 or 1); it takes one full second to transmit a single binary digit, and the channel is open for only one second. Obviously, only one binary digit can be transmitted. How much information can we communicate about the placement of the marker?

It may appear that one can transmit only 1 bit of information over this channel, but this is incorrect. The truth of the matter is that one can only *average* 1 bit of information. I can, on a specific occasion (given the right code) succeed in transmitting much more than 1 bit of information with my single binary digit. For example, by prearrangement we can agree that I will transmit a 1 if (and only if) the marker is on square 2, and a 0 if the marker is on one of the other 63 squares. When s_2 is realized (a happy accident) and I transmit a 1, 6 bits of information are transmitted about the location of the marker. This particular signal carries

6 bits of information from s to r as a reference to formula (1.5), and formula (1.8) will verify:

(1.5) $I_s(r) = I(s)$ – equivocation

Since we are concerned with the amount of information carried by a particular signal (the 1), we must subtract the equivocation associated with this particular signal from the quantity $I(s)$ (which, in this case, equals 6 bits). Since the arrangement is that a 1 will be transmitted *only if* the marker is on square 2, and assuming that a 1 will be received only if a 1 is transmitted, the conditional probabilities defining equivocation (1.8) are all either 1 or 0. Hence, $E = 0$. There is no equivocation associated with the receipt of a 1 at the receiver. In accordance with formula (1.5), then, we may conclude that the amount of information transmitted by this digit equals 6 bits:

$$I_s(1) = 6 - 0$$
$$= 6 \text{ bits}$$

I cannot *average* this rate of transmission, of course, since more often than not one of the other possibilities will be realized (the marker will *not* land in square 2). When the marker is located in one of the other 63 squares, I must transmit a 0. When this occurs, I succeed in transmitting only a fractional amount of information. The amount of equivocation associated with the receipt of a 0 at r is very great. Using formula (1.8) again, we find that $E(0) = 5.95$ bits (approximately). Hence, the arrival of a 0 at the receiver carries only about .05 bit of information about the location of the marker. Using this code, we can *average* only about .095 bit of information per message [formulas (1.9) and (1.5)].

On the average, then, with this method of encoding information, I will succeed in transmitting only about .095 bit of information with each message. This is very inefficient. To maximize the average amount of information I transmitted with each symbol, I would have been better advised to adopt a different code. If, for example, I let a 1 stand for the marker's being on a red square, and a 0 for the marker's being on a black square, then each transmission would have carried 1 bit of information (reducing the possibilities at s from 64 to 32) and the average rate of transmission would have been 1 bit.

As we have repeatedly stressed, in most applications of information theory the important quantity is the *average* amount of information generated at a source and the *average* amount of information transmitted about this source. Engineers are interested in devising the most efficient code for *maximizing the average* rate of communication. Of the two methods for encoding information about the placement of the marker, the communications engineer would obviously prefer the second. Over the long haul much more information will be communicated by this method than by the first. Nevertheless, we give up something by maximizing the average. What we give up is the possibility of being told by the transmitted signal exactly where the marker is. In the first method we transmit 6 bits of information very infrequently (1/64th of the time), but this particular signal carries *all* the information associated with the marker's being on square 2. We strike out most of the time, but when we do connect we hit a home run. If we adopt the second method, letting a 1 stand for the marker's being on a red square and a 0 for the marker's being on a black square, we consistently transmit 1 bit of information, but *no* signal carries 6 bits of information. Hence, no signal is capable of telling the recipient exactly where the marker is. For someone interested in finding out exactly where the marker is, the first method of encoding information is to be preferred. It does not tell you what you want to know very often, but at least it *sometimes* tells you. To adopt the other strategy, the most efficient strategy from the engineer's point of view, is to give up the possibility of ever learning, from any signal, exactly where the marker is. To *find out* exactly where the marker is (i.e., which square), one must abandon the engineer's ideal coding system and adopt a much less efficient one.

The same point can be illustrated by the game of Twenty Questions. Usually one has twenty questions (answerable by either "yes" or "no") to discover what one's partner in the game is thinking about. Usually questions are devised to maximize the amount of information provided by each "yes" or "no" answer. One tries to reduce the remaining possibilities by one-half with each question. On information-theoretic grounds this is the most efficient strategy since, on the average, one will obtain the most information by proceeding in this way. Suppose, however, that we change the game slightly and give you only *one* question. Your strategy must now change. It will no longer do to begin with such a question as, "Is it larger than a bread box?" since one *cannot* win this way. One's quota of questions will be exhausted before one ever reaches the key question—e.g., "Is it this pencil?" In this modified game one must simply "shoot in the dark" and begin by asking the only kind of question that can make one a winner: "Is it this pencil?" or "Is it my cat?" The average amount of information one gets from the answers to these questions will be very low (since the answer will almost always be "no"), but the possibility exists of receiving a "yes" answer. And when one receives a "yes" answer, one has succeeded in reducing an indefinitely large number of possibilities to one with a single lucky question. The "yes" answer carries a vast amount of information—*enough* information to make one a winner in this learning enterprise.

All the interesting theorems in communication theory depend on "information" being understood as *average information*. For example, Shannon's fundamental theorem[12] is expressed in terms of a channel's capacity for transmitting information. It must be understood, however, that this theorem is concerned only with the channel's limitations for achieving a certain *average* rate of transmission. Channel capacity is, for this reason, an important magnitude in the study of communication systems, but it is, for the same reason, largely irrelevant to the application of information theory to the study of information as ordinarily understood. For, as we have seen, information is a question of what, and how much, can be learned from a particular signal, and there simply is *no limit* to what can be learned from a particular signal about another state of affairs. As the above example with the marker shows, we can learn from a signal exactly where the marker is even though 6 bits of information is associated with the position of the marker and the channel's "capacity" for transmitting information is 1 bit. Channel capacity (as understood in communication theory) represents no limit to what can be learned over a channel (from a specific signal) and therefore represents no limit to the amount of information (in the ordinary sense) that can be transmitted.[13]

If, then, we want a proper measure for information, we must look to the amount of information contained in particular signals. Communication theory can be exploited to give us a measure of this quantity. Indeed, I have already used this theory (contrary to its intent) to compute the amount of information associated with *individual* signals. With respect to the location of the marker, it was said that a 1 carried 6 bits of information about the marker. A 0 carried only a fraction of 1 bit. These can be viewed as the information-theoretic measures of the amount of information carried by these particular signals, and it is these measures, I submit, that provide us with a convenient measure of the amount of information contained in particular signals. Although the *surprisal* of a given event, $I(s_2)$, and the amount of information carried by a particular signal [e.g., $I_s(1)$] are not significant quantities in engineering applications of information theory (except, perhaps, as mathematical intermediaries for the calculation of entropy), these *are* the important quantities for the study of information, as commonly understood, and hence for the kind of cognitive studies that depend on a semantically related concept of information.

The quantities of interest, then, are the amount of information generated by a particular event or state of affairs s_a:

(2.1) $$I(s_a) = \log 1/p(s_a)$$

and the amount of information carried by a particular signal r_a about s_a:

(2.2) $$I_s(r_a) = I(s_a) - E(r_a)$$

where $E(r_a)$ is understood to be the equivocation associated with the particular signal r_a [defined in accordance with (1.8) from Chapter 1]—hereafter referred to as simply the equivocation of the signal r_a.

It should be emphasized (if only for the benefit of those who will accuse me of *mis*representing, or *mis*understanding, communication theory) that the above formulas are now being assigned a significance, given an interpretation, that they do not have in standard applications of communication theory. They are now being used to define the amount of information associated with particular events and signals. Such an interpretation is foreign to (but, I would urge, perfectly consistent with) orthodox uses of these formulas. In standard applications of communication theory the interest centers on the *source* of information and the *channel* for transmitting this information, and for purposes of describing these aspects of communication, there is no reason to be interested in the particular messages transmitted. But we are here concerned with the particular messages, the particular content, the *information*, that gets transmitted from a source over a channel. And for understanding this commodity it is, I submit, formulas (2.1) and (2.2) that hold the key.

COMMUNICATION RESTRICTIONS ON THE FLOW OF INFORMATION

It may seem as though (2.1) and (2.2) are not very useful tools. Aside from contrived examples involving games (or in applications to telecommunications systems in which there is some theoretically restricted range of possibilities with their associated probabilities) the use of these formulas to compute amounts of information seems hopeless. How, for example, do we calculate the amount of information generated by Edith's playing tennis? And how much information about her activities is contained in the light reaching Herman—a casual spectator?

In order to answer questions like this in accordance with (2.1) and (2.2) one needs to know: (1) the alternative possibilities (e.g., Edith's eating lunch, Edith's showering); (2) the associated probabilities of all these alternative possibilities; (3) the conditional probabilities (given the configuration of photons reaching Herman's visual receptors) of each of these alternative possibilities. Obviously, in most ordinary communication settings one knows none of this. It is not even very clear whether one *could* know it. What, after all, are the alternative possibilities to Edith's playing tennis? Presumably there are some things that are possible (e.g., Edith going to the hairdresser instead of playing tennis) and some things that are not possible (e.g., Edith turning into a tennis ball), but how does one begin to catalog these possibilities? If Edith might be jogging, shall we count this as *one* alternative possibility? Or shall we count it as more than one, since she could be jogging almost anywhere, at a variety of different speeds, in almost any direction?

These difficulties in applying (2.1) and (2.2) to concrete situations (situations of interest to someone, like myself, trying to formulate a theory of knowledge) may seem formidable indeed, but as we shall see, they represent obstacles only to an overambitious use of these formulas. If one seeks an *absolute measure*, a *definite numerical figure*, for the amount of information generated by an event or carried by a signal, one must be in a position to determine the range of possibilities and their associated probabilities. In some engineering applications of communication theory these conditions are met.[14] But in most ordinary situations in which information is transmitted we can only make clumsy guesses about the amount of information being generated and transmitted. Even this is an exaggeration. There may not be an answer to the question: How much information is being transmitted? There may not be answer to this question because there may be no *well-defined* range of alternative possibilities in terms of which this figure could be calculated.

Despite these limitations, formulas (2.1) and (2.2) have an important use. They can be used to make *comparisons*, in particular comparisons between the amount of information generated by the occurrence of an event and the amount of information a signal carries about that event. Such comparisons can be made without ever determining absolute values for either magnitude. That is, one can use these formulas in the way one would use a piece of string that is not marked off in inches and feet. One can use the string to determine whether A is longer than B without ever determining the length of either A or B.

For example, if I tell you that Denny lives on Adams Street in Madison, Wisconsin, I give you *more information* than if I tell you, simply, that he lives in Madison, Wisconsin. In order to use (2.2) to authenticate this intuitive judgment it is not necessary to know the number of possible places that Denny can live—not even the number of possible places he can live in Madison, Wisconsin. All one has to know is that the number of possible places to live in Madison, Wisconsin, is greater than the number of possible places to live on Adams Street in Madison, Wisconsin. If this is so, and I do not see how it can fail to be so (knowing what I do about Madison), then the equivocation associated with the first message is *less than* the equivocation associated with the second. Therefore, (2.2) tells us that the first message carries *more information* about where Denny lives than does the second.

Or consider another possible use of formula (2.2)—a use that is of crucial importance to our (eventual) definition of a signal's *informational content*. We want to know, not how much information is generated by the occurrence of s_a, *not* how much information

r_a carries about the occurrence of this event, but whether r_a carries *as much* information about s_a as is generated by its occurrence. In order to answer this question, one does not have to know the value of $I(s_a)$ or the value of $I_s(r_a)$. Inspection of formula (2.2) shows that all one has to know is whether the equivocation is zero or not. If the equivocation $E(r_a)$ is 0, the signal carries *as much information* about the source as is generated at the source by the occurrence of s_a. If, on the other hand, the equivocation is positive, the signal carries *less information* than that associated with s_a's occurrence.

This *comparative* use of formula (2.2) is the only essential use to which it will be put throughout this essay. The epistemological application of communication theory, and in particular the use of this theory in developing an account of a signal's *informational content* (the *message* it bears), does not require that we know whether a subject has received 20, 200, or 2,000 bits of information. All it requires (quantitatively) is that the subject receive *as much information* as is generated by the state of affairs he knows to obtain. For a proper determination of these matters the absolute values of $I(s_a)$ and $I_s(r_a)$ are irrelevant. What we want to know is whether $I_s(r_a)$ is less than or equal to $I(s_a)$.

It cannot be stressed too strongly, however, that the set of conditional probabilities defining the equivocation between source and receiver are meant to be *objective* features of the communication system. We may not *know* what these conditional probabilities are, we may not be *able* to determine what they are, but this is irrelevant to the actual value of the equivocation and therefore irrelevant to whether the signal carries as much information as the source generates.[15] Our earlier example should help to make this clear. When the employees agreed to name Herman on their note to the boss if Shirley was selected, it was said that the note carried *only* 2 bits of information about the outcome of the selection process. The note reduced the number of possibilities from 8 to 2 (Herman or Shirley). The employer, of course, *believed* that the note was unequivocal. In information-theoretic terms he believed the note carried 3 bits of information. He was simply wrong. How much information a message carries is *not* a function of how much information the recipient thinks it carries. It is a function, simply, of the actual possibilities that exist at s and the conditional probabilities of these various possibilities after the message has been received. In another example, the messenger lost the memo and composed a new one with the name "Herman" on it. It was said that this memo carried *no* information about the employees' decision. Once again, the value of $I_s(r_a)$ is independent of what the recipient of r_a happens to *believe* about r_a's informational content.

We shall, later in this essay, and in conformity with many information-processing models of human cognition, think of an organism's sensory systems as channels for the receipt of information about their external environment. At the appropriate time, the question of skepticism will have to be faced. But skeptical issues should not be allowed to intrude prematurely. They are *not* relevant to what information, or how much information, has been received. Even if, following Hume, we regard the organism as trapped within the circle of its own perceptions, we cannot conclude that these perceptions are devoid of information. Even if one agrees with Hume that:

> The mind never has anything present to it but the perceptions, and cannot possibly reach any experience of their connection with objects. The supposition of such a connection is, therefore, without any foundation in reasoning,[16]

one cannot conclude, as apparently F. J. Crosson does conclude, that according to Hume's theory one cannot regard the senses as information channels because "we have no independent access to the input data and their probabilities, and hence no conditional probabilities."[17] The *most* that follows from Hume's theory is that we can never *determine* what the conditional probabilities are—hence, never determine whether our perceptions *do* contain information about our surroundings. But this is quite compatible with our perceptual experience being rich in information about our physical surroundings. A signal from a distant, and rapidly receding, galaxy is not devoid of information simply because we are incapable of determining what the relevant conditional probabilities are, and hence what information (or *how much* information) the signal contains. For the amount of information contained in the signal depends, *not* on the conditional probabilities that *we can independently verify*, but on the conditional probabilities themselves.

Neither is the information contained in a signal dependent on the receiver's actually learning something from that signal.[18] The recipient may not be able to *decode* or *interpret* the message. Or he may *think* he can decode it but do so incorrectly. If I may be allowed to use my old example once again, the employees could have communicated with their employer in code. They might have arranged to write the name "Herman" on the memo if Shirley was selected, the name "Shirley" if Doris was selected, the name "Doris" if Emil was selected, and so on. When the memo arrives on the employer's desk with the name "Barbara" (code name for Herman) on it, the memo *contains the same amount of information* about the outcome of the selection process as it did when the employees were using the conventional code ("Herman" for Herman).[19] But if the employer is not apprised of the code, he will mistakenly conclude that Barbara was the nominee. He will *misinterpret* the message. But his misinterpretation does not mean that the memo did not unequivocally specify the nominee, did not contain the information about who was selected. One simply has to know the code to extract this information.[20]

With these preliminaries out of the way we are finally in a position to articulate a principle about the flow of information, a principle that will, when supplemented by what we already know about communication theory, guide us in the formulation of a genuine semantic theory of information in the next chapter.

Xerox principle: If *A* carries the information that *B*, and *B* carries the information that *C*, then *A* carries the information that *C*.

I take this to be a regulative principle, something inherent in and essential to the ordinary idea of information, something that any *theory* of information should preserve. For if one can learn from *A* that *B*, and one can learn from *B* that *C*, then one should be *able* to learn from *A* that *C* (whether one *does* learn it or not is another matter).

I have named the principle to suggest its most obvious illustration. Xerox copies of a pamphlet (containing the information that *C*) carry the same information (i.e., that *C*) as does the original pamphlet as long as they are accurate copies—as long as the copies carry accurate information about the words, diagrams, and figures in the original pamphlet. One does not *lose* information by duplicating something that contains information—not, at least, if the duplicates carry accurate information about the original vehicle of information. This is really all the xerox principle says. If a stream of photons carries the information that the light is on, and the light's being on carries the information that the switch is closed, then the stream of photons carries the information that the switch is closed.

The xerox principle is absolutely fundamental to the *flow* of information. The acoustic waves emanating from a radio speaker carry information about what is happening at the broadcasting studio *because* they carry accurate information about what is happening in the audio circuit of the receiver; these events, in turn, carry information about the modulation of the electromagnetic signal arriving at the antenna; and the latter carries information about the manner in which the microphone diaphragm (in the broadcasting studio) is vibrating. The microphone's behavior, in turn, carries information about what the announcer is saying. This whole chain of events constitutes a communication system, a system whose output carries information about its input, because of iterated applications of the xerox principle. The same principle finds an application in ordinary oral communications. I receive information about your activities last summer, and thereby learn that you visited Italy, in virtue of the fact that (if you are honest) your utterances carry information about your beliefs and (if you know whereof you speak) your beliefs carry information about what you did last summer.[21] Without the xerox principle the links in these communication chains could never hold the ends together.

I shall assume, then, without further argument, that any account of the information carried by a signal must preserve the validity of the xerox principle. What does this tell us about the informational content of a signal? It tells us that if a signal is to carry the information that s is F (where s denotes some item at the source), then the *amount* of information that the signal carries about s must be equal to the amount of information generated by s's being F. If s's being F generates 3 bits of information, no signal that carries only 2 bits of information about s can possibly carry the information that s is F.

For suppose, contrary to what we wish to show, that a signal could carry information in the face of positive equivocation, could carry the information that s is F despite carrying *less* information than that associated with s's being F. This would mean that A could carry the information that B, and B could carry the information that C, despite the fact that there was positive equivocation between A and B and positive equivocation between B and C. A little information is lost in the transmission from C to B (but not *enough* is lost to interfere with the transmission of the information that C), and a little information is lost in the transmission from B to A (but not enough is lost to interfere with the reception, at A, of the information that B). These losses can be made to add up.[22] The amount of information at A about C can easily be made *less than* the amount of information at B about C. As we add links to this communication chain in this fashion, the amount of information available about C grows progressively smaller. The distant links in the communication chain will carry virtually *no* information about C (an amount of information as close to zero as we please), but they will carry *enough* information about the preceding link to keep the message intact according to the xerox principle. Communication theory tells us that the distant links of this communication chain will carry progressively smaller amounts of information about C (since the small equivocations that exist between the adjacent links accumulate to make a large amount of equivocation between the end points). Our xerox principle tells us, on the other hand, that if each link in the chain carries the appropriate piece of information about its predecessor (A carries the information that B, B carries the information that C), then the *final link* will carry the *same information* about the first link (viz., that C) as does the second link B. The only way to preserve the xerox principle in the face of the vanishing amount of information is to concede that a signal can carry a message (e.g., the information that C) despite an overwhelming amount of equivocation, despite the fact that the signal carries only a *negligible amount* of information about the source. But this is absurd.

It is absurd because it means that *no* degree of correlation, *no* amount of dependency, between source and receiver is necessary for the transmission of a message. *Any* correlation (short of complete randomness) between source and receiver is good enough

KNOWLEDGE AND THE FLOW OF INFORMATION

for the communication of content. As we have seen, a signal carries *some* information about s if there is some degree of dependency between it and what takes place at s, if it alters (in any small way) the distribution of probabilities of the various possibilities at s. But we must surely resist the idea that a signal can carry the information, say, that s_2 (one of a hundred different equally likely possibilities) occurred if it raises the probability of s_2's occurring from .01 to .02 and lowers the probability of the remaining 99 possibilities commensurately. Such a signal *cannot tell* you what happened at the source. Even if s_2 *did* occur, you *cannot learn* from a signal of this sort that it did occur. The signal carries *some* information about the source, but *not enough* to carry the message that s_2 occurred.

What communication theory (together, of course, with the xerox principle) tells us is that for the communication of *content*, for the transmission of a *message*, not just any amount of information will do. One needs *all* the information associated with that content. If an event's occurrence generates X bits of information, then a signal must carry at least X bits of information if it is to bear the information that that event occurred. Anything short of X bits is *too little* to support this message. Any attempt to settle for less than X bits implies either a rejection of the xerox principle or acceptance of the view that informational content (a message) can be transmitted *no matter how little* information (greater than zero) is conveyed. Since both alternatives are objectionable, we conclude that for a signal to carry an X-bit message about a source (e.g., the message that s is F where s's being F generates X bits of information), the signal must carry at least X bits of information about s.

Getting a message through is like being pregnant—an all or nothing affair. When dealing with *amounts* of information, one can speak of any amount one pleases; it makes sense to say that 0, 43, or 100 percent of the information generated at the source reaches the receiver. But when dealing with the message itself, the information that comes in these amounts, the information is either transmitted in toto or it is not transmitted at all. When talking about *content*, it does not make sense to speak of transmitting 99 percent of the information *that* it is raining.

This does not mean that a signal must tell us *everything* about a source to tell us *something*. A signal can be equivocal and still carry a message. In one of the situations described in the first chapter, the employees decided to name Herman on their note to the employer if either Herman or Shirley was selected. When the note arrived on the employer's desk bearing the name "Herman," it was said that it carried only 2 bits of information about which employee was nominated. Since Herman's selection generated 3 bits of information, the memo had an equivocation of 1 bit. This is how much information was lost. It was hinted at the time (and we are now in a position to see why) that therefore the memo did not carry the information *that Herman was selected*. The 2-bit memo could not carry this 3-bit message. Nevertheless, in accordance with our present vantage point, the memo can carry a 2-bit message. This, in turn, conforms nicely with our intuitive judgment that the memo carried the information *that either Herman or Shirley was selected*. For the state of affairs described by "Either Herman or Shirley is selected" is a state of affairs that has an informational measure of 2 bits (constituting a reduction of 8 equally likely possibilities to 2). Hence, our memorandum, though equivocal about exactly who was selected, is capable of carrying the information that it was either Herman or Shirley.

What this indicates is something that should be perfectly obvious on other grounds; viz., that whether or not a signal is equivocal depends on how we carve up the possibilities at the source. My king is on KB-3. Its being on this particular square generates (let us say) 6 bits of information, since there are 64 possibilities. We could also describe the position of this piece in a less determinate fashion. We could, for instance, describe my king as being on a black square. In this case we are talking about a state of affairs (king's being on a black square) that has an informational measure of only 1 bit (there being only two possibilities: black square or white square). A signal might carry only 1 bit of information about the position of my king. Is the signal equivocal? Relative to the first description (king on KB-3), yes. Relative to the second description (king on black square), no. Relative to the first description, the signal has 5 bits of equivocation; relative to the second description it has 0 bits of equivocation. But in *both* cases it carries 1 bit of information about the location of the king.

What communication theory tells us about the information in a signal is *not* that the equivocation of that signal must be 0 in order to carry a message. For whether or not the equivocation is 0 will depend on how we specify the possibilities at the source. It is relative to *how we describe* the event at the source about which information is being transmitted. What communication theory tells us is that the *amount of information* a signal carries about a source sets an upper bound on *what information* a signal can carry about that source. The 1-bit signal described above can carry the message that my king is on a black square, but it *cannot* carry the message that it is on KB-3. This consequence is independent of how finely we divide up the possibilities at the source. By multiplying the number of possibilities at the source (by more detailed and specific descriptions of the ensemble of possibilities) one increases the equivocation E of potential signals, but one also increases the value of $I(s)$—the information generated at the source. Since the amount of information *transmitted* [see formula (1.5)] is $I(s)$ *minus* E, the amount of information transmitted is unaffected. And it is this magnitude that is instrumental in determining the kind of informational content that can be transmitted.[23]

This result, so tediously arrived at, may strike some readers as trivial. If being trivial means being obviously *true*, I hope it impresses *all* readers this way. For we shall, in the next chapter, use this result to render an account of a signal's informational *content*. Once this is achieved, we will be in a position to provide a unified, information-theoretic analysis of a number of key epistemological ideas. However trivial the present result may seem, it has remarkably powerful consequences for a variety of stubborn epistemological problems. After examining these consequences, readers may wish to reevaluate whatever concessions they are now prepared to make.

Chapter 3
A Semantic Theory of Information

Our discussion in the last chapter revealed two conditions that a definition of information must satisfy. The first, the communication condition, is that if a signal carries the information that s is F, then it must be the case that

(A) The signal carries as much information about s as would be generated by s's being F.

So, for example, if s's being a particular color generates 2 bits of information, no signal can carry the information that s is a particular color (red, say) unless it carries *at least* 2 bits of information. Obviously, however, this condition, though necessary, is not sufficient. A signal can carry 2 bits of information about s's color without carrying the information that s is red. For if (contrary to fact) s was blue, the signal would carry 2 bits of information about s's color *without* carrying the information that s was red. In such a case the signal does not carry the information that s is red despite carrying as much information (2 bits) about the color of s as would be generated by s's being red. A further condition is required. If a signal carries the information that s is F, it must be the case that:

(B) s is F

Recall, Herman's selection generates the same amount of information (3 bits) as would be generated by the selection of any other employee. To be told that the memo to the employer carries 3 bits of information is *not* to be told that it carries the information that Herman was selected. For the memo could carry 3 bits of information without Herman's having been selected. It could carry the information that Shirley was selected. In order to carry the information that Herman was selected, it must be the case that Herman *was* selected.

(A) and (B), then, are individually necessary. But they are not jointly sufficient. Suppose s is a red square. Its being red generates 3 bits of information and its being square generates 3 bits of independent information. A signal is transmitted carrying the information that s is square but not the information that s is red. In this case the signal carries as much information about s as would be generated by s's being red, and s is red, but the signal lacks this information.

Something else is needed. The trouble is that although a signal carries X bits of information about s, and although s's being F generates X bits of information, the signal, as it were, carries the *wrong* X bits to carry the information that s is F. A signal must not only carry enough information; it has to carry the *right* information. To rectify this deficiency, something like the following condition must be met:

(C) The quantity of information the signal carries about s is (or includes) that quantity generated by s's being F (and not, say, by s's being G).

(B) and (C) together constitute what I shall call the semantic conditions on information. The formulation of (C) leaves much to be desired. It is not clear, for example, what it could mean to say that one quantity (amount of information the signal carries) is (or includes) another quantity (amount of information generated) when this is meant to imply something more than a numerical comparison. Nevertheless, (C) will do for the moment. It is not meant to be a clarification of anything. It is merely intended to mark, in a suggestive way, the need for something beyond (A) and

(B)—a need that should be apparent from the fact that (A) and (B) do not *suffice* to determine the information carried by a signal.

What follows is a definition of the information contained in a signal that simultaneously satisfies these three conditions. It also picks up a feature of information that was briefly alluded to in Chapter 2—the fact that what information is transmitted may depend on what the receiver already knows about the possibilities existing at the source. In formulating this definition, I will speak of a *signal* carrying information, but it should be understood that r can be any event, condition, or state of affairs the existence (occurrence) of which may depend on s's being F. It will be assumed, furthermore, that s's being F is always a condition that has some positive amount of information associated with it (there are possible alternatives to s's being F). We will return to the question of necessary or essential properties, properties whose possession by s generates zero information, in a later chapter.

> *Informational content*: A signal r carries the information that
> s is F = The conditional probability of s's being F, given r
> (and k), is 1 (but, given k alone, less than 1)

The parenthetical k will be explained in a moment. It is meant to stand for what the receiver already knows (if anything) about the possibilities that exist at the source. So, for example, if one already knows that s is either red or blue, a signal that eliminates s's being blue as a possibility (reduces this probability to 0) carries the information that s is red (since it increases this probability to 1). For someone who does not know that s is either red or blue (given what they know, it could be green), the *same signal* might *not* carry the information that s was red.

This definition is, I submit, the only one that will simultaneously satisfy conditions (A), (B), and (C). The definition satisfies (A) because if the conditional probability of s's being F (given r) is 1, then the equivocation of this signal must be 0 and [in accordance with formula (1.5)] the signal must carry *as much* information about s, $I_s(r)$, as is generated by s's being F, $I(s_F)$. Condition (B) is satisfied because if the conditional probability of s's being F is 1, then s *is* F.[1] And condition (C) is satisfied because whatever *other* quantities of information the signal may carry about s, our definition assures us that the signal includes the *right* quantity (the quantity associated with s's being F) in virtue of excluding just those situations that motivated the imposition of this requirement.

Of course, the fact that our definition satisfies these three conditions does not imply that it is the *only* definition of informational content that will satisfy them. I think it is evident, however, that nothing else will do. It may be thought, for example, that one could lower the demands by requiring only a conditional probability of, say, something greater than .9 (or .99 or .999). This modified definition would not satisfy condition (B), since a state of affairs (s's being F) need not exist to have a probability of .9 (or .999). This defect might be repaired by appending, as a separate clause in the definition, a stipulation to the effect that s *be* F, but condition (A) would still remain unsatisfied. For if a signal could carry the information that s is F while raising the probability of s's being F to *only* .9 (or .999), then the signal could carry this information while carrying *less* information (quantitatively) than is generated by s's being F—a clear violation of (A).[2] There may be other ways to formulate the above definition, but if the definition satisfies conditions (A), (B), and (C) it will, I submit, be found equivalent to the one already given.

The informational content of a signal is being expressed in the form "s is F" where the letter s is understood to be an *indexical* or *demonstrative* element referring to some item at the source. What the definition gives us is an account of what philosophers might call the signal's *de re* informational content, a content that might (more revealingly) be expressed by saying that r carries the information *of* or *about s* that it is F. This content is called a *de re* (versus a *de dicto*) content because what is being described when we describe a signal's informational content is a relation between what is expressed by an open sentence ("... is F") and some individual s.[3] A lowercase constant (usually s to suggest *source*) is used in the verbal expression of a signal's informational content to emphasize that we are concerned, *not* with the manner in which we may happen to describe or refer to this individual, but with the individual s itself. A signal's *de re* informational content is determined by two things: (1) the individual s about which the signal carries information, and (2) the information (determined by the open sentence "... is F") it carries about that individual. What descriptive phrase we happen to use (in the verbal expression of a signal's informational content) to refer to the individual about which information is carried is irrelevant. So, for example, if we describe the information carried by a signal as the information that my grandmother is smiling, it should be understood that the signal need not carry the information that the person is my grandmother (or even that she is *a woman* or *a person*). Rather, the signal is being described as carrying information *about* my grandmother, information to the effect that she is smiling. Of course, the signal might also carry the information that she is my grandmother. In this case the signal carries the information that *s* is my grandmother and is smiling—information we might express by saying that the signal carries the information that my grandmother is smiling. But, generally speaking, it is *only* the descriptive or conceptual elements embodied in the *predicate* expression (". . . is *F*") that reflect the informational content of the signal. The subject term merely attaches that content to a particular individual.

Signals can therefore differ in the information they carry in two ways. If r_1 carries the information that *s* is *F* and r_2 carries the information that *s* is *G*, then (assuming *F* and *G* give expression to independent features or characteristics) they carry different pieces of information. In addition, however, r_1 may carry the information that *s* is *F* while r_2 carries the information that *t*, a different individual, is *F*. This also constitutes a different piece of information. The information that *this* is white differs from the information that *that* is white as long as *this* is not identical to *that*.[4]

Throughout this work attention will be restricted to propositional contents of the *de re* variety. When we turn to the analysis of knowledge and belief, cognitive attitudes that take a propositional content, we will similarly be concerned with these contents in their *de re* manifestations. That is, we will be concerned with knowing or believing *of* something that it is *F* where the something which is known or believed to be *F* is determined by perceptual factors (see Chapter 6 under 'The Objects of Perception'). This restriction allows us to sidestep some thorny problems associated with the analysis of *de dicto* propositional contents—contents of the form "The *S* is *F*" where the content is, in part at least, a function of the meaning of the term or phrase ("The *S*") used to designate the item which is *F*. Nevertheless, although certain

problems are avoided by this maneuver,[5] the present account as-
pires to a degree of completeness. For it is assumed, and in later
chapters will be argued, that *de re* beliefs and knowledge are more
fundamental than their *de dicto* counterparts. And, as I hope to
show, a theory of a signal's *de re* information content suffices for
the analysis of our *de re* beliefs and knowledge.

A survey of the examples already used will show that the above
definition of a signal's informational content gives an intuitively
satisfying result in each case. One example, in particular, should be
mentioned, since it illustrates the rather subtle discriminations of
which our definition is capable. When Herman was selected by the
employees, but they had decided to name Herman on their note
to the employer if *either* Herman or Shirley was selected, communication theory told us that the note carried only 2 bits of
information about which employee had been selected (1 bit of
equivocation). But although this theory tells us *how much* information the note carries, it does not tell us *what* information it
carries. As far as this quantitative theory is concerned, the memo
could carry a variety of different messages as long as these messages have a measure of 2 bits. So, for example, the memo might
carry the information *that either Herman or Shirley was selected*
(2 bits) or it might carry the information *that either Herman or
Donald was selected* (2 bits). Both these possible messages are *true*
(since Herman was selected). Hence, both qualify as *information*
the memo might carry. Our definition of a signal's propositional
content neatly distinguishes between these two possible messages.
It fixes on *Herman* or *Shirley* as the content rather than *Herman*
or *Donald* because the former possibility (given the name appearing on the memo) has a probability of 1 while the latter possibility
has a probability of only .5. This meshes nicely with our pre-
analytic intuitions that the memo carries the information that
either Herman or Shirley was selected. It does not carry the information that either Herman or Donald was selected despite the fact
that either Herman or Donald *was* selected and the memo carries
(quantitatively) *enough* information (2 bits) to handle this message.

Up to this point examples have been carefully chosen so as to
always yield an identifiable content. Not all signals, however, have
an informational content that lends itself so neatly and economi-
cally to propositional expression. Suppose that *s* can be in any one

of four different states, each of which is equally likely: A, B, C, and D. Suppose, furtheremore, that s occupies state B and a signal r carries 1 bit of information about the situation at s. There are a variety of ways a signal can carry 1 bit of information about the condition of s. It might, for example, reduce the probability of A and D to 0, leaving B and C equally likely. In this event the signal carries 1 bit of information and (according to our definition) carries the information that s is in either state B or C. But the signal might also shift the configuration of probabilities in such a way as to yield 1 bit of information. If, for example, the conditional probabilities are:

$$P(A/r) = .07$$
$$P(B/r) = .80$$
$$P(C/r) = .07$$
$$P(D/r) = .06$$

then an application of formula (1.8) reveals that the equivocation of r is 1 bit. Hence, r carries 1 bit of information about the condition of s. What is the *content* of this signal? What is the message? We obviously cannot suppose that the signal carries the information that s is in state B because, even though s *is* in state B, this condition generates 2 bits of information and our signal carries only 1 bit. Neither can we suppose that the signal carries the information (say) that s is in either state B or state C. For although s *is* in either state B or state C, and although this condition has a measure of only 1 bit, our definition tells us that this is *not* the 1 bit of information that the signal carries (since the probability of this state is less than 1). There is not, in fact, any unqualified way of expressing the information carried by this signal. The best we can do in such cases is to say that the signal carries the information that s is *probably* in state B. This comes the closest to satisfying our definition of informational content, since (we may suppose) the conditional probability of s's *probably being* B, given r, is unity. I am not sure it makes sense to talk this way. It is silly, of course, to think of s's *probably being* B as itself a condition of s that we could receive information about, as something that could have a conditional probability of 1 and therefore qualify as the informational content of a signal. But this is not the point. When there is no sentence describing the situation that does exist at the

source which satisfies our definition of informational content, and
we nonetheless wish to give propositional expression to the quantity of information that is transmitted, we are forced to adopt the
expedient of talking about the fact that *something is probably so*
as the informational content of a signal.

This result should not be viewed as a weakness of our definition
of a signal's informational content. Quite the contrary. It reflects,
I think, a common practice in expressing the information we receive. Some bridge partnerships, for example, *never* open the bidding in a major suit (hearts or spades) unless they have at least five
cards in that suit. An opening bid of "1 heart" from a member of
such a pair therefore carries the information they have *five or
more* hearts. Other pairs will occasionally open a major suit with
as few as four cards in the suit. Their bid tells you that they have
four or more cards in that suit—*less* information than in the first
case, but still a significant piece of information. Some players,
however, occasionally indulge in "psychic" bids (having little or
nothing corresponding to the conventional meaning of their bid).
A bid of "1 heart" from such a player tells you even less about the
character of the hand. Even if they *normally* have five (or more)
hearts for their bid, their occasional psychic bids degrade the information carried by their bid to such a point that it is difficult to
say exactly what information is communicated. The most one can
say about it is that the person *probably* has five (or more) hearts,
perhaps as few as four, and *possibly* none. By way of giving propositional expression to the information communicated by such a
bid, this is about the best one can do.

It is important to notice that, generally speaking, it makes little
sense to speak of *the* informational content of a signal. For if a
signal carries the information that s is F, and s's being F carries, in
turn, the information that s is G (or t is H), then this same signal
also carries the information that s is G (or t is H). For example, if
r carries the information that s is a square, then it also carries the
information that s is a rectangle. This is so because if the conditional probability (given r) of s's being a square is 1, then the conditional probability (given r) of s's being a rectangle is also 1.
Furthermore such a signal will also carry the information that s is
a quadrilateral, a parallelogram, *not* a circle, *not* a pentagon, a
square *or* a circle, and so on. Similarly, if the mercury's expansion

carries the information that the temperature is rising, then any signal carrying the information that the mercury is expanding also carries the information that the temperature is rising. This is what makes thermometers useful devices for telling the temperature. In general, if there is a natural law to the effect that whenever s is F, t is G (thus making the conditional probability of t's being G, given s's being F, 1), then no signal can bear the message that s is F without also conveying the information that t is G.

This point may be expressed by saying that if a signal carries the information that s is F, it also carries all the information *nested in s's being F*. This follows immediately from our definition of a signal's informational content and the following definition of the nesting relation:

The information that t is G is nested in s's being F = s's being F carries the information that t is G.

I shall occasionally find it convenient to distinguish between information that is *analytically* nested in a state of affairs and information that is *nomically* nested in a state of affairs (nested in virtue of certain *natural laws*). In using this terminology I mean nothing very deep or profound. I certainly do not intend to be adopting a position on the philosophically controversial analytic-synthetic distinction. This terminology is merely a device to mark certain apparent differences in the way information can be nested. Whether these apparent differences are really differences in kind, or merely differences along some continuous dimension of a single kind, is of no importance for anything that follows. For present purposes what is important is *that* one piece of information can be nested in another, not *how* it is nested. The terminology is suggestive, however, and it will prove useful in our discussion of belief and concept formation in Part III. For this reason I will frequently distinguish between these two forms of the nesting relation even when nothing much depends on the distinction. So, for example, I will say that the information that s is a rectangle (or *not* a circle, or *either* a square *or* a circle) is analytically nested in s's being a square. On the other hand, the fact that I weigh over 160 pounds is nomically nested (if it is nested at all) in the reading of my bathroom scale.

It makes little sense, therefore, to speak of *the* informational content of a signal as though this was unique. Generally speaking, a signal carries a great variety of different informational contents, a great variety of different pieces of information, and although these pieces of information may be related to each other (e.g., logically), they are nonetheless *different* pieces of information. The acoustic signal that tells us someone is at our door carries not only the information that someone is at the door but also the information that the door button is depressed, that electricity is flowing through the doorbell circuit, that the clapper on the doorbell is vibrating, and much else besides. Indeed, all the information that is nested (analytically or nomically) in these states of affairs is also part of the acoustic signal's informational content. No single piece of information is entitled to the status of *the* informational content of the signal. The receiver of the signal may be more *interested* in one piece of information than he is in any other, he may succeed in *extracting* one piece of information without another, but these differences are irrelevant to the information the signal contains.

This feature of information serves to distinguish it sharply from the concept of *meaning*—at least the concept of meaning relevant to semantic studies of language and belief. The statement "Joe is at home" may be said to mean that Joe is at home (whatever the person who made it happened to mean or intend by making it). It certainly does not mean that Joe is either at home or at the office. The statement *implies* that Joe is either at home or at the office, but this is not what it means. On the other hand, if the statement carries the information that Joe is at home, it thereby carries the information that Joe is either at home or at the office. It cannot communicate the one piece of information without communicating the other. The one piece of information is analytically nested in the other.

The distinction between meaning and information becomes even more evident when we examine cases of nomically nested information. Assuming it to be a law of nature that water expands upon freezing, no signal can carry the information that some body of water is freezing without carrying the information that this body of water is expanding. But the statement, "This body of water is freezing" can *mean* that this body of water is freezing without *meaning* that this body of water is expanding.

It may seem as though the informational content of a signal is threatening to overflow. Our discussion has revealed that when a signal *r* carries the information that *s* is *F*, it also carries the information that *s* (or *t*) is *G* when the fact that *s* (or *t*) is *G* is nested (either analytically or nomically) in *s*'s being *F*. Signals, it seems, are pregnant with information. And so they are. Nevertheless, there is obviously an enormous amount of information that a signal fails to carry. We have already encountered numerous instances of this. Under one set of circumstances the memo to the employer carried *no* information about who the employees selected. In another instance, although Herman was selected, and although the memo carried the name "Herman," it failed to carry the information that Herman was selected. It carried only the information that either Herman or Shirley was selected.

Any signal that contains the information that *s* is water thereby contains the information that *s* is composed of H_2O molecules. This assumes that the conditional probability of *s*'s being composed of H_2O molecules, given that it is water, is unity, but there is every reason to make this assumption. As long as the assumption is true, regardless of whether we know it to be true, the fact that *s* is composed of H_2O molecules is information that arrives with every signal carrying the information that *s* is water. But, even if the water is salty, a signal need not carry the information that *s* is salty water just because it carries the information *s* is water. For the conditional probability of *s*'s being *salty* water may be less than 1 despite the fact that the conditional probability of *s*'s being water is 1 and *s* is, as a matter of fact, salty.

The last example is instructive because it reveals that truth alone, even when the truth in question is a perfectly *general* truth expressing an exceptionless uniformity, is not sufficient for the purposes of transmitting information. Correlations, even pervasive correlations, are *not* to be confused with informational relations. Even if the properties *F* and *G* are perfectly correlated (whatever is *F* is *G* and vice versa), this does not mean that there is information in *s*'s being *F* about *s*'s being *G* (or vice versa). It does not mean that a signal carrying the information that *s* is F also carries the information that s is G. For the correlation between F and G may be the sheerest coincidence, a correlation whose persistence is not assured by any law of nature or principle of logic. All Fs can be G without the probability of s's being G, given that it is F, being 1.

To illustrate this point, suppose that all Herman's children have the measles. Despite the "correlation," a signal might well carry the information that Alice is one of Herman's children without carrying the information that Alice has the measles. Presumably the fact that all Herman's children (living in different parts of the country) happened to contract the measles at the same time does not make the probability of their having the measles, given their common parentage, 1. Since this is so, a signal can carry the information that Alice is one of Herman's children without carrying the information that she has the measles despite the fact that all Herman's children have the measles. It is this fact about information that helps to explain (as we will see in Part II) why we are sometimes in a position to see that (hence, know that) s is F *without being able* to tell whether s is G despite the fact that every F is G. Recognizing Alice as one of Herman's children is not good enough for a medical diagnosis no matter what *happens* to be true of Herman's children. It is diagnostically significant only if the correlation is a manifestation of a *nomic* (e.g., genetic) regularity between being one of Herman's children and having the measles.

The same point is, perhaps, easier to appreciate if one thinks of two communication systems: A-B and C-D. A transmits to B and C transmits to D. Quite by chance, and at exactly the same time, A pecks out exactly the same message (sequence of dots and dashes) to B that C does to D. Assuming that no other messages are ever transmitted, and assuming that the channels are perfectly reliable (B receives accurate replicas of what A transmits and D receives accurate replicas of what C transmits), there is a perfect correlation (over all time) between what A transmits and what D receives. Yet, despite this correlation, D receives *no* information from A. To make this even more vivid, we could imagine system A-B separated by hundreds of light-years from system C-D. Physically, there is no basis for communication. Still, the correlation between what transpires at A and D is perfect (at least as perfect as what transpires between A and B). The conclusion is inescapable that perfect correlation does not suffice for the transmission of information. The reason A does *not* communicate with D, but *does* communicate with C, is that there is a *nomic dependence* between what occurs at A and B, but not between what occurs at A and D, and it is these *nomic dependencies* that determine the amount of information (and, hence, indirectly *what* information) flows between two points. If the conditional probability of C's transmitting a dash, given that A transmits a dash, is such as to make this a matter of pure chance (as we assumed in supposing that A's and C's transmission of the same message was purely coincidental), then the conditional probability of D's receiving a dash, given that A transmitted one, is also such as to make *this* a matter of pure chance. Hence, the equivocation between A and D is at a maximum despite the perfect correlation. No information gets through.

This fact tells us something of fundamental significance about the informational content of a signal. If a signal carries the information that s is F, it does not necessarily carry the information that s is G despite the *extensional* equivalence of "F" and "G." Even though "F" and "G" are true of exactly the same things (have the same *extension*), the information that s is F is different from the information that s is G.

Philosophers have a special terminology for describing such phenomena: *intentionality* (or, if we are speaking of the *sentences* used to describe such phenomena: *intensionality*). One of the ways a sentence can qualify as an intensional sentence is if the replacement of predicate expressions by coextensive predicate expressions alters (or *can* alter) the truth value of the sentence as a whole. So, for example, "He believes that s is F" is an intensional sentence (and the attitude or state it describes is an intentional state) because even if "F" and "G" are coextensional (true of exactly the same things), one cannot substitute "G" for "F" in this sentence without risking a change in truth value. That is, "He believes that s is G" may be false even though everything that is F is G and vice versa. There are a great variety of intensional sentences (and corresponding intentional states). Many of these sentences describe what are commonly thought of as mental or psychological phenomena. Intending, believing, knowing, hoping, wishing, planning, and imagining are intentional attitudes, states, or processes. The sentences that describe what a person intends, believes, knows, hopes for, wishes, plans, and imagines are all intensional in one way or another.

This is suggestive. For, as we have just seen, the flow of information exhibits a similar sort of intentionality. Just as sentences describing what a person knows or believes are intensional, so are the sentences describing what information a signal carries. Just as we cannot conclude from the fact that S believes that s is F (and the fact that "F" and "G" are coextensional) that S believes that s is G, so we cannot conclude from the fact that a signal carries the information that s is F (and the fact that "F" and "G" are coextensional) that the signal carries the information that s is G. What information a signal carries exhibits the same kind of intentionality as what we believe or know. This suggests that we may be able to understand the peculiar intentional structure of our cognitive states as symptoms of their underlying information-theoretic character. Perhaps, that is, the intentionality of our cognitive attitudes (the way they have a unique *content*), a feature that some philosophers take to be distinctive of the mental, is a manifestation of their underlying information-theoretic structure.

I intend to develop these suggestions, but not now. This will be the subject of Part III. For the present it will suffice to note that our definition of information does yield something with intentional characteristics and to this degree parallels our ordinary, semantic idea of information. Just as we ordinarily distinguish the information that s is F from the information that s is G, despite the fact that all (and only) Fs are G, our definition of a signal's informational content yields the same distinction. That is, our definition of information *distinguishes* between *extensionally equivalent* pieces of information. In this respect, and to this degree, statements describing the information carried by a signal are intensional descriptions, and the phenomena they describe qualify as *intentional* phenomena.

The ultimate source of the intentionality inherent in the transmission and receipt of information is, of course, the *nomic regularities* on which the transmission of information depends. The transmission of information requires, not simply a set of de facto correlations, but a network of nomic dependencies between the condition at the source and the properties of the signal. The conditional probabilities used to compute noise, equivocation, and amount of transmitted information (and therefore the conditional probabilities defining the informational content of the signal) are all determined by the lawful relations that exist between source and signal. Correlations are irrelevant unless these correlations are a symptom of lawful connections. And since a lawful connection between two properties or magnitudes is itself an intentional phenomenon, information inherits its intentional feature from the nomic regularities on which it depends.[6]

Information inherits its intentional properties from the lawful regularities on which it depends. But (it may be asked) whence comes the intentional character of laws? This is a controversial topic in the philosophy of science, a controversy in which we need not embroil ourselves. For what is controversial is not *whether* laws have intentional characteristics, but how this is to be understood. There is wide disagreement about how best to analyze this peculiar feature of natural laws but almost universal agreement that laws *have* this peculiar feature. For example, if it is a law of nature that all *A*s are *B*, the fact that "*B*" and "*C*" are coextensional does *not* imply that there is a law of nature to the effect that all *A*s are *C*. The most that is implied is that all *A*s are (as a matter of fact) *C*—not that all *A*s *must* be *C*. This feature of natural laws is often described by saying that laws have a *modal* quality (they tell us what *must* be the case or what *cannot* happen) that is absent from simple statements of exceptionless correlations. The fact that all *A*s are *B* (exceptionless correlation) does not imply that any *A must* be *B*, it does not imply that if this non-*B were* an *A*, it *would* also be a *B*. But genuine laws of nature *do* imply this. They tell us what *would* happen if certain conditions were realized (were the metal to be heated, it would expand) and what could not happen whatever our efforts might be (e.g., making an object travel faster than the speed of light). It is precisely this modal quality of laws that constitutes one of the chief philosophical problems about them. But the problem is not whether laws have this modal, intentional quality, but where they get it (how to analyze it). For our purposes it is not important *where* natural laws acquire this puzzling property. What is important is *that* they have it. For we have traced the intentional aspects of information to the intentional aspects of natural laws, and we are prepared to leave the matter there with a reminder that the ultimate clarification of our idea of information (in particular its intentional or semantic aspect) rests with a clarification of the modal authority of natural laws.[7]

One point remains to be clarified. Our definition of informational content makes reference to what the receiver *already knows* (*k*) about the possibilities existing at the source. To illustrate, suppose that there are four shells and a peanut is located under one of them.[8] In attempting to find under which shell the peanut is located, I turn over shells 1 and 2 and discover them to be empty. At this point you arrive on the scene and join the investigation. You are *not* told about my previous discoveries. We turn over shell 3 and find it empty. How much information do you receive from this observation? How much do I receive? Do I receive information that you do not receive?

Intuitions may differ on how best to characterize such a situation in informational terms. On the one hand the observation of shell 3 tells *me* where the peanut is but it does not tell *you*. Since I was able to learn something from this observation that you were not, the observation must have been more pregnant with information for me than for you. I must have received *more information* from this single observation than you. Yet, on the other hand, we know it is not just this single observation that "told" me where the peanut was. All I was "told" by this single observation was that the peanut was *not* under shell 3—the same thing the observation told you. What allows me to determine the whereabouts of the peanut is this third observation *together with* my previous two discoveries. According to this second line of reasoning, then, the single observation (the one we made together of shell 3) carries the same information to both of us. The explanation for why I learned more from it than you (viz., that the peanut is under shell 4) is that *I knew more to begin with*. The information that the peanut is under shell 4 is a piece of information that is carried by the composite set of *three* signals—not by any *single* observation. Hence, it is not true that I learned more *from the third observation* than did you. I learned something you did not, but only because I received *three* information-bearing signals and you received only one, and what was learned depended (in this case) on the receipt of all three.

In discussing a similar sort of example, Daniel Dennett concludes that: "the information received by people when they are spoken to depends on what they already know and is not amenable to precise quantification."[9] I propose to follow Dennett in relativizing the information contained in a signal because I think this accurately reflects our ordinary ways of thinking about such matters. But, unlike Dennett, I do not believe this means that we cannot precisely quantify the amount of information contained in a signal. Nor does it mean that we must abandon our analysis of what information a signal contains. This should be apparent from the above example. Having already examined shells 1 and 2, I know they are empty. The peanut is under either shell 3 or 4. When we turn over shell 3 and find it empty, the two possibilities are reduced to one. Hence, the third observation provides me with 1 bit of information as to the whereabouts of the peanut. You, however, undertake the examination of shell 3 in ignorance of the results of the first two observations. For *you* there are four possibilities and the examination of shell 3 reduces these four possibilities to three. Hence, you receive only .42 bits of information as to the whereabouts of the peanut. Since there are 2 bits of information associated with the peanut's being under shell 4, you receive *too little* information to locate the peanut. All you learn is that shell 3 is empty (.42 bits). On the other hand, the third observation supplies me with the information that shell 3 is empty (1 bit) *and* the information that the peanut is under shell 4 (1 bit). The latter piece of information is (for me) nested in the former piece of information. For you it is not.

This constitutes a *relativization* of the information contained in a signal because *how much* information a signal contains, and hence *what* information it carries, depends on what the potential receiver already knows about the various possibilities that exist at the source. The amount of information generated by the peanut's being under shell 4 depends, of course, on what the possible alternatives are. If I know that it is not under shells 1 and 2, then there are only two possibilities and $I(s)$, the amount of information associated with the peanut's being under shell 4, is 1 bit. For you, however, there are still four possibilities (all equally likely), and so the amount of information associated with the peanut's being under shell 4 is 2 bits. This neatly explains (at least in quantitative terms) why the third observation "told" me where the peanut was but did not tell you. It "told" me where the peanut was because the observation supplied me with the full 1 bit of information associated with the peanut's being under shell 4. The same observation supplied you with only .42 bits of information—something far short of the 2 bits of information associated (for you) with the peanut's being under shell 4. Your greater ignorance requires a commensurately greater amount of information to repair. This greater amount of information (2 bits) is not available to you in your examination of the third shell. Hence, you remain ignorant of the whereabouts of the peanut. I learn where the peanut is because I receive enough information (1 bit) from this third observation to get the information that the peanut is under shell 4. Knowing what I do, it requires less information (quantitatively) to deliver this piece of information to me than it does to you.

Up to this point we have indulged in the harmless fiction that the number of possibilities existing at the source (and their respective probabilities) was fixed *independently* of what anyone happened to know. This fiction allowed us to develop the information-theoretic framework without distracting complications. Furthermore, the fiction is often rendered harmless by the fact that the assessment of the information contained in a signal (both *how much* information and *what* information) is carried out against a background of communally shared knowledge in which individual differences are submerged.[10] That is, what is known about the various possibilities at the source (the k in our definition of informational content) is the same for all relevant receivers, and the discussion can proceed (for practical purposes) as though the commodity in question was *absolute* and *fixed*. We do the same sort of thing when discussing such relative magnitudes as weight, velocity, and simultaneity. Only when there is a *shift* of reference systems does the need arise to make explicit the relative nature of the quantity under consideration. Information is no different. This *is* a relative quantity, but for the purpose of many discussions there is little to be gained by distracting reminders of this point. For, often enough, a common frame of reference is understood. Every relevant party knows the same thing about the possibilities existing at the source. When this is so, we can proceed with the calculations as though we were dealing with an absolute quantity.

As the example indicates, a receiver's background knowledge is relevant to the information he receives (both *how much* information and *what* information) only to the extent that it affects the value of $I(s)$—the amount of information generated at the source by the existence of a specific state of affairs. If the receiver's knowledge does not affect the value of $I(s)$, then it is irrelevant to how much information he is receiving and what information he is receiving. In particular, it makes no difference if one person *knows* that the signal he is receiving is reliable and the other does not. As long as the signal *is* reliable, whether or not it is *known* to be reliable, $I_s(r)$, the amount of information reaching the receiver about the source, equals $I(s)$, the amount of information generated at the source. What makes $I_s(r)$ a relative quantity is not what the receiver knows about the channel over which he gets information about the source, but what the receiver knows about the situation *at* the source about which he is getting information.

We shall return to this important point in Part II when we discuss the nature of the communication channel over which information is received. At that time a question will be raised about what constitutes a legitimate *possibility* for the calculation of information transmitted and received. This issue is temporarily postponed because its proper treatment takes one to the very heart of skeptical questions about the possibility of knowledge, questions about whether information (involving as it does a conditional probability of 1) can be transmitted from place to place. Such issues are best raised when we examine the relationship between knowledge and the receipt of information.

I hope enough has been said in this chapter, however, to make plausible the claim that our theoretical characterization of a signal's informational content *does* provide us with a precisely defined idea that corresponds strikingly well with our ordinary, intuitive understanding of information. Our definition not only yields a concept of information that satisfies the quantitative demands of communication theory, it also explains the cognitive importance of information by revealing the nature of the connection between information and truth; it enables us to understand the source (the intentionality of natural laws) of the *semantic* character of information;[11] and it reveals the extent to which, and the reason why, the information one receives is a function of what one already knows. What remains to be shown is how this commodity, as theoretically understood, helps us to understand the common view that information is something that makes *learning* possible, as something that is required for *knowledge*. This is the task of Part II.

PART II
   KNOWLEDGE AND PERCEPTION

Chapter 4
Knowledge

What is knowledge? A traditional answer is that knowledge is a form of justified true belief. To know that s is F is to be fully justified in one's (true) belief that s is F. Normally, these conditions are interpreted so as to be independent of one another. Beliefs can be false, and the truth may not be believed. Furthermore, one can be fully justified in believing that s is F without s's being F (in which case, of course, one does not know) and have a full justification for something one does not believe.

Although still used as a touchstone for epistemological discussion, this orthodox account is no longer deemed satisfactory. It must be either abandoned or severely qualified to withstand a variety of crippling objections. Aside from objections, however, the account remains seriously incomplete insofar as the concept of *justification* is left unanalyzed. It is of no help to be told that knowledge depends on having an adequate justification if, as is so often the case, one is not told what constitutes an adequate justification.[1]

I propose to replace this traditional account with an information-theoretic analysis. This chapter is a first step in that enterprise. What follows is a characterization of knowledge in terms of information and belief. Later (Part III) belief itself will be resolved into its informational components, but for the time being, I will use this concept as an auxiliary device to abbreviate matters and postpone issues that can only be attended to later.

When there is a positive amount of information associated with s's being F,[2]

> K knows that s is F = K's belief that s is F is caused (or causally sustained) by the information that s is F.

It should be emphasized at the outset that this is intended to be a characterization of what might be called *perceptual knowledge*, knowledge about an item s that is picked out or determined by factors other than what K happens to know (or believe) about it. That is, following our discussion of *de re* informational contents in the last chapter, we are concerned with knowing *of* something that it is F where the something known to be F is fixed by perceptual (noncognitive) factors. We shall, in a later chapter, discuss the nature of the perceptual object—what it is we see, hear, and smell. There it will be argued that the perceptual object is, so to speak, the *focus* of the information relations holding between the subject and the sources from which he or she receives information. But until this point can be clarified, I must ask the reader to understand s to be something K perceives, something at an informational source *about which* K receives information. If K has a belief *about* this object, the belief that it is F, then this belief qualifies as knowledge if and only if that belief is caused (or causally sustained) by the information that it is F.

The analysis may appear circular. Knowledge is identified with information-produced (or sustained) belief, but the information a person receives (Chapter 3) is relative to what he or she *already knows* about the possibilities at the source. Since there is a covert reference to knowledge on the right-hand side of the equation (concealed within the idea of information), the equation does *not* tell us, as it purports to tell us, what knowledge is. Rather, it presupposes that we already understand what knowledge is in its use of the concept *information*.

This objection overlooks the *recursive* character of our equation. Whether a person can learn that s is F may depend on what *else* he knows about s, but it does not depend, and is not said to depend, on his knowing that s is F. Take, for example, our shell game. The peanut is known to be under one of the four shells. The investigator has already examined the first two shells and found them empty. Given what he knows, there are only two possibilities left. When he turns the third shell over and finds it empty, the observation carries the information that the peanut is under the fourth shell (thereby enabling him to *learn* the whereabouts of the peanut) *because* of what he already knows about the first two shells. If we are interested in whether he really does know that the first two shells are empty, we can reapply our formula to this *different* piece of knowledge. Did the observation of the first shell carry the information that it was empty? If it did, and this information caused him to believe it was empty, then he knows the first shell is empty. The same with the second shell. If these pieces of information (that the first shell is empty, that the second shell is empty) depend, in turn, on something the investigator already knows, then we can continue applying the formula to this collateral knowledge. Eventually we reach the point where the information received does not depend on any prior knowledge about the source, and it is this fact that enables our equation to avoid circularity.

What is meant by saying that a belief is caused (or causally sustained) by a piece of information? How can an abstract commodity like information be causally efficacious?

Suppose a signal r carries the information that s is F and carries this information in virtue of having the property F'. That is, it is r's *being F'* (not, say, its being G) that is responsible for r's carrying this specific piece of information. Not just any knock on the door tells the spy that the courier has arrived. The signal is three quick knocks followed by a pause and another three quick knocks. It is this particular *sequence* that carries the vital piece of information that the courier has arrived. It is not the amplitude or pitch of the sounds that is significant. It is not the time of day at which the knocks occur. It is the temporal pattern of knocks that constitutes the information-carrying feature (F') of the signal. The same is obviously true in telegraphic communication.

When, therefore, a signal carries the information that s is F *in virtue* of having property F', when it is the signal's *being F'* that carries the information, then (and only then) will we say that the information that s is F *causes* whatever the signal's being F' causes.

So, for example, if the particular spacing of the knocks (that spacing that carries the information that the courier has arrived) causes the spy to panic, then the information that the courier has arrived will be said to have caused the spy to panic. If, on the other hand, it is merely a knock on the door that causes the spy to panic (two quick knocks would have had the same result), then the information that the courier has arrived is *not* the cause of the panic. Similarly, if it is the particular spacing of the knocks that causes the spy to believe that the courier has arrived, then his belief is caused or produced by the information that the spy has arrived. If the belief is brought about merely as a result of several knocks at the door (their pattern being irrelevant to the effect), then although the spy believes the courier has arrived, and although this belief is brought about by the courier's knock, it is not produced by the information that the courier has arrived.[3]

I assume that this talk of events having certain effects *in virtue of* having certain properties is clear enough. Although a substance may dissolve in a liquid, it may not be the liquidity of the solvent that is causally responsible for the effect. The substance dissolves in the liquid in virtue of the liquid's being an acid, *not* in virtue of the liquid's being a liquid. Similarly, a flying object may break the glass, but that in virtue of which it has this effect is not its being a flying object. Flying cotton balls do not have this effect. What causes the glass to break is the object's having a certain momentum (combined mass and velocity). It is the object's having *a sufficiently great momentum*, not its having *a momentum*, that causally explains the breakage. This is not to say that an object's hitting the glass did not cause it to break. Of course it did. But what it was about the object's hitting the glass that made the glass break was not its being an object (i.e., something with mass) that hit the glass, not its hitting (with some velocity) the glass, but its hitting the glass with a sufficiently great combination of mass and velocity. This is why flying bricks break windows but falling leaves do not.[4]

It is a bit trickier to say what is meant by a piece of information *causally sustaining* a belief. The reason for including this parenthetical qualification in the characterization of knowledge is to capture an obvious fact about knowledge and the generation of belief —the fact, namely, that a person can know that *s* is *F* without his belief having been caused, or in any way brought about, by reliable means. To illustrate, suppose K believes that s is F because an ignorant meddler told him s was F. The ignorant meddler knows nothing about the matters whereof he speaks, but K, unaware of this, believes him. After acquiring this belief, K undertakes an examination of s and observes it to be F (i.e., comes to *know* that it is F by perceptual means). In such a case K knows that s is F (having observed it to be F), but his belief that s is F was not caused or produced by the *information* that s is F. Rather, this belief was caused or produced by the ignorant meddler's assurances, and these assurances *lacked* the relevant information. The reason we say K (now) knows is not because his belief was originally caused by the relevant piece of information, but because his belief is (now) *supported* or *sustained* by the relevant piece of information (obtained through his observation of s).

I hope this example gives the reader an intuitive idea of the kind of case we mean to be talking about when we speak of information causally sustaining a belief. It is like adding a second piece of string to support an object that is already being suspended by a first piece of string. The object is now being held up by *two* pieces of string. They both bear some of the weight. Yet, neither piece of string (taken by itself) is necessary since the other piece of string is (by itself) sufficient unto supporting the full weight of the object. In such a case we cannot say that the second piece of string is supporting the object—at least not if this is taken to imply that if we removed it, the object would fall. For, of course, if we removed the second piece of string, the first piece would resume its former role as *sole* supporter of the object.

What we must say about the second piece of string is that it is *helping* to support the object and that it *suffices* for support of the object. It is having an effect on the object and, moreover, the sort of effect that would, in the absence of other means of support, suffice for the existence of the effect (suspension). Such, at least, is how I propose to understand a *sustaining cause*. K's belief that s is F is causally sustained by the information that s is F if and only if this piece of information affects the belief in such a way that it would, in the absence of other contributory causes, suffice for the existence of the belief. The information must play a a role similar to that of the second piece of string in our example.

K's belief that *s* is *F* qualifies as knowledge as long as his observation would have produced that belief in the absence of the ignorant meddler's assurances. If we suppose that *K* would not have trusted his observation without the prior assurances of the meddler (would not have believed, on the basis of the observation alone, that *s* was *F*), then the observation does not causally sustain the belief in the required sense (it is not, by itself, sufficient for the belief), and *K* does not (in such a case) know that *s* is *F*.

This definition (of one thing causally sustaining another thing) has technical flaws of which I am aware. However, I do not know how to *motivate* a search for a technical remedy, let alone *find* such a remedy, without a tedious digression on the nature of causal relations, causal sufficiency, overdetermination, and counterfactuals. I propose, therefore, to rest with what I have. It captures well enough the range of cases for which it is designed. It allows us to say of someone who receives the pertinent information *after* he has the belief that he nonetheless knows as long as this belief is suitably based on the new information—as long, that is, as the new information causally sustains the belief in the way a second piece of string may help to support an object.[5]

It should be clear from such examples that a belief that is caused (or causally sustained) by the information that *s* is *F* may not *itself* embody the information that *s* is *F*. Whether or not *K*'s belief that *s* is *F* carries the information that *s* is *F* depends on what else (besides the information that *s* is *F*) may cause *K* to believe this. In the above example a signal lacking the information that *s* was *F* (viz., the ignorant meddler's assurances) caused *K* to believe that *s* was *F*. *K* later learned *s* was *F* by observation. In this case *K*'s belief that *s* is *F* (after observing *s* to be *F*), though it qualifies as knowledge, does not itself carry the information that *s* is *F*. It does not carry this information because signals lacking this piece of information are capable of causing (in fact, *did* cause) this belief. Not everyone who knows that *s* is *F* is someone from whom one can learn that *s* is *F*. Whether one can learn that *s* is *F* from *K* depends, not only on whether *K* *knows* that *s* is *F*, but also on what else (besides the information that *s* is *F*) may induce such a belief in *K*. *K* is *not* a reliable informant, although he does *know*. This, indeed, is why one cannot define knowledge that *s* is *F* as a belief (that *s* is *F*) which carries this information; for some beliefs that qualify as knowledge do *not* carry the relevant piece of information.[6]

The idea of information causing (or causally sustaining) belief is intended to capture what is worth capturing in the doctrine that for a person's belief to qualify as knowledge, there must not only *be* evidence to support it, the belief must be *based on* that evidence. Insofar as the information that s is F causes K's belief that s is F, we can say that the belief is *based on* the information that s is F.

It is important to notice that this is *not* an inferential account of perceptual knowledge. If K sees s moving and, as a result, comes to the belief that s is moving, we need not suppose that this belief about s was reached via some inference. K's sensory state (whatever is required for him to see s moving) may embody the information that s is moving, and this information may cause K to believe that s is moving, without K's believing anything about his sensory state itself. His belief is based on (i.e., caused by) the sensory information he receives, but K need not (although he *may*) believe something about the intrinsic properties of his sensory state, those properties that carry the information about s. K need not believe, for example, that he is having a certain sort of *visual experience*, that he is being *appeared to* in such and such a way, or that things *look* so and so to him (where these are understood to be beliefs about the so-called phenomenal character of his experience). It is, of course, the intrinsic properties of the sensory state (those carrying the information that s is moving) that cause K to believe that s is moving, but if no intermediate belief is produced, the belief about s (that it is moving) has no causal ancestors that are themselves beliefs. The belief has no *discursive* derivation, and in this respect, it is acquired directly and without inference.

With these preliminaries out of the way we are ready to turn to a defense of our characterization of knowledge. It should be noted at the outset, however, that this is not intended to be a *definition* of knowledge, something that might be established by *conceptual* analysis or by an inquiry into the *meanings* of the terms "knowledge," "information," "belief," and "cause." It represents a coordination between our ordinary concept of knowledge (or, better, *perceptual* knowledge) and the technical idea of information developed in Part I. It is an attempt to describe, with the conceptual resources of information theory, the state that is ordinarily described with the verb "to know." In this respect the equation is analogous to a thermodynamic redescription of hot objects in terms of their heat capacity, conductivity, and temperature.[7] This is not what it *means* to be hot, but (thermodynamically speaking) what it is to *be* hot. We are, as it were, providing a bridge principle *between* conceptual schemes, not a truth *within* either scheme. What helps to obscure the *inter*conceptual nature of our equation is the occurrence in it of the word "information." If this word is interpreted in some ordinary sense, as meaning something akin to news, intelligence, instruction, or knowledge, then the characterization of knowledge as information-produced belief may appear trivial and unilluminating. But this is *not* how the word "information" is being used. This term is to be understood as meaning exactly what it was said to mean in the definition of a signal's information content in Chapter 3. Under this interpretation our information-theoretic characterization of knowledge is an epistemological thesis that is neither trivial nor obvious. Quite the contrary.

What, then, can be said in support of the idea that knowledge is information-produced belief? What follows is an attempt to mobilize the arguments in favor of this theoretical equation—in particular the arguments for the necessity of information. Later (Chapter 5) we will examine some possible objections.

Ordinary Judgments

One way to determine whether Y is necessary for X, when there are independent means for determining the presence of both X and Y, is to sample a number of different situations in order to see whether X ever occurs without Y. If it does, that settles the matter: Y is not necessary for X. If it does not, then, depending on the size of the sample and the variety of situations examined, one has inductive grounds for concluding that (probably) Y is a necessary condition for X.

This strategy can be employed in the present case only if we have independent means for determining when someone knows something. Since we obviously do not have clear and well-articulated criteria in this area (else philosophical efforts such as the present one would be otiose), one is forced to rely on ordinary, intuitive judgments. There may be disagreements about cases, of course, and when there is, this method will be inconclusive. But if there is a set of clear cases—clear, at least, to the theoretically unprejudiced judge—then they can be used to test the hypothesis. How convincing one finds the results will depend on one's agreement or disagreement with the intuitive sorting on which the results depend.

We may begin by citing the examples used in previous chapters. In every instance where the signals reaching the subject lacked the relevant piece of information (as defined in Chapter 3), the subject would be judged, on ordinary, intuitive grounds, *not* to know. When the messenger lost the memo and composed a new one with the name "Herman" on it, the memo carried zero information about who the employees had selected. Hence it did not carry the information that Herman was selected, and it is clear that whatever the employer was induced to believe by the receipt of this message, he did not know that Herman was selected—not if the only relevant communication was the corrupted memo bearing the name "Herman." Similarly, when the employees agreed to protect Shirley by naming Herman if she was selected (and otherwise correctly designating the nominee), the employer may have come to believe, and to believe *truly*, that Herman was selected, and he may have been caused to believe this by his receipt of a memo with the name "Herman" on it, but he did not thereby come to know that Herman was selected. The reason he did not is that the memo did not carry this information. Hence, the employer's belief could not have been caused by the information that Herman was selected.

The remaining examples give the same result. In searching for the peanut under the shells, the subject was described as first examining shells 1 and 2 and finding them empty. Clearly, he does not *yet* know where the peanut is. Only after finding the third shell empty (or a peanut under it) would we judge knowledge (of the whereabouts of the peanut) to be possible. The first two observations do not carry the information that the peanut is under shell 4, and this, I submit, is the basis for our ordinary judgment that at this stage of the investigation the subject cannot know where the peanut is. He has not *yet* received the requisite piece of information.

It may be supposed that the examples so far discussed are contrived, and that less artificial examples will prove less favorable.

The examples have certainly been contrived, but not for the purpose of verifying the present analysis. They have been carefully chosen to illustrate the fundamental ideas of communication theory. Other examples will do as well. In particular, consider a situation in which one might be tempted to suppose that knowledge is possible without the requisite piece of information. There are four possibilities (P, Y, B, and G) at the source. They are equally likely. A signal r arrives, altering the configuration of probabilities as follows:

$$P(P/r) = .9$$
$$P(Y/r) = .03$$
$$P(B/r) = .03$$
$$P(G/r) = .04$$

The signal raises the probability that s is P and simultaneously lowers the probability of all competing alternatives. Calculation shows that the equivocation of this signal is .6 bits. It carries only 1.4 bits of information about the state of s. Therefore, it does *not* carry the information that s is P even though s *is* P. Yet, it may be thought, one *can* learn from such a signal that s is P. Or, if the probability of s's being P is still deemed too low for knowledge, we can raise its probability to .99 and lower the probabilities of the competitors to .003, .003, and .004, respectively. Even at this level the signal fails to carry the information that s is P, since there remains a positive amount of equivocation. Surely, though, there is *some* sufficiently high probability for s's being P (short of 1) that will allow us to *know* that s is P. Or so it may be argued.

It is here that intuitions may begin to diverge. The use of this method to test our theoretical equation may therefore become unreliable. The best I can do is to state my own view of the matter. Consider a case that exemplifies the above set of conditional probabilities. You draw a ball from an urn containing 90 pink balls (P), 3 yellow balls (Y), 3 blue balls (B), and 4 green balls (G). Given that you are drawing a ball at random from an urn with this relative distribution of colored balls, the probability of drawing a pink ball is .9, the probability of drawing a yellow ball is .03, and so on. Suppose K receives a message containing the information that you randomly drew a ball from an urn having this distribution of colored balls (e.g., he observes you draw from an urn that he has, by prior inspection, determined to have this composition of colored balls). Assuming that you do, in fact, draw a pink ball, does *K know* that you did? *Can* he know that you did if all he has to go on is the fact that you drew at random from *that* urn? We may assume that he believes you drew a pink ball. He may be absolutely certain of it. He is, moreover, correct in this belief. But the question remains: does he know it? It seems clear to me that he does *not* know it. He may be ever so reasonable in believing it (or betting on it), but he is not in the position of someone who actually took a peek at the color of the ball you drew (who *saw that* it was pink). If you attempted to deceive *K* by telling him that you selected a yellow ball, he would not, unlike the person who peeked, know you were lying. And there is no significant change in this situation if we increase the relative proportion of pink balls. As long as the information is absent, as it always will be when there are any other colored balls in the urn, knowledge is impossible.[8]

The same intuitions operate in more routine contexts. Some neighborhood dog runs off with the steaks *K* is grilling in his back yard. *K* catches a glimpse of the dog bounding off with the steaks in his mouth. There is enough information embodied in that brief observation to permit an identification of the dog as a golden retriever. Now, if you have the *only* golden retriever in the neighborhood, you can expect *K* at your doorstep insisting that your dog took his steaks. Whether he knows this or not may still be a matter for dispute (did he actually see the steaks in the dog's mouth?), but one thing seems clear. If there is *another* golden retriever on the block, usually tied up but occasionally allowed to run free then *K*, despite his protests, does not know that *your* dog was the culprit. He may be right in thinking it was your dog, but cross examination should reveal that he does not know it was not the other dog. After all, the other dog, though usually tied, is *occasionally* allowed to run free. If *K* cares to make the effort, he may acquire information to the effect that the other dog was tied at the time of the incident. Upon receipt of such information, he may *then* be said to know that it was your dog who took his steaks. But this judgment merely confirms the information-theoretic condition. For the two pieces of information, visual and (say) acoustic, *taken together*, contain the information that it was your dog that ran off with the steaks, information that neither signal, taken by itself, contains.

I do not expect universal agreement about the way I have described these cases. There may be honest differences of opinion over the question of whether an individual (such as K in the last few examples) knows, or does not know, what he is described as knowing and not knowing. There is little to be gained by matching intuitions over controversial cases. A white bird is not a satisfactory test case for the hypothesis that all ravens are black if investigators cannot agree about whether the bird is a raven or not. When disagreement persists, the only reasonable thing to do is either look for other examples, examples about which agreement can be obtained, or seek out more general, systematic considerations that bear on the validity of the hypothesis in question. For the remainder of this chapter I propose to do the latter. What follows are some theoretical considerations favoring an information-based theory of knowledge. The following chapter will examine some of the most serious arguments against such an analysis—in particular those relating to the possibility of receiving information of the required sort and, hence, the possibility of knowing anything about an independent source. We will return to cases later.

The Gettier Problem

In a well-known and much discussed article, Edmund Gettier gives two examples that purport to show that knowledge is not, or is not merely, justified true belief.[9] Many philosophers have found these examples convincing. It is worth mentioning, therefore, as a point in favor of the present view that Gettier-type difficulties cannot be raised against an analysis that makes knowledge conditional on the receipt of information.

Gettier's examples were designed to apply to those analyses in which the sense of "justified" was such that one could be justified in believing something that was false. If knowledge is viewed as a form of justified true belief, and the justification required for this knowledge is fallible (i.e., one can, in this sense, be justified in believing something false), then this view of knowledge is seriously defective. For one can, in this sense, be justified in believing something that is true without knowing it. For suppose that K is justified in believing that a marker is on square 2 of a checkerboard, but suppose that it is, in fact, on square 3. If we assume that K comes to the belief that the marker is on *either* square 2 or square 3 on the basis of his justified belief that it is on square 2, and assume that justification is inherited by the known logical consequences of what one is justified in believing, then K's belief that the marker is on either square 2 or square 3 is not only true, but he is justified in believing it. Clearly, however, he does not know it. This example (an adaptation of Gettier's second case) reveals that it is not enough to justifiably believe something that is true. For the truth of what one believes may be quite unrelated to one's grounds (justification) for believing it.

The present analysis is immune from such difficulties. The immunity derives from the fact that one cannot receive the information that s is F when s is *not F*. K (in the above example) did not receive a message containing the information that the marker was on square 2 because it was not on square 2. He may have received enough information about the location of the marker to justify him in believing it was on square 2, but he could not have received the information that it was on square 2. Hence, even if we accept the principle that K is justified in believing everything he knows to be a logical consequence of what he is justified in believing,[10] the most we can infer is that K is justified in believing that the marker is on square 2 or square 3. We cannot reach the conclusion that K's justified true belief (that the marker is on square 2 or square 3) constitutes knowledge. And we cannot reach this conclusion because we have not been told whether K has received the information that the marker is on square 2 or square 3—something that, on the present analysis, is necessary to his knowing.

There is, of course, the possibility that K receives the information that the marker is on square 2 or square 3 (but neither the information that it is on square 2 nor the information that it is on square 3) and comes to the (mistaken) belief that it is on square 2 on the basis of this information. He does not know it is on square 2, but we may suppose that he is justified in believing this (the message he received may have made it very probable that the marker was on square 2). K then infers that the marker is on square 2 or square 3. He now has a justified *true* belief ("true" because the marker *is* on square 2 or square 3), but this true belief was derived from the false belief that the marker was on square 2. Since

K has received the information that the marker was on square 2 or square 3, can we conclude (according to the present analysis) that he *knows* the marker is on square 2 or square 3?

If a subject receives a signal containing the information that *s* is *H* (e.g., *F* or *G*) and, on the basis of this message, comes to the false belief that *s* is *F*, we can say immediately that the subject does not know that *s* is *F*. But if the subject then comes to believe that *s* is *H* (e.g., *F* or *G*) on the basis of his belief that it is *F*, does he know or does he not know? There is no *general* answer to this question. We need more details about the particular case.[11] For what is crucial is just how the intermediate (false) belief figures in the generation of the resultant (true) belief. Suppose I observe you smoking what I take to be cigars (actually, they are fat brown cigarettes). Later, when someone inquires about whether or not you smoke, I remember seeing you smoke (what I mistakenly take to be) cigars and answer, "Yes he does." Do I know that you smoke? Do I know that someone left the party early if I reach this (true) conclusion from the fact, or what I take to be a fact, that I saw Betty leaving early? If I am wrong in my belief that it was Betty leaving early (the woman I saw leaving looked just like Betty), does this disqualify me from knowing that *someone* left early? Of course not. Everything depends on what is causing me to believe that someone left early. Is it the information (which I received in watching a guest depart early) that someone left early? If so, then even if this signal produces in me a false belief (that Betty is leaving early), I nonetheless know that someone left early. This is so because the causal influence of the information (that someone left early) reaches *through* the intermediate false belief, making it (the intermediate false belief) causally dispensable. Even if it is true (and this is not entirely clear from the way I have described the case) that I believe that someone left early because I believe that Betty left early, still, I do not believe that someone left early *only* because I believe that Betty (in particular) left early. Were I to discover that it was not Betty I saw leaving early, the belief that someone left early would remain intact, for this belief is (in the imagined situation) anchored in the information I received in watching someone leave early. When this is so, knowledge that *s* is *H* is possible even though it is produced in association with a false belief that *s* is *F*.

Situations can easily be imagined, however, in which the resultant true belief is not brought about, or sustained, by the appropriate piece of information. Suppose I am convinced that no one would leave early *except* Betty. What leads me to believe that someone left early are not just those features of the signal that carry the information that someone is leaving early, but those features that I (mistakenly) take to be carrying the information that *Betty* is leaving early. If told that it was not Betty I saw to be leaving early, I would abandon my belief that someone left early (the person must have stepped outside for some reason). In this case the belief that someone is leaving early is *not* causally sustained by the information that someone is leaving early, even though this information is being received. The belief is being caused by those more specific aspects of the signal that I (mistakenly) take to be indicative of Betty's leaving early. In such a case the resultant true belief does not qualify as knowledge.

The Lottery Paradox

If you have a ticket in a lottery and millions of other people also hold a ticket, the odds against your winning are enormous. Someone must win (let us say), but the odds against any particular person's winning are overwhelming. Yet, though the probability of your losing be ever so close to unity, it seems wrong to say that you know you are going to lose. For if *you* know you are going to lose, everyone else who holds a ticket should be similarly qualified, since the odds against their winning are the same. Yet, not everyone can know they are going to lose, since someone is going to win. Can we say that everyone knows they are going to lose *except* the person who is going to win? This sounds odd. For there is absolutely nothing to distinguish the eventual winner from the eventual losers except the fact that he is going to win. He has the same evidence as everyone else.[12]

From an information-theoretic standpoint each of the one million participants in the lottery (assuming it to be a fair lottery in which every ticket holder has an equal chance of winning) is in the same position. The amount of information associated with their holding a *winning* ticket is nearly 20 bits and the amount of information associated with their holding a *losing* ticket is very nearly zero. But although the amount of information associated with their holding a losing ticket is *very nearly zero*, it is not *equal to zero*. Hence, unless the participants have special information about the eventual outcome of the lottery, none of them have received that (quantitatively) small piece of information which, according to the present view of knowledge, is essential to their knowing they are going to lose. The information-theoretic condition on knowledge neatly explains why nobody *knows* he is going to lose in a fair lottery.[13] Everyone is justified in being pessimistic, but no one has access to the information that would permit them to know they are going to lose.

One can, of course, reject the information-theoretic analysis of knowledge without endorsing the strange view that everyone (except the eventual winner) knows he is going to lose in the lottery.[14] Perhaps there are alternative conceptions of knowledge that handle such cases in an equally elegant way. This possibility must be conceded. Nevertheless, there is a related point that I believe gives the competitive edge to an information-based analysis.

Suppose that knowledge does *not* require the receipt of information. Then K can know that s is F without having received the information that s is F. Suppose, therefore, that K *does* know that s is F without having received this piece of information. Since this entails that any signals K may have received bearing information about s were equivocal to some degree, let e_F stand for this positive amount of equivocation. Suppose, furthermore, that K knows that t is G and he knows this without having received the information that t is G. Let e_G represent the positive equivocation of those signals (if any) that K has received with respect to t's being G. Since equivocation is additive when the sources are independent of one another, the total equivocation of the ensemble of signals K has received about s and t is $e_F + e_G$. Question: given (by hypothesis) that K knows that s is F and knows that t is G, does he know that s is F and t is G? That is, does he know the *conjunction* of those things that (taken individually) he knows? The equivocation of the conjunction is greater than the equivocation of either conjunct. And it is easy to see that as one conjoins propositions, each of which, taken individually, is an expression of what K knows to be the case, the total equivocation will continue to increase. It can be made as large as one pleases.

If one accepts the principle that if K knows that P and knows that Q, then he knows that P and Q (call this the conjunction principle), then one will be forced to answer the above question in the affirmative. That is, K *does* know that s is F and t is G because he knows that s is F and he knows that t is G. But, given our opening assumption (that one could know without having received the information), this means that one can know things *no matter how large the equivocation becomes*, no matter how much information is lost between source and receiver. For as one continues to conjoin propositions (each of which is an expression of what K knows), the equivocation of the conjunction reaches a point where it "swamps" whatever positive information one is receiving. To illustrate, consider the lottery example. K buys a ticket in the lottery. He then learns that 1 million other tickets have been sold. The receipt of this piece of information makes it overwhelmingly likely that K will lose. The amount of equivocation that remains is negligible (but not, of course, zero). But the same may be said for K's friends who also (as it turns out) hold losing tickets. If K can know that he is going to lose in the face of such negligible equivocation, then (by parity of reasoning) he can know that his friend J is going to lose, since the equivocation associated with J's losing is exactly the same as for K (and J, like K, *is* going to lose). Hence, we conclude (in accordance with the conjunction principle) that K knows that *both* he and J are going to lose. But K has thousands of unlucky friends. *All* of them hold losing tickets. If negligible equivocation is no obstacle to knowledge, then K can know of *each* of his friends that they are going to lose. But if he knows it of *each*, then (by the conjunction principle) he knows it of *all*. But the equivocation associated with knowing that all his friends are going to lose is no longer negligible. Depending on the number of his unlucky friends, it can be very substantial indeed. If (to take an extreme case) he has 500,000 unlucky friends, the amount of equivocation associated with this (conjunctive) proposition completely overwhelms the small amount of information K has about the truth of each conjunct. In effect, K receives *no information* about whether or not the conjunction is true (this is 50–50), despite the fact that he has positive information about the truth of each conjunct. We are led to the absurd result that K can know something about which he has received no information—that he can, for example, know that none of his (500,000) friends are going to win the lottery—despite the fact that (given the information he has received) the probability of this result is only 50 percent.

The only way to avoid this consequence (while retaining the conjunction principle) is to abandon the hypothesis that K can know that s is F without having received the information s is F. The knowledge that s is F requires, not simply information *about* s, but, specifically, the information *that* s is F. Since this requirement is imposed by our information-based analysis of knowledge, I conclude that, to this extent at least, the analysis is satisfactory.

It may be supposed that this conclusion could be avoided by abandoning the conjunction principle. And so it could. But it seems to me that this principle is absolutely fundamental. I am not even sure how to argue for it. It should be emphasized, however, that the conjunction principle does *not* say that if one knows that P and knows that Q, then one knows what is logically implied by P and Q. It may be possible, for instance, for K to know that A is larger than B, and to know that B is larger than C, without knowing that A is larger than C. The conjunction principle does *not* rule out this possibility. Neither does it imply that if one knows that P and knows that Q, then one believes, knows, or would be prepared to acknowledge that one knows both P and Q. The latter "principles" have their defenders, but I think they should be rejected. At least they should be distinguished from the conjunction principle itself. And when the principle is carefully distinguished from its more suspicious relatives, I think it becomes clear that the price one pays for abandoning it is exorbitant.[15]

Communication

Part of our ordinary conception of knowledge is that it is something that can be imparted by communication between knowledgeable parties. If Herman knows that s is F, then he can, by either word or deed, bring it about that Shirley knows that s is F. He can *tell* her. Of course, if Herman is dishonest, or is believed to be such by his listeners, then his utterances may not have their usual cognitive upshot.[16] No one will believe him. But if communication and learning of the ordinary sort is to occur, there must be some relationship between individuals that can serve as the basis for instruction, for imparting knowledge. We may try to summarize this by saying that when a speaker knows that s is F, sincerely asserts that s is F with the purpose of informing his listeners of what he knows to be the case, is generally reliable and trustworthy about such matters, and is reasonably believed to be such by his listeners, then listeners can learn (come to know) that s is F on the basis of what the speaker tells them. I do not really know whether this is a sufficient basis for imparting knowledge by verbal means. But whatever the actual conditions must be, our ordinary practice manifests a conviction that these conditions are frequently realized in our daily intercourse. For we commonly suppose that this is *how* we learned something: we heard it from Herman, read it in a book, saw it in the newspapers, or heard it on the evening news.

Consider, now, what happens to communication of this sort if one denies that the information that s is F is essential to learning that s is F. We can imagine a chain of communication in which there is a small amount of equivocation between adjacent links in the chain. The equivocation between adjacent links is *small enough*, however, not to interfere with a link's learning what is occurring at the immediately preceding link. K_1 receives a signal from the source s, and although the information that s is F is not communicated, the amount of equivocation is small enough to permit K_1 to know that s is F. K_1 now turns to K_2 in order to tell him what he (K_1) knows to be the case: viz., that s is F. In order to communicate this information, K_1 says, "s is F." Since the amount of equivocation between K_1 and K_2 is small enough not to interfere with K_2's learning what it is that K_1 is saying, we may suppose that K_2 comes to know what it is that K_1 is saying. Though the auditory signal K_2 receives does not make the probability of K_1's having said "s is F" equal to unity, though (as a consequence) this signal does not carry the information that K_1 said, "s is F," the equivocation of this signal is sufficiently low to permit K_2 to know that K_1 said that s was F. Since we may suppose that communication conditions are ideal in every other respect, there is nothing to prevent our concluding that K_2 could come to know in this way, not only that K_1 *said* that s was F, but that s *was* F. After all, K_1 knows that s is F, what he said was an honest expression of what he knew, K_2 has a well-grounded trust in K_1's veracity and reliability, and more-

KNOWLEDGE AND THE FLOW OF INFORMATION   104

over, K_2 knows that K_1 *said* that s was F. Surely this is the kind of situation in which knowledge is imparted.

There is, however, a fly in the ointment. The equivocation between the individual links in the communication chain *accumulates* so that, generally speaking, the equivocation between A and C will be *greater than* the equivocation between A and B or between B and C. What this means in terms of our example is that, although the amount of equivocation between K_1 and the source may be very small (small enough, we are supposing, so as not to interfere with K_1's coming to know that s is F), and although the amount of equivocation between K_2 and K_1 is also very small (small enough, we are supposing, so as not to interfere with K_2's coming to know what is happening at K_1), the equivocation between K_2 and the source is *larger than* either of these two small equivocations. That is, K_2 gets *less information about the source* than does K_1. And when K_2 passes the message along to K_3 (over a channel similar to that linking K_1 and K_2), K_3 receives even less information about s (although, once again, enough information *about* K_2 to know what is going on there). As we reach the more distant links of this communication chain, K_n will be receiving a negligible amount of information *about* s. The information about s will gradually evaporate, nibbled to death by the small equivocations existing between adjacent links in the communication chain.

Eventually, of course, we reach links in the communication chain in which there is virtually no information about the source. The signal K_{n+1} receives from K_n will still carry enough information (about K_n) to let K_{n+1} know what K_n is saying (about s), but it will carry virtually no information about s itself. Since the information about s can be made as small as we please (by going to sufficiently distant links in the communication chain), we must suppose that there is some point in the chain of communication where it is impossible to learn that s is F from the arriving signals. After all, the probability of s's being F, given the arriving signal (from the preceding link in the communication chain), can be as close to the chance level as we care to make it.

This obviously constitutes a dilemma, and it constitutes a dilemma for anyone subscribing to the opening assumption that knowledge does *not* require the receipt of the appropriate piece of information. The dilemma is *not* that as we pass a message from one person to another we may reach a point at which the receiving parties no longer learn what the initiating parties knew (and communicated), but that *it is hard to say just where this point is*. This is not an instance of the sorites paradox.[17] The dilemma is, rather, that somewhere in the chain of communication the student (K_{n+1}) cannot learn from his instructor (K_n) what K_n knows to be the case, and he cannot learn it from him even though they are communicating over a channel that is just as good as the one over which K_n learned. K_n has a piece of incommunicable knowledge, a piece of knowledge that he cannot share with his students even though he is linked to them by a channel of communication that was good enough to permit *him* to learn from *his* teacher. This constitutes a dilemma because one is at a loss to say what the difference is between, say K_1 and K_n. They both know that s is F. They are communicating with their listeners over identical channels. Their respective students know and understand what it is they are saying. Both may be assumed to be reliable informants. Yet, K_1 succeeds in imparting knowledge to his student (K_2), while this is impossible for K_n.

The source of this dilemma is, of course, the assumption that K_1 could learn (come to know) that s is F without having received the information that s is F. The difficulty this presents to communication is really the same difficulty we witnessed in connection with the lottery paradox a few pages back. If one admits the possibility of knowing that s is F *without* the information that s is F, one is immediately confronted by the fact that the missing information (equivocation), although presumably acceptable when considered in isolation, can be made to *accumulate* to unacceptable levels very quickly. No matter how *little* equivocation (greater than 0) one is prepared to tolerate, the fact remains that these negligible amounts of equivocation can be made to add up to something intolerable. And this has the consequence that one cannot know the conjunction of those things that (taken individually) one knows and one cannot impart to others the knowledge that one has. To avoid these consequences, we must accept the view (built into our characterization of knowledge) that the knowledge that s is F requires (because it is required as a cause of belief) the information that s is F.

Although I consider these arguments in favor of the information-theoretic analysis persuasive, I do not think they are decisive. The ultimate test of a theory lies in its usefulness in organizing and illuminating the material to which it is applied. And of equal importance to the voices speaking in its favor are the voices that fail to speak against it. I turn, therefore, to a consideration of the more serious objections to the present analysis and, in particular, the challenge of skepticism.

Chapter 5
The Communication Channel

Knowing that something is so, unlike being wealthy or reasonable, is not a matter of degree. Two people can both be wealthy, yet one be wealthier than the other; both be reasonable, yet one be more reasonable than the other. When talking about people, places, or topics (*things* rather than *facts*), it also makes sense to say that one person knows something *better* than another. He knows the city better than we do, knows more Russian history than any of his colleagues, but does not know his wife as well as do his friends. But *factual* knowledge, the knowledge *that s* is *F*, does not admit of such comparisons. If we both know that the ball is red, it makes no sense to say that you know this better than I. A rich man can become richer by acquiring more money, and a person's belief can be made more reasonable by the accumulation of additional evidence, but if a person already knows that the ball is red, there is nothing he can acquire that will make him know it better. If he already knows it, additional evidence will not promote him to a loftier form of knowledge. One can raise the temperature of boiling water beyond its boiling point, but one is not thereby boiling it better. One is just boiling it at a higher temperature.

In this respect factual knowledge is *absolute*. Those who view knowledge as some form of reasonable or justified belief acknowledge this fact by speaking, not simply of justification, but of *full*, *complete*, or *adequate* justification. These qualifications on the sort of justification required for knowledge constitute an admission that knowledge is, whereas justification is not, an absolute notion. For these qualifiers are meant to express the idea that there is a certain *threshold of justification* that must be equaled or exceeded if knowledge is to be obtained, and *equaling or exceeding this threshold* is an absolute idea. I can have a better justification than you, but my justification cannot be more adequate (more sufficient) than yours. If my justification is complete in the intended sense, then your justification cannot be more complete.

Generally speaking, philosophers who view knowledge as some form of justified true belief are reluctant to talk about this implied threshold of justification. Just how much evidence or justification is *enough* to qualify as an adequate, a full, or a complete justification? If the levels (or degrees) of justification are represented by real numbers between 0 and 1 (indicating the relative probability of that for which we have evidence or justification), any threshold less than 1 seems arbitrary. Worse yet, any threshold less than 1 seems to be *too low*. For examples can quickly be manufactured in which that particular threshold is exceeded without the evidence being good enough to know. Recall the example (from the last chapter) of the lottery or the example of someone drawing colored balls from an urn *most* (but not *all*) of which are pink.

Our information-based account of knowledge traces the absolute character of knowledge to the absolute character of the information on which it depends. Information itself is not an absolute concept, of course, since we can get more or less information *about* a source. Information *about* s comes in degrees. But the information *that* s is F does not come in degrees. It is an all or nothing affair. One cannot get the information that s is F *better* than someone else, or *more* than someone else, because the receipt of this information requires the equivocation of the signal (relative to s's being F) to be zero. Not *close* to zero. Not *very near* to zero. But zero. This leaves no room for degrees. Once the information that s is F has been received, there is *no more* information to be had about whether or not s is F. Everything else is either redundant

THE COMMUNICATION CHANNEL

or irrelevant. You cannot know that s is F *better than* I because you cannot get *more* information than I must already have in order to know.

This is not a view that will generate much enthusiasm among philosophers and psychologists. Philosophers will view it as a manifestation of skepticism.[1] Psychologists are likely to regard it as betraying an appalling ignorance of psychophysics.[2] Both reactions are inspired by what are taken to be the *facts* of the case. For it will certainly be objected that if the knowledge that s is F requires, not just *some* information about s (a "sufficient" or "adequate" amount), but the information *that s is F* (as this has been defined), then precious little can ever be known. For in most practical situations the conditional probabilities are always less than one. There is always *some* equivocation.

Peter Unger has an interesting discussion of absolute concepts, and I believe he identifies what it is about such concepts that proves troublesome.[3] He illustrates the problem by using the concept *flat*. This, he argues, is an absolute term in the sense that a surface is flat only if it is *not at all bumpy or irregular*. Any bumps or irregularities, however small and insignificant they may be (from a practical point of view), mean that the surface on which they occur is not really flat. It may be almost flat, or very nearly flat, but (as both these descriptions imply) it is not really flat. We do, it seems, compare surfaces with respect to their degree of flatness (e.g., this surface is flatter than that), but Unger argues, persuasively, that this must be understood as a comparison of the degree to which these surfaces approximate flatness. They cannot both be flat and yet one be flatter than the other. Hence, if A is flatter than B, then B (perhaps also A) is not really flat. Flatness does not admit of degrees, although a surface's nearness to being flat does.

Unger concludes that not many things are really flat. For under powerful enough magnification almost any surface will exhibit some irregularities. Hence, contrary to what we commonly say and believe, these surfaces are not really flat. When we describe them as being flat, what we say is literally false. Maybe *nothing* is really flat. So be it. According to Unger, this is the price we pay for operating with absolute concepts.

If knowledge is an absolute concept of this sort, a similar line of reasoning will lead to the conclusion that most of our knowledge claims are false. At least this is the fear of many philosophers. Powerful magnification (i.e., critical inquiry) will reveal small "bumps" and "irregularities" in those situations to which we commonly apply the concept *knowledge*. Indeed, there are reasons to think that such irregularities are everywhere, infecting even what we regard as our most immediate and secure forms of knowledge. To admit that knowledge is an absolute concept, then, would be to flirt with the idea that perhaps *nothing* is really known.

This skeptical conclusion is unpalatable. Unger endorses it. Knowledge, according to him, is an absolute concept that, like flatness, has very little application to our bumpy, irregular world. I have already indicated my agreement with Unger. Knowledge *is* an absolute idea. It inherits this quality from the information on which it depends.[4] Unlike Unger, however, I do not derive skeptical conclusions from this fact. I will happily admit that *flat* is an absolute concept, and absolute in roughly the way Unger says it is, but I do not think this shows that nothing is flat. For although nothing can be flat if it has any bumps or irregularities, what *counts* as a bump or irregularity depends on the type of surface being described. Something is empty (another absolute concept according to Unger) if it has nothing in it, but this does not mean that my pocket, or the abandoned warehouse, is not really empty because there is *something* in it. Dust and air molecules do not count when determining the emptiness of pockets and warehouses. This is not to say that, if we changed the way we used warehouses (e.g., as giant vacuum chambers), they still would not count. It is only to say that, given the way they are now used, molecules do not count. Similarly, a road can be perfectly flat even though one can feel and see irregularities in its surface, irregularities which, were they found on the surface of a mirror, would mean that the mirror's surface was not really flat. Large mice are not large animals, and flat roads are not necessarily flat surfaces.[5] The Flat Earth Society may be an anachronism, but they are not denying the existence of hills and valleys.

Knowledge exhibits a similar logic. Although it is an absolute concept, an absoluteness it inherits from the information on which it depends, this does not mean that knowledge is unobtainable. Information of the requisite sort can be transmitted. The irregularities the skeptic purports to find in the communication of information are not irregularities at all. At least they do not count as such for purposes of communication. Such, at least, is the point I mean to clarify in the remainder of this chapter.

CHANNEL CONDITIONS

The view that the information requirement on knowledge is too severe, that it cannot (in most practical situations) be satisfied, ultimately rests on the confusion between: (1) the information (about a source) a signal carries, and (2) the channel on which the delivery of this information depends. If one mistakenly supposes that a signal's dependence on a source is less than optimal insofar as it is conditioned by factors about which the signal carries no information, one will regard *all* communication as impossible—and, hence, as impossible the knowledge that (according to the present view) depends on the transmission of information.

Consider, though, a simple measuring instrument: a voltmeter attached to a resistor in an electric circuit. The function of this instrument is to measure differences in voltage—in this case the voltage drop across the resistor. Let us suppose that the voltage drop across the resistor is 7 volts. When the meter is attached, this voltage difference generates a current flow through the internal circuit of the instrument. The current flow sets up a magnetic field; the magnetic field exerts a twisting force (torque) on an armature; the armature turns (against the force of a restraining spring), and a pointer (affixed to the armature) moves up an appropriately calibrated scale on the face of the instrument. The pointer comes to rest on 7.

This instrument (indeed, *any* measuring instrument) may be regarded as an information-processing device. When the instrument is in proper working order, the information generated at the resistor by the 7-volt difference across its leads is communicated to the face of the instrument. The *position* of the pointer carries information about the voltage across the resistor. If, for the sake of the example, we think of the voltage as having only ten possible values,[6] then approximately 3.3 bits of information are generated at the source. If, as assumed, the instrument is functioning properly, the equivocation between source (voltage across resistor) and receiver (position of pointer) is zero: the pointer's registering 7 volts carries the information *that* the voltage drop across the resistor is 7 volts. And this, according to the present account, is what enables the user to *tell* (know) what the voltage across the resistor is.

Notice, however, that although the pointer carries this information about the voltage across the resistor, although the equivocation is zero, or is alleged to be zero, when the instrument is functioning properly, the position of the pointer, even *when* the instrument is functioning properly, depends on a great many things besides the voltage at the source. If, for example, we exchange the leads connecting the instrument to the circuit, substituting wires with a different resistance, the *same* voltage drop across R (the resistor) will generate a different current flow through the meter, a different magnetic field, a different torque on the armature, and a different position for the pointer. There is a restraining spring attached to the armature that is precisely calibrated to resist the twisting action of the magnetic field and to allow the armature to stop rotating at the desired point. If we modify this spring, if it fatigues (or breaks), the pointer will come to rest at the wrong point. Thus, the state of affairs existing at the receiver (the position of the pointer) depends on a great many factors other than those associated with the source (the voltage across R). We could, in fact, arrange to obtain the same reading (7 volts) by tinkering with these other variables. We could reduce the voltage across R to 5 volts and weaken the spring proportionately, and the instrument would still register 7 volts.

Given these facts, and the same sorts of facts could be recited about *any* channel of communication, it may seem that our claim to have perfect communication in this situation was exaggerated. How *can* the pointer reading carry the information that the voltage across R is 7 volts? Given the definition of a signal's carrying the information that s is F, the pointer carries this piece of information only if, given the position of the pointer (and k: things known to obtain on independent grounds[7]), the conditional probability of a 7-volt drop is *unity*. But, as we have just seen, the *same* reading can be produced by a 5-volt drop *with* a weakened restraining spring. What excludes *this* possibility? There is, after all, nothing in the position of the pointer itself to indicate that the restraining spring has not suddenly weakened. Even if the spring was checked before the instrument was used, what excludes the possibility of its having weakened *since* being checked? If there is nothing in the signal (position of pointer) to indicate the spring has not weakened, how can the probability, given the pointer reading, of a weakened spring be zero? But if this probability is not zero, then the probability that the 7-volt reading is being brought about by a 5-volt difference at R *together with* a weakened spring is not zero either. Hence, the conditional probability (given the pointer reading) of a 7-volt drop at R cannot be 1. The equivocation must be greater than zero even when the instrument is in perfect working order—unless, of course, the instrument is *known* (on independent grounds) to be in perfect working order.

The conclusion of this line of reasoning is that voltmeters and other measuring devices never deliver the information they are designed to deliver. The signal *always* depends on conditions other than s's being F, conditions whose value is not known at the time the instrument is used to deliver information about s's being F. Hence, the signal is always equivocal about the source. If a signal is transmitted over a channel in condition C, and there are possible states of the channel C^* which are such that the *same* type of signal can be transmitted over C^* *without* s's being F (as there always are), then the signal does not carry the information that s is F unless the channel is *known* to be in condition C at the moment the signal is received.

Philosophers will immediately recognize this objection as the information-theoretic analog of a shopworn skeptical thesis—the thesis, namely, that if our sensory experience depends, not only on the character of the objects we perceive, but also on the condition of our sensory apparatus, on the nature of the illumination, intervening medium, and so on, then the sensory experience itself cannot (or *should* not) be trusted to tell us about the properties of the objects we perceive. The sensory state, taken by itself, is always equivocal. It is equivocal even when all systems are functioning optimally—as well as they can function.

From an information-theoretic point of view the skeptical thesis amounts to the claim that for purposes of reckoning equivocation between source and receiver, for purposes of determining *how much* (and therefore what) information a signal carries about a source, no actual condition (unless known to obtain on independent grounds) can be taken as fixed. *Everything* is a potential source of equivocation. Even if the restraining spring in our volt-meter is specially designed to retain its elasticity, manufactured so as *not* to weaken with prolonged use, this fact cannot be taken for granted in determining the amount of dependency (hence equivo-cation) between pointer reading and voltage. For as long as the sig-nal (pointer reading) does not itself exclude the possibility of a weakened spring,[8] a weakened spring must be counted as a possi-bility from the point of view of this signal. But if *this* is a possibil-ity from the point of view of the signal, then it is also a possibility that the voltage across R is *not* 7. Hence, unless there is something in the signal that precludes an abnormal state of the channel vari-ables, or these are known (on independent grounds) to be in a normal state, the signal will not carry the required information about the source.

The skeptical recipe for determining the amount of information a signal carries about a source nourishes the view that a signal can-not carry the information that s is F unless it (or some simulta-neous auxiliary signal) also carries the information that the channel (over which the signal is being received) is *not* in one of those states in which such signals can be received without s's being F. According to the skeptical formula, information-bearing signals must be self-authenticating. In order to carry the information that s is F, a signal must also bear witness to the fact that what it car-ries is information, that it (the signal) *does* depend (in the requisite, unequivocal way) on conditions at the source.

There is little to be gained by quarreling with the skeptic on this matter. For his position combines a discovery of sorts with a recommendation, and although the discovery is real enough, it does not sustain the recommendation. It does not show what he takes it to show—any more than the discovery of small cracks in the surface of a road shows that the road is not really flat. The skeptic's discovery is that a signal bearing information about a source typically depends, not only on the source, but on a variety of other circumstances of which we are (normally) ignorant. The recommendation is that we treat this fact as showing that the sig-nal does not *really* carry the kind of information about the source that it is normally taken to carry. The discovery does not sustain the recommendation because some existing conditions (on which the signal depends) generate no information, or no *new* information, for the signal to carry. This, indeed, is what constitutes the channel of communication:

The channel of communication = that set of existing conditions (on which the signal depends) that either (1) generate no (relevant) information, or (2) generate only redundant information (from the point of view of the receiver).

This is why a signal, though depending on conditions both at the source and on the channel, carries information about *only* the source. Among the conditions on which the signal depends, *only the source* is a generator of new information.

Consider the voltmeter once again. The leads by means of which the instrument is connected (electrically) to various points of a circuit have a certain resistance. What the meter registers depends on this resistance, since the pointer's deflection depends on the amount of current flowing through the meter and this, in turn, depends on the resistance of the leads (among other things). If the resistance of the leads varied from moment to moment, or from day to day, the position of the pointer would vary correspondingly without any change in the voltage being measured. Hence, *if* the resistance of the leads varied, the position of the pointer would be *equivocal* with respect to the voltage being measured. But the resistance of these leads cannot be made to vary in the way envisaged by this hypothesis.[9] The resistance of a wire is a function of its physical constitution and dimensions, and these properties are not capricious. We can, of course, *cut* the wire or it can break, but as long as the leads remain intact, a stable value for their resistance is not something that itself generates information. That the leads are *not* changing their resistance, that they have the *same* resistance today that they had yesterday (or last week), is not a condition that generates information because there are no (relevant) possible alternatives. This is a channel condition because it generates no information for the signal (transmitted over the wires) to carry.

Periodic calibration and adjustment of such instruments is necessary, of course, since springs lose their elasticity over prolonged periods, wires break, soldered connections work loose, and so on. But this is simply to say that before using the instrument to measure voltage one must get information about the electrical-mechanical integrity of the system whose responsibility it is to convey

information about voltage differences. Once the instrument has
been initially calibrated and adjusted, certain procedures become
wholly redundant. Repeated checking of the leads (to see whether
they have changed their resistance), daily tests of the spring's
elasticity (to see whether it has unpredictably changed its coefficient of elasticity), recounting the number of windings on the
internal electromagnets (to make sure the same current flow will
generate the same magnetic field) is unnecessary. When carried to
an extreme, it becomes neurotic. It is like the man who keeps
going back to the door to make sure it is locked. Such a person
does not keep getting *new* information (viz., that the door is still
locked) since the door's *still* being locked generates no new information, no information he did not already have (20 seconds ago)
when he got the information that it was *then* locked. Given that it
was locked 20 seconds ago, every revisit to the door is *informationally redundant.* Redundancy may be psychologically reassuring,
and to this extent it may be epistemologically relevant (i.e., insofar as it affects one's preparedness to believe), but it is otherwise
of no epistemological significance.

There are an enormous number of conditions whose permanence,
whose lack of any (relevant) possible alternative state, qualifies
them as channel conditions. The amount of current that will flow
through a wire of a given resistance upon the application of a given
voltage, the amount of magnetic flux that will be created by a
given current flowing through a certain coil, the amount of torque
that will be exerted on a given armature by this magnetic field,
and the amount of rotation that this armature will undergo as the
result of this torque acting against the restraining action of a particular spring—all these are conditions that have no relevant possible
alternatives. Even though the signal depends on these relationships
being as they are, in the sense that *if* they were different, or *if*
they changed erratically, the signal would be equivocal, these conditions contribute nothing to the actual equivocation, since they
generate no information for the signal to carry. Since they are the
origin of no information, these conditions qualify as the framework *within which* communication takes place, not as a source
about which communication takes place.

As I have already indicated, however, some conditions have
genuine possible alternative states. They *do* generate information.

Wires *can* break, soldered connections work loose, points corrode, springs fatigue and lose their elasticity, and moving parts stick or bind. When such possibilities are genuine (I will have more to say in a moment about what constitutes a "genuine" or "relevant" alternative possibility), and the signals received over a channel do not themselves exclude such possibilities, then they must be excluded on independent grounds. In the case of measuring instruments, this means that periodic checking and calibration is required. We examine the leads before we use the instrument, adjust the zero setting, and check for electrical continuity. If the instrument has been lying idle for a long period, greater precautions may be necessary. It may have to be recalibrated. That is, one uses the instrument to measure *known* values of a quantity in order to see if the instrument registers correctly, if what it indicates corresponds to what one knows, on independent grounds, to be the correct value. If it is known that Q has a value of 6, and the instrument registers 6, then this provides information about the instrument's reliability—information to the effect that the restraining spring has *not* weakened, that the leads are *not* broken, that the pointer is *not* sticking, and so on. In ordinary use the instrument acts as a channel for transmitting information about Q. During calibration, known values of Q are used to get information about the instrument. It is important to notice, however, that we can obtain information *about* the instrument only by abandoning it (temporarily) as a channel for relaying information about Q. We cannot use the instrument simultaneously to collect information about Q and about its own reliability. *Something* has to function as the channel in order for something to qualify as the source. The same phenomenon is illustrated when we "test" a friend about whom we have become suspicious. We ask him to tell us about a situation of which we are already informed. His response tells us (gives us information) about *him*, not about the situation he is (perhaps accurately) describing. To suppose that we could receive information about the reliability of a channel at the same time as the channel is functioning *as a channel* is like supposing that a speaker could give his listeners information about his own reliability by appending, "and everything I have said is true" at the end of all his statements. This does not give one information about the reliability of the speaker; at best it gives the listeners a piece of *redundant information* (i.e., zero *new* information) about what the speaker has already described.

Once these preliminary tests and checks have been performed, the conditions about which one has received information become *fixed*, and thereby qualify as part of the channel, for as long a period as there exists no genuine possibility of their changing into some alternative state. That is, they function as part of the channel for as long a period as their *persistence* in the fixed condition generates no new information—information that was not obtained during the initial test. A few simple operations, operations that most technicians perform routinely, suffice to fix the state of many channel conditions: things are connected properly, the leads are not broken, the pointer does not stick, and so on. If initial checks determine that the spring has not broken, worked loose, or lost its elasticity, then the integrity of the spring qualifies as a channel condition for (at least) hours, probably days, and perhaps even months (this will depend on the *quality* of the instrument). This becomes a channel condition because for hours, probably days, and perhaps even months, the actual state of the spring generates no new information, no information that was not already obtained during preliminary checks. Springs do not change their coefficient of elasticity from one moment to the next any more than locks spontaneously become unlocked. To insist on rechecking this condition every twenty minutes is to behave as neurotically as one who pulls on the door every twenty seconds to reassure himself that it is still locked. Springs wear out, yes, but they do not (during normal use) do so overnight. They sometimes *break*, but information about this is carried by the signal itself (a pointer slamming against the full-scale stop).

Things (trees, people, flowers) change their size, but they do so at varying rates. Your niece grows up, but she does not do so between breakfast and lunch. If you saw her yesterday (or last week), then, her size today can function as a channel condition for transmission of information about, say, her distance even in the absence of other cues (texture gradients, etc.). Seeing her yesterday (in familiar surroundings where information about her size was available) was, in effect, a recalibration. It is quite true that under reduced viewing conditions (immobile monocular viewing with other cues removed) the incoming signals are, in a sense, equivocal.

The angle subtended by the incoming light rays, hence the size of the retinal image, depends on two things: the actual *size* of the object being viewed and the *distance* of this object from the viewer. This, however, does not mean that the signal is equivocal. Whether it is or not depends on whether the object's size generates any (new) information, whether the size of the object has been fixed and is thereby functioning as a channel condition by means of which information about distance is being transmitted. If one has "recalibrated" with respect to the size variable in the recent past (*how* recent is recent *enough* will depend, among other things, on what the object is: a person, an oak tree, or a dandelion), then incoming signals carry unequivocal information about the object's distance.[10]

The situation is exactly parallel to some test instruments that operate on an internal battery that gradually loses its strength under normal operating conditions. With such instruments it is necessary to adjust the settings (compensating thereby for any loss of battery strength) before using it, before it can deliver the kind of information it is designed to deliver. Such semipermanent, slowly varying conditions must be fixed so that they can serve as part of the channel. For short periods (after adjustment) the *actual* condition of the battery generates no information, since like the locked door, its *retention* of its original state has no relevant alternatives.

It is important to emphasize that what qualifies a condition as a channel condition is not that it is *known* to be stable, not that it is *known* to lack relevant alternative states, but that it *is* stable, *lacks* relevant alternative states, *in fact* generates no (new) information. We can imagine a technician who refused to trust his instrument. Every few minutes elaborate tests would be repeated: the resistance of the leads measured, the number of windings verified, the spring recalibrated, and so on. The point to be made about such precautions is that for purposes of transmitting information they are unnecessary.[11] An instrument for which these tests are not performed (every few minutes) transmits as much information as one for which they are performed. If such precautions are necessary for the technician to trust his instrument, well and good. Let him perform the tests. But if, as we have been supposing, the tests are genuinely redundant, if the information he already has (whether he knows it or not) excludes whatever genuine possibilities exist for these conditions, then such tests are superfluous. One cannot squeeze more information out of an instrument by monitoring conditions whose actual state generates no new information any more than one can *make* a bridge safe to cross by checking the strength of its supports. Given the technician's mistrust, the information delivered by a suspected instrument may not have its usual effect, it may not cause the technician to *believe* what the instrument indicates, but the information would be there nonetheless.

There are, of course, conditions (on which the signal depends) that are too variable to qualify as channel conditions. They are a *steady source* of information. In such cases it is essential to the delivery of information (about the source) that information also be transmitted about these variable conditions. We often arrange to monitor such parameters by a *separate* channel. If the signal depends, say, on the charge of the battery, and the battery's retention of an appropriate charge is not something that can be relied on from moment to moment, then we can introduce an auxiliary meter to register battery strength. Information about the source is now being delivered by means of a *composite signal*: the (main) pointer's position *plus* the indication of the auxiliary meter. Nature has seen fit to install such monitoring devices in our sensory channels. Consider, for example, the way we detect movement. When we are looking at a moving object, the proximal stimulus (pattern of light on the retina) sweeps across the densely clustered rods and cones. A signal is sent via the optic nerve to the brain, which carries information about these retinal events. But the eyes, head, and body are also capable of moving. Their position is not a stable condition. If the eyes move, the proximal stimulus once again sweeps across the retina even if one happens to be viewing a stationary object. Yet, interestingly enough, under normal conditions we do not see the object as moving when the change in retinal stimulation is brought about by our *own* movement. Objects look stationary despite the occurrence of an event (a change in the position of the retinal image) which is the same as when we see the object as moving. How is this possible? We are told that this is made possible by a device that serves the same purpose as the auxiliary meter on our battery-operated instrument.[12] The brain not only receives information about the movement of the image across the retina, it also receives information about the state of the retina. If the eye (head, body) moves, the nervous system *takes account* of this movement in evaluating the signals arriving from the retina. If all the movement of the retinal image is accounted for by the movement of the eye or head, then the signal that is eventually produced cancels the ostensible information from the retina and we experience no sensation of movement. If the monitoring device signals no movement of the head or eyes, then a movement of the retinal image will signal (because it goes uncanceled) a movement of the object. In information-theoretic terms this is an exact analog of a battery-run instrument with a separate channel for monitoring battery strength. If we suppose that information about battery strength is used to adjust the position of the main pointer so as to compensate for any loss of battery strength (instead or having a separate indicator), we have, in the position of the main pointer, a rough model of the way our sensory experience carries information about an object's movement.

There is, of course, a limit to how completely a communication system can be monitored. Auxiliary channels may be introduced to track some variable aspect of the system (e.g., the movement of the eye), but unless the whole process is repeated, *ad infinitum*, for each of the auxiliary channels, some channel will necessarily go unsupervised. Hence, if information could not be transmitted through a system without simultaneously transmitting information (via auxiliary channels) about the system's reliability, it would be impossible to transmit information at all. Fortunately, however, there is also a limit to what conditions *need* be monitored in order to transmit information. Only those aspects of a communication system whose actual state generates information need be monitored. The others are part of the channel.

As the above-mentioned regress shows, there is a limit to our ability to monitor the channels over which we receive information. But this limit does not represent an obstacle to our receiving information over these channels. Rather, it represents an obstacle to receiving that higher-order information that the signals being received do indeed carry information about the source. In the case of movement perception, for example, the brain monitors the input channel over which information is received about the motion of objects. The brain does not, however, monitor the fidelity of this auxiliary channel. It seems likely that the way the brain monitors this main channel (concerning the movement of the eyes, head, and body) is by recording the commands sent by the central nervous system to the motor centers.[13] As long as things work properly, a command to move the eyes serves as information that the eyes *are* moving. Hence, the brain can integrate this information about what the eyes are doing with information received from the retina (concerning movement of retinal image) to compose a message bearing information about the movement of the object. Nevertheless, the eye muscles can be paralyzed and prevented from moving when told to move. In this case there is a breakdown in the auxiliary system. The brain gets misinformation about the movement of the eyes (it "tells" the eyes to move, but they do not move). As a result, objects seem to move even though everything (object *and* eyes) remains stationary. The signal is misleading because the sensory system has no way of monitoring the reliability of its auxiliary channel—no way of checking to see that the eyes perform in the way they are told to perform.

It would be a mistake to conclude, because the brain has no "backup" system to monitor the reliability of its auxiliary system (nothing to tell it that its commands to the eye muscles are being obeyed), that, therefore, the entire sensory channel over which we receive information about the movement of objects is unreliable or equivocal. Whether or not the sensory signals are equivocal depends on whether the coordination between central commands and motor performance, a coordination essential to unequivocal sensory signals, is itself a *channel condition*. It depends on whether there exist genuine alternative possibilities for this aspect of the auxiliary system. Even if we suppose that a breakdown in this auxiliary system *is* a real possibility, even if we suppose that under normal operating conditions the continued reliable performance of this auxiliary system generates positive information, there is no reason to think that the perceptual system as a whole is not continuously calibrated with respect to the integrity of this condition. Paralysis of the eye muscles may make it appear as though X is moving when it is not, but it also makes it appear as though *everything* is moving (even those things which it is known, on independent grounds, *not* to be moving). A malfunction in this auxiliary system is as apparent in the abnormal character of the signals being received as is a broken restraining spring in the erratic movement of a voltmeter's pointer.

RELEVANT POSSIBILITIES AND SKEPTICISM

The discussion reveals the source of that seemingly paradoxical fact that a person can know that s is moving (say), and know this by sensory means (she can *see* that it is moving), without knowing that her sensory system, the mechanism by means of which she *tells* that s is moving, is in satisfactory working order. The explanation of this "paradox" lies in the fact that the information that s is moving can be communicated over a channel without the receiver's knowing (or believing) that the channel is in a state such as to transmit this information. The receiver may be quite ignorant of the particular mechanisms responsible for the delivery of information—holding no beliefs, one way or the other, about the conditions on which the signal depends. One does not have to *know* that one's eyes are *not* paralyzed in order to see that something is moving. The channel is that set of existing conditions that have no relevant alternative states, that in fact generate no (new) information. Whether the receiver is ignorant of these particular conditions or not is beside the point. As long as the conditions of which he or she is ignorant (holds no beliefs about) are conditions which in fact have no relevant alternative states—or, if they do, have alternative states that have been excluded (whether this is known or not) by information already received by prior test and calibration —then these conditions function as the *fixed framework* (channel) within which equivocation (and hence information) is reckoned. They are not a *source* of equivocation (information). Information (and therefore knowledge) about a source depends on a reliable system of communication between source and receiver—not on whether it is *known* to be reliable.

This point is important enough to be illustrated in somewhat greater detail. For this purpose I offer the following example.[14] A sensitive and completely reliable instrument (a pressure gauge) is used to monitor the pressure within a certain boiler. Since the boiler pressure is a critical quantity, in that too much pressure can result in a dangerous explosion, the gauge is made from the finest materials, to the most exacting standards, by the most careful methods. These instruments have always been completely reliable.

The gauge is located on a console. An attendant checks it period-ically. No one has the slightest hesitation about saying that the attendant *knows* what the boiler pressure is when he consults the gauge. The gauge delivers the relevant information.

Nevertheless, despite an impeccable performance record, a ner-vous engineer becomes concerned about a possible failure in the pressure-sensing mechanism and the consequent accuracy of the gauge. He decides to install an auxiliary system whose function it is to detect malfunctions in the main channel of communication (the pressure-sensing system). If things go wrong with the pressure gauge, a small light will flash on the attendant's console, alerting him to the problem.

The auxiliary system is installed, but before the attendant can be told about the additional precautions that have been taken, a failure occurs in the auxiliary device. The warning light flashes on the attendant's console, but the pressure gauge, operating in its old reliable way, indicates a completely normal boiler pressure. We may suppose that the attendant either does not see the flashing light or sees it but (ignorant of its purpose) ignores it in coming to the belief (on the basis of the pressure gauge reading) that the boiler pressure is normal. Question: does the attendant *know* that the boiler pressure is normal?

From an information-theoretic point of view there is only one way to judge this case. If the attendant knew about the boiler pressure *before* the installation of the auxiliary device, *before* peo-ple became concerned about its possible malfunction, and knew this on the basis of the pressure gauge, then (since the gauge on which he *now* relies is *still* perfectly reliable) he *still* knows that the pressure is normal. He cannot be robbed of this knowledge by the introduction of a malfunctioning (and therefore misleading) device that is either unobserved or totally ignored. If the sensor was delivering information about boiler pressure *before* the instal-lation of the auxiliary system, it is *still* delivering this information since its reliability (and hence the unequivocality of the signals transmitted over it) is not diminished by the presence of a mal-functioning auxiliary system. And since it is the information de-livered to the pointer on the pressure gauge that is causing the attendant to believe that the pressure is normal, the attendant *knows* that the boiler pressure is normal.

There is, however, another way of interpreting situations of this sort. The second evaluation is influenced by the same considerations that motivated the nervous engineer, the same considerations that prompted expenditure of time and money on the installation of an auxiliary system. Despite the spotless performance record of the pressure gauge, despite the acknowledged remoteness of any malfunction, the boiler pressure is such a critically important quantity that even *remote possibilities* should be guarded against. Even remote possibilities become *relevant* possibilities. The pressure gauge is not, after all, an infallible instrument. Even if (as a matter of fact) it has never malfunctioned (and never will), circumstances can be imagined in which it would cease to be reliable. Every precaution has been taken to eliminate these possibilities in the manufacture and installation of the pressure-sensing mechanism, but the stakes are high enough to warrant *additional* precautions.

The reader will doubtless have recognized our nervous engineer as the skeptical wolf in sheep's clothing. If he can prevent the attendant from knowing that the boiler pressure is normal while changing *neither* the attendant's beliefs *nor* the reliability of the mechanisms producing these beliefs, he has caught the shepherd napping. The whole flock is endangered. For there is now nothing to prevent him from attacking indiscriminately—impugning the reliability of whatever auxiliary systems we introduce to allay suspicions about the main channel of communication. There is no reason, after all, to think that the auxiliary mechanisms are any *more* reliable, any *more* capable of delivering genuine information, than was the carefully manufactured pressure-sensing mechanism. We need warning lights and auxiliary gauges for each of the auxiliary systems. Before long we have a control console cluttered with an array of useless gauges—useless because their net effect (from an epistemological point of view) is zero. The attendant still cannot tell, by consulting all the gauges, what the boiler pressure is. This information cannot get through because there always remain some possibilities (simultaneous malfunctioning of *all* systems) that the composite signal does not eliminate.

As a practical matter, of course, our engineer would be assigned to the shipping (or philosophy) department long before his employers committed thousands of dollars to humoring his lively imagination. But the point he is making, he will insist, is not just a practical point. It is a theoretical point about who knows and when.

What makes the nervous engineer a sympathetic character, at least to many people, is the fact that he begins his crusade in a perfectly reasonable way. This *is* an imperfect world. We do, sometimes, take a channel to be reliable when it is not. Clocks run slow, witnesses lie, gauges break, letters are fake, books (purporting to be genuine history) are frauds, and experiences are illusory. Furthermore, some information is of sufficiently great importance to us that we take extraordinary precautions about the channel over which we receive it. When Abner tells me it is 3 o'clock, I rush off (like the naïve attendant) *knowing* I am late. When Abner denies having had a drink after sideswiping four parked cars, the prosecuting attorney (like the nervous engineer) insists on a lie-detector test. I once worked in a power-generating station in which there were three gauges (plus an elaborate system of mirrors) to allow an attendant (three stories below) to monitor a critical quantity (water level in a boiler drum). Yet, engineers install *one* gauge of *lesser* quality in every automobile so that we can *see* how much gas we have in our tank from the driver's seat. If *one* gauge is enough to transmit information about the amount of gas I have in my tank, enough to let me see (and therefore know) that I am low on gas, why is it not enough for the engineers at the power station? It would appear that either we common folk never know how much gas we have (since a single gauge is not enough to bring us the relevant information) or the power station has gone to considerable expense to install redundant gauges—*one* would have been enough to see whether the water level was normal.

It is a mistake, however, to conclude that because *your* watch is slow, *my* watch cannot be trusted, that because *some* gauges are inaccurate, *all* gauges are unreliable, that if *some* people lie, *no one* is dependable, that if *any* newspaper (book, document) has ever been in error, *no* newspaper (book, document) conveys information of the sort required for knowledge. It is, furthermore, a mistake to suppose that if there are good practical reasons for installing multiple channels of communication between a source and a receiver, then no *one* of these channels carries the relevant information. Redundancy has its uses. It is psychologically reassuring, and insofar as such assurance is needed for trusting the signals one receives, it is epistemologically relevant (since relevant to the signal's efficacy for producing belief). The skeptic is certainly right in pointing out that there *may* be equivocation on a channel, equivocation of which we are unaware. There may be genuine alternative possibilities that we, through ignorance or carelessness, have failed to recognize. *If* such possibilities exist (whether or not they actually occur is immaterial), then we do not know. We do not know because we do not get the relevant piece of information. But there is another side to this coin. *Taking* something to be a possibility, as a source of equivocation, does not make it so. If we later find that a condition we took to be erratic, unstable, or untrustworthy is (and *was*) perfectly reliable, we may revise our estimates *upward* of what people knew. I may be indignant if someone claims to know that I am nervous if they rely, simply, on my twitching cheek muscle. Nonetheless, if I later find that this twitching is completely involuntary, that I cannot deliberately make it occur (at least not in the same way), and that it occurs only when I am nervous, I may (or *should*) belatedly concede that the person knew whereof he spoke. The twitching, unbeknownst to me, carried information about my mental state. And someday we may have to revise our estimates of what various psychics *now* know. We will revise these estimates when (but only when) we discover that they had access to, and in fact relied upon, information that we presently have reason to believe is unavailable to them.

What this means is that the flow of information, and the status of those beliefs produced by this information (their status *as* knowledge) are relatively immune from the dissolving effects of skeptical doubts. If (as originally assumed) the pressure gauge on which the attendant relies *is* perfectly reliable, then it carries information about the boiler pressure *whatever* people may happen to believe, or disbelieve, about the operation of the instrument. The engineer's doubts about the reliability of the gauge are just that—doubts. They do not *make* the gauge unreliable. They do not *create* equivocation. What makes a bridge unsafe are facts about the bridge (e.g., structural defects), not the fears of people who cross it. And what makes a communication system equivocal are facts about the system itself, not the suspicions (however well grounded) of potential receivers. No one may *cross* the bridge if his fears become great enough, and no one may *use* (or trust) a communication channel if his suspicions are sufficiently aroused, but these facts are as irrelevant to the quality of the communication channel as they are to the safety of the bridge.

Our engineer's doubts may induce others to mistrust the gauge. If this happens, *they* will be prevented from knowing what the attendant knows. *They* will be prevented from knowing, not because the information is unavailable to them, but because the information that the pressure is normal (available to them, as to the attendant, in the reading of the gauge) fails to produce *in them* the requisite belief. If these suspicions (about the reliability of the gauge) are communicated to the attendant, it may no longer be reasonable for him to *claim* to know (since no longer reasonable for him to think he is getting the information required to know), but if he should stubbornly (and, perhaps, unreasonably) persist in trusting the gauge, he would know what no one else knows—that the boiler pressure is normal. When suspicions affect neither the cause (information) nor the effect (belief), they are powerless to destroy the resulting knowledge. At best, they undermine our knowledge, or reasons for believing, *that we know*.

Nevertheless, despite the immunity of information (and hence knowledge) from skeptical doubts about the presence of information (or knowledge), there is a valid point to be made about the integrity of the channel. I have tried to acknowledge this point by describing the alternative possibilities (the absence of which define a channel condition, and the elimination of which defines information) as *relevant* or *genuine* possibilities. Philosophical suspicions may already have been aroused by my glib use of these qualifications. What, after all, is a *relevant* possibility? When does an existing condition have *genuine* alternative states? If one has, by initial calibration, determined a condition to be in state C, how long does its persistence in this state generate no *new* information (thus qualifying as a channel condition). If it is informationally redundant to return to the locked door every twenty seconds, when does one start getting *new* information—information to the effect that the door is *still* locked? Twenty minutes? Twenty days? Twenty years?

There is nothing particularly original in the idea that knowledge involves the exclusion of *relevant alternatives* (to what is known). What may be somewhat novel is the suggestion that knowledge inherits this property from information-theoretic sources, the idea that the distinction between a relevant and an irrelevant alternative (as this relates to *cognitive* studies) is just the distinction between a *source* (about which information is received) and a *channel* (over which information is received). The source, as a generator of information, is the locus of relevant alternative possibilities, since it is these possibilities that the signal is called upon to eliminate. The channel, being that set of conditions (on which the signal depends) that have no relevant alternative states—thus generating no information—constitutes the fixed framework within which dependency relations between source and receiver are determined. In articulating his own analysis of knowledge, for instance, Alvin Goldman alludes to the importance of relevant alternatives.[15] A relevant alternative, according to Goldman, is one the knower must be in an evidential position to exclude if he is to have the knowledge attributed to him. As the terminology suggests, this means that there are some irrelevant alternatives which the knower need not be in a position to exclude in order to know. Goldman illustrates the point by imagining the following sort of situation. While driving through the Wisconsin countryside I recognize (come to know) some buildings to be barns while remaining fully aware that I am in no position to exclude the possibility that what I am seeing are elaborate facsimiles constructed by Hollywood specialists for the purposes of deceiving casual tourists. For most situations, however, this possibility is not a relevant alternative. *If* such facsimiles happened to exist, however, and existed in various places in the Wisconsin countryside (not just on Hollywood sets), then such an alternative would become a relevant possibility. I would *then* have to be in a position to tell that the building I was looking at was not a cleverly contrived facsimile—something I am ordinarily *not* in a position to tell. Furthermore, the question of when an irrelevant alternative becomes relevant is a matter of degree. If such facsimiles existed in Iowa but not in Wisconsin, could one (by casual observation from the road) tell that something was a barn in *Wisconsin*? What if the facsimiles existed only in Sweden?

Or consider the following sort of case.[16] You take your son to the zoo, see several zebras, and when questioned by your son, tell him they are zebras. Do you know they are zebras? Well, most of us would have little hesitation in saying that we did know this. We know what zebras look like and, besides, this is the city zoo (not Disneyland) and the animals are in a pen clearly marked "Zebras." Yet, something's being a zebra implies that it is not a mule and, in particular, not a mule cleverly disguised by the zoo authorities to look like a zebra. Do you know that the animals are *not* mules cleverly disguised by the zoo authorities to look like zebras? Can you rule out this possibility? Are you getting *this* piece of information? If not, how can you be getting the information (and therefore know) that they are zebras? And if deception by the zoo authorities is not a relevant possibility, why is it not? What if the zoo director is a notorious practical joker?

Such examples may seem silly, but they illustrate an important truth about all information-carrying signals. *No* signal can rule out *all* possibilities if possibilities are identified with what is consistently imaginable. No signal, for instance, can eliminate the possibility that it was generated, not by the normal means, but by some freak cosmic accident, by a deceptive demon, or by supernatural intervention. If such contingencies are counted as *genuine* possibilities, then *every* signal is equivocal.

The way communication theory avoids this result is by taking what does (and does not) happen (over a sufficiently long run) as an index to what can (and cannot) happen. This guide is by no means infallible, of course, since rare, but perfectly genuine, possibilities may fail to materialize in the course of any finite sample. If Elmer has correctly identified one hundred playing cards drawn at random in a distant room, this may *suggest* that he is (somehow) getting information about the cards, it may be taken as *evidence* that he is, but it certainly does not constitute a *demonstration* that he is. He may, after all, get the next one hundred wrong. Nevertheless, the procedure, though not infallible, does have the merit of taking the question of what is possible, of what constitutes genuine equivocation of a signal, out of the hands of idle speculators (skeptical or otherwise) and putting it where it belongs—*in* the communication system whose reliability is in question. It has the effect of making a communication channel innocent until proved guilty. This is not to say that a signal is unequivocal until shown to be equivocal. Rather, it means that a signal is not equivocal merely because it has not been shown, and perhaps *cannot* be shown, to be unequivocal. The fact that we can imagine circumstances in which a signal would be equivocal, the fact that we can imagine possibilities that a signal does not eliminate, does not, by itself, show that the signal is equivocal. What has to be shown is that these imagined circumstances *can* occur, that these imagined possibilities do obtain. If a given type of signal *has* occurred only when s was *F*, the presumption, at least, is that it *can* occur only when s is *F*. This presumption may be in error, but it takes something more than a lively imagination to show that it *is* in error. The burden of proof has been shifted to those who would impugn the reliability of a hitherto reliable channel.

The question of when a channel is secure enough to transmit information of the sort required for knowledge (zero equivocation) is, by and large, an empirical question. It cannot be settled by *imagining* possibilities or by *ignoring* possibilities. To qualify as a relevant possibility, one that actually affects the equivocation of (and therefore information in) a signal, the possibility envisaged must actually be realizable in the nuts and bolts of the particular system in question. If, in the past, signals of kind *R* have arrived when s was not *F* (whether or not this is known is immaterial), that settles the matter.[17] Signals of kind *R* are equivocal with respect to s's being *F*, and they are equivocal whether or not, on *this* occasion, s happens to be *F*. But if, in the past, signals of type *R* have arrived *only* when s was *F*, the issue is less clear. Insofar as we are aware of the past regularity, there will be a presumption that the signal is unequivocal. And it will take some positive, countervailing, consideration to undermine the reasonableness of believing that *R* does indeed carry the information that s is *F*. But none of this is conclusive. How, after all, is one to assess the claim that this particular gauge's reading, that particular person's testimony, or that particular sensory experience *could* be in error, *is* equivocal, if there is no past record of such errors by *that* gauge, *that* person (on this topic, in these circumstances), or *that kind* of sensory experience. If Elmer has never hallucinated french fries on his dinner plate, is the fact that *others* have (if not french fries on their dinner plate, then squiggly things on their arm) enough to make this a real possibility for Elmer? Is this *enough* to show that Elmer's experience of french fries on his dinner plate is equivocal and, therefore, lacks the information that he has french fries on his dinner plate? Is the fact that the pointers on some gauges *have* stuck enough to show that the pointer on *this* gauge *might* be sticking? Why does it not simply show that *some* gauges are not reliable?

It is precisely at this point that our evaluation of a communication system begins to betray what some philosophers call a "social" or "pragmatic" aspect. A number of investigators have emphasized the context-dependent, interest-relative dimension of knowledge.[18] Whether someone knows something (not: is *said*, or *reasonably thought*, to know something) seems to depend on such extraneous factors (extraneous, at least, from an information-theoretic standpoint) as what everyone *else* knows or takes for granted, on the importance of *what* is known (or the importance of someone's *knowing* it) and the proximity or availability of evidence (information) one does not possess. All these considerations are matters of *degree* and, in this respect, appear to violate the absolute requirements of an information-based theory of knowledge. If the technician knows what the voltage is by using a newly acquired, recently calibrated, instrument, how long can he continue to use it (without recalibration or checking) and continue to know? How long will it continue to deliver the requisite information? If lying idle in the shop for twenty years is too long (contacts may have become corroded, parts may have rusted, etc.), when does the information cease to get through? How can knowledge be identified with information-produced belief if knowledge has this social, relative, pragmatic dimension to it while information does not?

The answer, of course, is that information has this very same character. Whether or not a signal carries a piece of information depends on what the channel is between source and receiver, and the question of whether an existing condition is stable or permanent *enough* to qualify as part of the channel, as a condition which itself generates no (new) information, is a question of degree, a question about which people (given their differing interests and purposes) can reasonably disagree, a question that may not have an objectively correct answer. When a possibility becomes a *relevant* possibility is an issue that is, in part at least, responsive to the interests, purposes, and, yes, values of those with a stake in the communication process. The flow of information, just like the cognitive exploits it makes possible, is a process that exhibits some sensitivity to the variable purposes of those who send and receive this information.

The point to notice, however, is that this relativity does not conflict with the alleged absoluteness of knowledge or the information on which it depends. To be empty is to have nothing in it, and in this respect, the emptiness of something is not a matter of degree. Nonetheless, whether something *counts* as a thing for purposes of determining emptiness *is* a matter of degree, a question about which people (given their differing interests and purposes) might easily disagree, a question that may not have an objectively correct answer. To be empty is to be devoid of *all relevant things*. The concept, though absolute, has a built-in plasticity (in the idea of a "relevant" thing) that is responsive to the interests and purposes of people applying it. Knowledge and information are no different. To know, or to have received information, is to have eliminated *all relevant alternative possibilities*. These concepts are absolute. What is not absolute is the way we apply them to concrete situations—the way we determine what will qualify as a relevant alternative.

The social or pragmatic dimensions of knowledge, then, are not incompatible with either the letter or the spirit of an information-theoretic analysis. On the contrary, this dimension to our concept of knowledge (and related cognitive concepts: recognition, perception, discovery, etc.) is to be *explained* by tracing it to its source in communication theory. Knowledge exhibits this pragmatic character *because* a communication system, *any* communication system, presupposes a distinction between a source *about which* information is received and a channel *over which* this information is received. The source is the generator of (new) information. The channel is that set of existing conditions that generates no (new) information. To say that an existing condition generates no new information, however, is to say that it has no relevant alternative states (at least none that have not been eliminated by information already received). It is in the determination of what constitutes a relevant alternative, a determination that is essential to the analysis of *any* information-processing system (whether it results in knowledge or not) that we find the source of that otherwise puzzling "flexibility" in our absolute cognitive concepts.[19]

Chapter 6
Sensation and Perception

Information-processing models of mental activity tend to con-flate perceptual and sensory phenomena on the one hand with cognitive and conceptual phenomena on the other. Perception is concerned with the pickup and delivery of information, cognition with its utilization. But these, one is told, are merely different stages in a more or less continuous information-handling process.[1] Recognition, identification, and classification (cognitive activities) occur at every phase of the perceptual process. Seeing and hearing are low-grade forms of knowing.

I think this is a confusion. It obscures the distinctive role of *sensory experience* in the entire cognitive process. In order to clarify this point, it will be necessary to examine the way informa-tion can be delivered and made available *to* the cognitive centers without itself qualifying for cognitive attributes—without itself having the kind of structure associated with knowledge and belief. For this purpose we must say something about the different ways information can be coded.

ANALOG AND DIGITAL CODING

It is traditional to think of the difference between an analog and a digital encoding of information as the difference between

135

a continuous and a discrete representation of some variable property at the source. So, for example, the speedometer on an automobile constitutes an analog encoding of information about the vehicle's speed because different speeds are represented by different positions of the pointer. The position of the pointer is (more or less) continuously variable, and each of its different positions represents a different value for the quantity being represented. The light on the dashboard that registers oil pressure, on the other hand, is a digital device, since it has only two informationally relevant states (on and off). These states are discrete because there are no informationally relevant intermediate states. One could, of course, exploit the fact that lights have a variable intensity. This continuous property of the signal could be used to represent the *amount* of oil pressure: the brighter the light, the lower the oil pressure. Used in this way the light would be functioning, in part at least, as an analog representation of the oil pressure.

The analog-digital distinction is usually used to mark a difference in the way information is carried about a variable property, magnitude, or quantity: time, speed, temperature, pressure, height, volume, weight, distance, and so on. Ordinary household thermometers are analog devices: the variable height of the mercury represents the variable temperature. The hands on a clock carry information about the time in analog form, but alarm clocks convert a preselected part of this into digital form.

I am interested, however, not in information about properties and magnitudes and the various ways this might be encoded, but in information about the instantiation of these properties and magnitudes by particular items at the source. I am interested, in other words, not in how we might encode information about temperature, but in how we might represent the *fact* that the temperature is too high, over 100°, or exactly 153°. What we want is a distinction, similar to the analog-digital distinction as it relates to the representation of properties, to mark the different way *facts* can be represented. Can we say, for example, that one structure carries the information that s is F in digital form, and another carries it in analog form?

For the purpose of marking an important difference in the way information can be encoded in a signal or structure, I propose to use the familiar terminology—analog vs. digital—in a slightly unorthodox way. The justification for extending the old terminology to cover what is basically a different distinction will appear as we proceed.

I will say that a signal (structure, event, state) carries the information that s is F in *digital* form if and only if the signal carries no additional information about s, no information that is not already nested in s's being F. If the signal *does* carry additional information about s, information that is *not* nested in s's being F, then I shall say that the signal carries this information in analog form. When a signal carries the information that s is F in analog form, the signal always carries more specific, more determinate, information about s than that it is F. Every signal carries information in both analog and digital form. The most specific piece of information the signal carries (about s) is the only piece of information it carries (about s) in digital form.[2] All other information (about s) is coded in analog form.

To illustrate the way this distinction applies, consider the difference between a picture and a statement. Suppose a cup has coffee in it, and we want to communicate this piece of information. If I simply *tell* you, "The cup has coffee in it," this (acoustic) signal carries the information that the cup has coffee in it in digital form. No more specific information is supplied about the cup (or the coffee) than that there is some coffee in the cup. You are not told *how much* coffee there is in the cup, how large the cup is, *how dark* the coffee is, what the shape and orientation of the cup are, and so on. If, on the other hand, I photograph the scene and show you the picture, the information that the cup has coffee in it is conveyed in analog form. The picture tells you that there is some coffee in the cup by telling you, roughly, how much coffee is in the cup, the shape, size, and color of the cup, and so on.

I can say that A and B are of different size without saying how much they differ in size or which is larger, but I cannot picture A and B as being of different size without picturing one of them as larger and indicating, roughly, how much larger it is. Similarly, if a yellow ball is situated between a red and a blue ball, I can *state* that this is so without revealing where (on the left or on the right) the blue ball is. But if this information is to be communicated pictorially, the signal is necessarily more specific. Either the blue or the red ball must be pictured on the left. For such facts as these a picture is, of necessity, an analog representation. The corresponding statements ("*A* and *B* are of different size," "The yellow ball is between the red and the blue balls") are digital representations of the same facts.

As indicated, a signal carrying information in analog form will always carry some information in digital form. A sentence expressing *all* the information a signal carries will be a sentence expressing the information the signal carries in digital form (since this will be the most specific, most determinate, piece of information the signal carries). This is true of pictures as well as other analog representations. The information a picture carries in digital form can be rendered only by some enormously complex sentence, a sentence that describes every detail of the situation about which the picture carries information. To say that a picture is worth a thousand words is merely to acknowledge that, for most pictures at least, the sentence needed to express all the information contained in the picture would have to be very complex indeed. Most pictures have a wealth of detail, and a degree of specificity, that makes it all but impossible to provide even an approximate *linguistic* rendition of the information the picture carries in digital form. Typically, when we describe the information conveyed by a picture, we are describing the information the picture carries in analog form—abstracting, as it were, from its more concrete embodiment in the picture.

This is not to say that we cannot develop alternative means of encoding the information a picture carries in digital form. We could build a device (a buzzer system, say) that was activated when and only when a situation occurred at the source that was *exactly* like that depicted in the picture (the only variations permitted being those about which the picture carried no information). The buzzer, when it sounded, would then carry exactly the same information as the picture, and both structures (the one pictorial, the other not) would carry this information in digital form. Computer recognition programs that rely on whole-template matching routines approximate this type of transformation.[3] The incoming information is supplied in pictorial form (letters of the alphabet or geometric patterns). If there is an exact match between the input pattern and the stored template, the computer "recognizes" the pattern and labels it appropriately. The label assigned to the input pattern corresponds to our buzzer system. The output (label) carries the same information as the input pattern. The information the picture carries in digital form has merely been physically transformed.

As everyone recognizes, however, such template-matching processes have very little to do with genuine recognition. As long as what comes out (some identificatory label) carries *all* the information contained in the input pattern, we have nothing corresponding to stimulus generalization, categorization, or classification. What we want, of course, is a computer program that will "recognize," not just a letter A in *this* type font, in *this* orientation, and of *this* size (the only thing the stored template will *exactly* match), but the letter A in a variety of type fonts, in a variety of orientations, and a variety of different sizes. For this purpose we need something that will extract information the input pattern carries in *analog* form. We want something that will disregard irrelevant features of this particular A (irrelevant to its being an instance of the letter A) in order to respond to those particular features relevantly involved in the pattern's being an instance of the letter A. We want, in other words, a buzzer system that is responsive to pieces of information the pictures (patterns) carry in analog form.

To understand the importance of the analog-to-digital conversion, and to appreciate its significance for the distinction between perceptual and cognitive processes, consider the following simple mechanism. A variable source is capable of assuming 100 different values. Information about this source is fed into an information-processing system. The first stage of this system contains a device that accurately registers the state of the source. The reader may think of the source as the speed of a vehicle (capable of going from 0 to 99 mph), and the first stage of our information-processing system as a speedometer capable of registering (in its mobile pointer) the vehicle's speed. This information is then fed into a converter. The converter consists of four differently pitched tones, and a mechanism for activating these different tones. If the source is in the range 0 to 14, the lowest-pitched tone is heard. A higher-pitched tone occurs in the range 15 to 24, a still higher pitch from 25 to 49, and the highest at 50 to 99. These different ranges may be thought of as the approximate ranges in which one should be in first, second, third, and fourth gear, and the converter a device for alerting novice drivers (by the differently pitched tones) of the need to shift gears. The flow of information looks something like Figure 6.1.

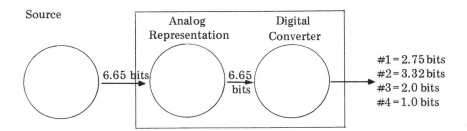

Figure 6.1

What I have labeled the "Analog Representation" (the speedometer) carries all the information generated by the variable source. Since the source has 100 different possible states (all equally likely), the speedometer carries 6.65 bits of information about the source. It carries the information that the vehicle is going, say, 43 mph. This information is fed into a converter, and (assuming a speed of 43 mph) the third tone is activated. Since the third tone is activated when, and only when, the vehicle has a speed in the range 25 to 49, this tone carries 2 bits of information about the speed of the vehicle (a reduction of 100 equally likely possibilities to 25).

The output of this system is always less, quantitatively, than the input. Although 6.65 bits of information get in, something less than this comes out. What is gained by this loss of information is a *classification* (in the various tones) of the *significant ranges* of the input variable. This is a form, albeit a fairly primitive form, of *stimulus generalization*. The output of this system ignores the difference between 43 mph and 32 mph. Both these values are treated as essentially the same. Both activate tone 3. From the point of view of the information the system is designed to communicate, the internal speedometer is an analog representation of the source because it carries more specific, more determinate information about the source than is required to control the system's output. The speedometer "says" that the vehicle is going 43 mph. Nested within this piece of information is the information that the vehicle is going *between* 25 and 50 mph. The digital converter is interested only in the latter piece of information. It "throws away" the more specific piece of information and passes along a piece of information (that the vehicle is going somewhere between 25 and 50 mph) that the speedometer carries in analog form. Of course, the speedometer carries the information that the vehicle is going 43 mph in digital form (since it carries no more specific information about the vehicle's speed), but relative to the information this system is designed to communicate (e.g., whether the speed is between 15 and 24 or between 25 and 49) the speedometer constitutes an analog representation of the state of the source. It is the information the speedometer carries in analog form that the system is *acting* on, that *drives* its motor centers (the various buzzers). The more specific pieces of information it carries are systematically ignored in order to achieve a uniform response to *relevant similarities*.

To describe a process in which a piece of information is converted from analog to digital form is to describe a process that necessarily involves the *loss* of information. Information is lost because we pass from a structure (the speedometer) of greater informational content to one of lesser information content. Digital conversion is a process in which irrelevant pieces of information are pruned away and discarded. Until information has been lost, or discarded, an information-processing system has failed to treat *different* things as essentially the *same*. It has failed to classify or categorize, failed to generalize, failed to "recognize" the input as being an instance (token) of a more general type. The simple system just described carries out this process in a completely mechanical way. Nevertheless, although it lacks some of the essential features of a genuine perceptual-cognitive system, it illustrates the information-theoretic processes underlying *all* forms of stimulus generalization, classification, and recognition.

Sensory vs. Cognitive Processes

The contrast between an analog and a digital encoding of information (as just defined) is useful for distinguishing between sensory and cognitive processes. Perception is a process by means of which information is delivered within a richer matrix of information (hence in *analog* form) *to* the cognitive centers for their selective use. Seeing, hearing, and smelling are different ways we have of getting information about *s* to a digital-conversion unit whose function it is to extract pertinent information from the sensory representation for purposes of modifying output. It is the successful conversion of information into (appropriate[4]) digital form that constitutes the essence of cognitive activity. If the information that *s* is *F* is never converted from a sensory (analog) to a cognitive (digital) form, the system in question has, perhaps, seen, heard, or smelled an *s* which is *F*, but it has not *seen that* it is *F*—does not *know* that it is *F*. The traditional idea that knowledge, belief, and thought involve *concepts* while sensation (or sensory experience) does not is reflected in this coding difference. Cognitive activity is the *conceptual* mobilization of incoming information, and this conceptual treatment is fundamentally a matter of ignoring differences (as irrelevant to an underlying sameness), of going from the concrete to the abstract, of passing from the particular to the general. It is, in short, a matter of making the analog-digital transformation.

Sensation, what the ordinary man refers to as the look (sound, smell, etc.) of things, and what the psychologist refers to as the *percept* or (in some contexts) the sensory information store (SIS),[5] is informationally profuse and specific in the way a picture is. Knowledge and belief, on the other hand, are selective and exclusive in the way a statement is. "The tapestry of awareness is rich, but the pattern recognition process, dependent on classification, is relatively impoverished in the detail with which it operates."[6] Our sensory experience embodies information about a variety of details that, if carried over in toto to the cognitive centers, would require gigantically large storage and retrieval capabilities.[7] There is more information in the sensory store than can be extracted, a limit on how much of this information can be exploited by the cognitive mechanisms.[8]

I do not mean to suggest by my comparison of sensory experience to pictures (or cognitive structures with statements) that our sensory experience is always (or *ever*) pictorial or imagistic in character—that the perception of things involves having little images (sounds, smells, tastes) in the head, or that cognitive activity is a linguistic phenomenon. It may be that the acquisition of language is essential to an organism's having the capacity to convert sensory information into digital form (hence the capacity to have beliefs and knowledge), but this, if so, is an empirical question, a question to which I will return in Part III. For the moment I merely wish to develop the idea that the difference between our perceptual experience, the experience that constitutes our seeing and hearing things, and the knowledge (or belief) that is normally consequent upon that experience is, fundamentally, a coding difference. In this respect the relation between sensory processes and cognitive processes is like the relation between the preliminary analog representation and the subsequent digital representation described in Figure 6.1. The speedometer carries the information that the vehicle is going between 25 and 50 mph, and it carries this information in analog form (embedded in the more specific information that the vehicle is going 43 mph), but the particular state of the system that carries this information (the position of the pointer) is not a picture of the vehicle's speed. It does not *resemble* the state of affairs about which it carries information. And the third tone, the one that carries (in digital form) the information that the vehicle is going between 25 and 50 mph, is not a *statement* or *linguistic representation* of the vehicle's speed. The conversion of information from analog to digital form *may* involve a conversion from picture to statement, but it need not. From a neurological point of view the transformation from sensory to cognitive coding takes place in the complete absence of either pictures or statements.

Unlike the simple, mechanical converter described in Figure 6.1, however, living systems (most of them anyhow) are capable of modifying their digital-conversion units. As the needs, purposes, and circumstances of an organism change, it becomes necessary to alter the characteristics of the digital converter so as to exploit *more*, or *different*, pieces of information embedded in the sensory structures. Shifts of attention need not (although they may) involve a change in the kind of information made available in the sensory representation. There need not be any change in the way things look, sound, or smell. It may only involve a change in what pieces of information (carried in analog form) are extracted from the sensory representation.

Similarly, learning a concept is a process in which there is a more or less permanent modification of a system's ability to extract analogically coded information from the sensory store. What the simple mechanical system already described lacks is the capacity to change its response characteristics so as to exploit more, or different, pieces of information embodied in the speedometer's registration. It cannot *learn*. There is no way for it to modify the way it digitalizes information so as to respond, say, with tone 3 (or an altogether different tone) when and only when the vehicle is going between 30 and 35 mph. This more specific piece of information *is* being picked up, processed, and fed into the converter (by the speedometer), but the system is incapable of "attending to" this fact, incapable of extracting this piece of information and "acting" on it. Contrast this with a young child, one whose receptor systems are fully matured and in normal working order, learning to recognize and identify items in her environment. Learning to recognize and identify daffodils, say, is not a process that requires the pickup of more information from (or about) the daffodils. Given the child's keen eyesight, she may already (before learning) be receiving more information from daffodils than her more experienced, but nearsighted, teacher. Still, the teacher *knows* that the flower is a daffodil and the child does not. The child knows only that it is a flower of some sort (perhaps not even this much). What the pupil needs is not more information of the sort that could be supplied by the use of a magnifying glass. She is not *perceptually* deficient. The requisite information (requisite to identifying the flower *as* a daffodil) is getting in. What is lacking is an ability to extract this information, an ability to decode or interpret the sensory messages. What the child needs is not more information about the daffodil but a change in the way she codes the information she has been getting all along. Until this information (vis., that they are daffodils) is recoded in digital form, the child *sees* daffodils but neither knows nor believes that they are daffodils.

The process of digitalization, and how it is related to learning and cognitive activity in general, will be examined at greater length in Part III. For the moment our concern is with the perceptual delivery systems—those systems whose function it is to make available, in our sensory experience, the information on which such cognitive activity depends.

It should perhaps be noted that I am greatly oversimplifying the process by means of which sensory information is extracted from the physical stimulus, integrated with collateral information, and coded in sensory form. I ignore the details of this process in order to highlight an important *difference* in the way this information is coded: a sensory (analog) form and a cognitive (digital) form. In particular, I simply ignore the fact that much of the information embodied in the sensory representation (our sensory experience) is the result of a temporal integration:

> evolution has tuned the human perceptual system to register not the low-grade information in momentary retinal images but rather the high-fidelity information in *sequences of images* (my emphasis) or in simultaneous complexes of images—the kind of information given by motion parallax and binocular parallax.[9]

James Gibson has argued persuasively that much of the information we manage to extract from our environment depends on a strategy of detecting higher-order invariants in a temporal series of signals—the kind of information we are able to pick up by *moving around* and registering the systematic alteration in patterns. textures, and relative positions.[10] To understand how certain sorts of information are registered, it is important to understand the way a sensory representation may be the result of a temporal summation of signals. To think of the processing of sensory information in static terms, in terms of the kind of information embodied in the stimulus *at a particular time*, is to completely miss the extent to which our sensory representations depend on an integrative process *over time*. Even a simple tachometer (depending, as it does, on the *frequency* of pulses) can be used to illustrate the importance of this phenomenon.

I am also ignoring the fact that our sensory representations often carry information derived from a number of different sensory channels. If we considered *only* the stimulus reaching the eyes (even if understood relative to some *temporal interval*), the conclusion would be inevitable that the stimulus is (very often at least) *equivocal*. It would be a mistake, however, to conclude from this that the sensory representation of the source is itself equivocal. For there is no reason to think that our visual experience of the source relies exclusively on the information arriving in the light reaching our *visual* receptors. Quite the contrary. Information about the gravitational orientation of objects is available in the sensory experience because the visual input is processed *jointly* with body-tilt information from proprioceptive sources. Signals specifying the position of the head in relation to gravity, the angular position and movement of the eyes in relation to the head, and the relative position and movement of all other relevant body parts play a role in determining *how* we experience what we experience. The wealth of information available in our sensory experience is to be explained, in part at least, by the fact that this experience embodies information gleaned *over time* from a *variety* of sources.

Important as it is for understanding the actual processes by means of which our sensory experience is produced, and the sorts of mechanisms responsible for the information to be found therein,[11] the details are not directly relevant to our characterization of the result—the sensory experience itself—and the manner in which it codes information. It will be necessary, later in this chapter, to look more closely at the machinery for delivering information in order to clarify the nature of the perceptual object and, in particular, the way the constancy mechanisms help to determine *what* we see, hear, and smell. But for present purposes these details can be set aside. Our immediate concern is with the analog character of our sensory experience.

Consider vision. You are looking at a fairly complex scene—a crowd of youngsters at play, a shelf full of books, a flag with all the stars and stripes visible. A reaction typical of such encounters, especially when they are brief, is that one has seen more than was (or perhaps *could be*) consciously noticed or attended to. There were (as it turns out) 27 children in the playground, and though you, perhaps, *saw them all*, you are unaware of how many you saw. Unless you had the time to count, you do not *believe* you saw 27 children (although you may certainly believe something less specific—e.g., that you saw *many* children or *over a dozen* children). You saw 27 children, but this information, precise numerical information, is not reflected in what you know or believe. There is no cognitive representation of this fact. To say one *saw* this many children (without realizing it) is to imply that there was *some* sensory representation of each item. The information *got in*. It was *perceptually* coded. Why else would it be true to say you saw 27 children rather than 26 or 28? Therefore, the information that *is* cognitively extracted from the sensory representation (the information, namely, that there are *many* children in the yard, or *over a dozen* children) is information that the sensory structure codes in *analog* form. The relationship between your *experience of* the children and your *knowledge of* the children is the same as that between the speedometer and the tone in Figure 6.1.

I do not mean to be suggesting that there is a psychophysical correspondence between the information contained in the physical stimulus (or temporal sequence of stimuli) and the information contained in the sensory experience to which that stimulus gives rise. There is obviously a *loss* of information between the receptor surfaces and the internal representation. And conversely, there occurs something that is called "restoration"—an insertion into the sensory experience of representationally significant features that have no counterpart in the physical stimulus (closure of boundaries, restoration of missing sounds, etc.).[12] If, for example, one saw all 27 children but saw some of them only peripherally (or at dusk), it seems unlikely that information about the color of their clothes would be available in the visual experience. If such color information, contained in the stimulus (light reaching the retina), does not fall on the color-sensitive cones of the fovea, it will obviously not be available in the resulting sensory experience.[13] But even with these peripherally seen children, information about their (rough) relative location, size, spacing, and number *will* be perceptually coded. We may suppose, along with many psychologists, that the preliminary operations associated with the pre-attentive processes (those which occur prior to the more elaborate perceptual processing associated with focal attention) yield only segregated figural units, units that lack the richness of information available in those portions of the visual field to which attention is given.[14] Still, there is certainly more information embodied in this configuration of "figural units" than we normally extract—

information about the spacing, relative size, and position of the objects represented. Typically, the sensory systems overload the information-handling capacity of our cognitive mechanisms so that not all that is given to us in perception can be digested. What *is* digested are bits and pieces—information the sensory structure carries in analog form.

There is a rule of seven which tells us that there is a certain limit to the rate at which human subjects can process information.[15] When information arrives at a rate that exceeds this "capacity," the organism fails to process it. We have already seen (Chapter 2, under The Proper Measure of Information) that the idea of "channel capacity" has no direct application to the amount of information that can be carried by a *particular* signal. It applies only to the *average* amount of information an ensemble of signals can carry. Nevertheless, understood in the correct way, this rule seems to have some rough empirical validity. Its significance should not be misinterpreted, however. If the rule applies at all, it must be understood as applying to our capacity for *cognitively* processing information. It does not apply, and there is no evidence to suggest that it applies (quite the reverse), to our *perceptual* coding of information. The rule represents some kind of limit to how much information we can extract *from* our sensory experience, not a limit to how much information can be contained *in* this experience. It assigns a limit to our capacity to convert information from analog to digital form. Recall the speedometer-buzzer system. A similar limitation applies to this system considered as a whole. Although the input contains 6.65 bits of information about the speed of the vehicle, the output contains, at most, 3.32 bits. The average output is something less than this. But this limit on the information-processing capabilities of this system is a limit that arises as a result of the analog-to-digital conversion mechanism. A full 6.65 bits of information *gets in*. There is an *internal representation* of the speed of the vehicle at all times. Nevertheless, this information is selectively utilized in order to obtain, in the output, a digital representation of certain relevant features of the input. If the rule of seven applies at all, it applies to the input-output relationship. It does not apply to that stage in the process which occurs prior to digital conversion. It does not apply to the sensory coding of information.

J.R. Pierce makes the same point in discussing the informational processing capacity of human subjects.[16]

Now, Miller's law and the reading rate experiments have embarrassing implications. If a man gets only 27 bits of information from a picture, can we transmit by means of 27 bits of information a picture which, when flashed on a screen, will satisfactorily imitate any picture? If a man can transmit only about 40 bits of information per second as the reading rate experiments indicate, can we transmit TV or voice of satisfactory quality using only 40 bits per second? In each case I believe the answer to be no. What is wrong? What is wrong is that we have measured what gets *out* of the human being, not what goes *in*. Perhaps a human being can in some sense only notice 40 bits/ second worth of information, but he has a choice as to what he notices. He might, for instance, notice the girl or he might notice the dress. Perhaps he notices more, but it gets away from him before he can describe it.

Pierce is making the point that to measure the amount of information that can flow *through* a subject is to measure the limitation on the *joint* operation of the perceptual and the cognitive mechanisms (not to mention the performative mechanisms). Whatever limits are arrived at by this technique will tell us nothing about the informational limits of our sensory mechanisms. It will give us, at best, the capacity of the *weakest link* in the communication chain, and there is no reason to think that sensation constitutes the weakest link. As Pierce notes, we cannot imitate a picture with only 27 bits of information even though 27 bits of information is about the most that one can *cognitively* process. Our own perceptual experience testifies to the fact that there is more information *getting in* than we can manage to *get out*.

The same point is revealingly illustrated by a set of experiments with brief visual displays.[17] Subjects are exposed to an array of nine or more letters for a brief period (50 milliseconds). It is found that after removal of the stimulus there is a persistence of the "visual image." Subjects report that the letters appear to be visually present and legible at the time of a tone occurring 150 milliseconds *after* removal of the stimulus. Neisser has dubbed this iconic memory—a temporary storage of sensory information in perceptual form.[18] We need not, however, think of this as the persistence of *an image*. What persists is a structure in which incoming information *about* a pictorial array is coded in preparation for its cognitive utilization. For it turns out that although subjects can identify only three or four letters under brief exposure, *which* letters they succeed in identifying depends on the nature of a later stimulus, a stimulus that appears only 150 milliseconds after removal of the original array of letters. The later stimulus (a marker appearing in different positions) has the effect of "shifting the subject's attention to different parts of the lingering icon." The later stimulus changes the analog-to-digital conversion process: different pieces of information are extracted from the lingering sensory representation.

What these experiments show is that although there is a limit to the rate at which subjects can *cognitively* process information (*identify* or *recognize* letters in the stimulus array), the same limitation does not seem to apply to sensory processes by means of which this information is made available to the cognitive centers. Although the subjects could identify only three or four letters, information about *all* the letters (or at least *more* of the letters) was embodied in the persisting "icon."[19] The sensory system has information about the character of all nine letters in the array while the subject has information about at most four. The availability of this information is demonstrated by the fact that after removal of the stimulus the subject can (depending on the nature of later stimulation) still extract information about *any* letter in the array. Hence, information about *all* the letters in the array must be available in the lingering icon. The visual system is processing and making available a quantity of information far in excess of what the subject's cognitive mechanisms can absorb (i.e., convert to digital form). Our sensory experience is informationally rich and profuse in a way that our cognitive utilization of it is not. Relative to the information we manage to *extract* from the sensory representation (whatever beliefs may be occasioned by having this kind of sensory experience), the sensory representation itself qualifies as an *analog* representation of the source. It is this fact that makes the sensory representation more like a *picture* of, and the consequent belief a *statement about*, the source.[20]

Consider, finally, an example from developmental studies.

Eleanor Gibson in reporting Klüver's studies with monkeys describes a case in which the animals were trained to the larger of
two rectangles.[21] When the rectangles were altered in size, the
monkeys continued to respond to the larger of the two
—whatever their absolute size happened to be. In the words of
Klüver:

> If a monkey reacts to stimuli which can be characterized as
> belonging to a large number of different dimensions, and if in
> doing so he reacts consistently in terms of one relation, let us
> say in terms of the 'larger than' relation, he may be said to
> "abstract."

Klüver's monkeys succeeded in abstracting the larger-than relation.
But how shall we describe the perceptual situation *before* they
learned to abstract this relation. Did the rectangles *look* different
to the monkeys? If not, how could they ever learn to distinguish
between them? What possible reinforcement schedule could get
them to react differently to perceptually indistinguishable elements? It seems most natural to say in a situation of this sort (and
the situation is typical of learning situations in general) that prior
to learning, prior to successful abstraction of the appropriate relation, the monkey's perceptual experience contained the information that it only later succeeded in extracting. It is possible, I
suppose, that the rectangles only *began* to look different to the
monkeys after repeated exposures, that the reinforcement schedule
actually brought about a perceptual (as well as a cognitive) change.[22]
This would then be a remarkable case of perceptual learning
(change in the *percept* or sensory representation as a result of
training).[23] Perceptual learning may certainly take place, especially with the very young and the newly sighted, and in mature subjects with ambiguous figures[24] but there is no reason to suppose
that it is occurring in *every* learning situation with mature subjects. What is taking place here is very much like what takes
place with the young child learning to recognize daffodils. The
flowers do not look any different; the subject merely learns how
to organize (recode) the information already available in its sensory experience.

The situation becomes even clearer if we present the monkeys with three rectangles and try to get them to abstract the

"intermediate-size" relation. This more difficult problem proves capable of solution by chimpanzees, but the monkeys find it extremely difficult.[25] Let us suppose that they are incapable of this more sophisticated type of learning. What shall we say about the perceptual situation with respect to the monkeys? Since they have already abstracted the larger-than relation, it may be assumed that they are receiving, and perceptually coding, the information that rectangle A is larger than B, and that B is larger than C. In ordinary terms this is a way of saying that the intermediate rectangle (B) *looks* smaller than the larger (A) and larger than the smaller (C). But information about which rectangle is intermediate, though obviously embedded (in analog form) in the perceptual experience itself, is not (and apparently cannot be) cognitively extracted by the animal. To say that the monkey cannot abstract the intermediate-size relation, therefore, is *not* to say anything about the way it perceptually codes information about figures. Rather, it is to say something about its cognitive limitations. The information is available in analog form in the experience the animal is having of the three rectangles, but the animal is unable to generate an appropriate on-off response, the kind of response characteristic of recognition or identification, to this piece of information. It does not *know* (think, believe, judge) that B is of intermediate size, even though this information is available in its sensory representation of A, B, and C.[26]

Although our speedometer-tone system cannot learn, its limitations can be usefully compared with those of the monkey. This simple mechanical system can receive, process, and generate an internal (analog) representation of the fact that the vehicle is going between 30 and 35 mph. The speedometer's registration of (say) 32 mph is an analog encoding of this information. As originally conceived, however, the system as a whole cannot be made to "respond" to this piece of information. We get the same tone whether the vehicle is going between 30 and 35 mph, slower (down to 25 mph), or faster (up to 49 mph). The problem lies in the system's built-in limitation for converting information from analog to digital form. It can "recognize" a speed as between 25 and 50 mph because this fact, the fact that the speed is within this interval, is information the system is designed to convert into digital form (a distinctive tone).[27] But the system is unable to "recognize" finer details, unable to make more subtle discriminations. It has no *concept* of something's being between 30 and 35 mph, no *beliefs* with this content, no internal structure with this kind of *meaning*.

To summarize, then, our perceptual experience (what we ordinarily refer to as the look, sound, and feel of things) is being identified with an information-carrying structure—a structure in which information about a source is coded in analog form and made available to something like a digital converter (more of this in Part III) for cognitive utilization. This sensory structure or representation is said to be an analog encoding of incoming information because it is always information *embedded in* this sensory structure (embedded within a richer matrix of information) that is subjected to the digitalizing processes characteristic of the cognitive mechanisms. Until information has been *extracted from* this sensory structure (digitilization), nothing corresponding to recognition, classification, identification, or judgment has occurred—nothing, that is, of any *conceptual* or *cognitive* significance.

If perception is understood as a creature's *experience* of his surroundings, then, perception itself is cognitively neutral.[28] Nevertheless, although one can see (hear, etc.) an *s* which is *F* (sensorily encode information about *s* and, in particular, the information that *s* is *F*) without believing or knowing that it is *F* (without even having the concepts requisite to such beliefs), perception itself depends on there *being* a cognitive mechanism able to utilize the information contained in the sensory representation. In this sense, a system that cannot know cannot see; but if the system is capable of knowing, if it has the requisite cognitive mechanisms, then it can see without knowing.[29] A sensory structure that carries the information that *s* is *F* is not to be confused with a belief about *s*, a belief to the effect that *s* is *F*, but to qualify as a *sensory* representation of *s* (an experience of *s*), this structure must have a certain function within the larger information-processing enterprise. It must make this information available to a suitable converter for possible cognitive utilization.

THE OBJECTS OF PERCEPTION

It has been argued that perception is a process (or, if you will, the result of a process) in which sensory information is coded in analog form in preparation for cognitive utilization. The sense modality (seeing, hearing, etc.) is determined, not by *what information* is encoded, but by the particular *way* it is encoded. I can *see* that it is 12:00 p.m. (by looking at a clock), but I can also get this information by auditory means (hearing the noon whistle). What makes one an instance of seeing and the other an instance of hearing is not the information carried by the two sensory representations (in this case the information is the same), but the differences in the vehicle by means of which this information is delivered—a difference in the representations (in contrast to what is represented).

I have argued, furthermore, that to pass from a perceptual to a cognitive state, to go from *seeing* Herman to *recognizing* Herman, from *hearing* the noon whistle to *knowing* that it is noon, from *smelling* or *tasting* a Moselle wine to *identifying* it as a Moselle wine (by the way it tastes or smells) is a process that involves a conversion in the way such information is encoded—a conversion from analog to digital. Cognitive states always, either explicitly or implicitly, have a specific propositional content. We know (or believe, or judge, or think) *that s is F* (identify, classify, or categorize *s* as *F*). We have a variety of ways to describe our cognitive states. Herman *realizes* that the wine has gone bad, *sees that* he needs a new typewriter ribbon, and *can hear* that there has been a change of key. Frequently the propositional content is not explicitly displayed in the nominal expression following the verb. We may say, for example, that Herman detects *a difference* between the two tastes, recognizes *his uncle*, or identifies *the object*. In each of these cases the propositional content is left unspecified, but there must always be some specific content if the attitudes in question are to qualify as cognitive. If Herman detects a difference between the two tastes, if he can distinguish between them, then he must know *that* the two tastes differ in some respect. Perhaps he only knows that they differ. If he recognizes his uncle, he must know that the man is such and such for some value of "such and such" (his uncle, the man who brings him candy, the stranger who kisses Mommy). And if he identifies the object, he must identify it as something—take it to be (and hence believe that it is) so and so for *some* value of "so and so."

Our perceptual states are different. We perceive (see, hear, smell, taste, and feel) *objects* and *events*. We see the man, smell the burning toast, taste the wine, feel the fabric, and hear the tree fall. What determines what we perceive (what object or event) is not what we believe (if anything) about what we perceive. For, as we have argued, one can see (say) a pentagon and think it is a square, taste a burgundy and take it to be a chianti, and hear a bell and believe one is hallucinating. Or one may have no relevant beliefs at all about the thing perceived. What is it, then, that determines the perceptual object? What makes it *Herman* I see when I mistake him for my Uncle Emil or see him under circumstances in which I fail to even notice him?[30]

Suppose you are sitting on a train and someone tells you that it is moving. You cannot feel it move, see it move, or hear it move. You learn that it is moving by being told that it is moving. The information that the train is moving is acquired auditorily. Yet, we do not say that you could hear the train moving. The train, or the movement of the train, is not the object of your perceptual state. We can say that you *heard that* the train was moving, indicating by this choice of words that the information was received by auditory means, but what you actually heard was your friend say, "The train is moving," or words to that effect. *That* the train is moving is the propositional object of your cognitive state, but the train's movement is not the object of your *perceptual* state.

A similar pattern is exhibited by all the sense modalities. When you read about an accident in the newspapers, you may come to know that a particular event occurred. Information is received by visual means, and we typically express this by the verb "to see"—you could see (by the newspapers) that there had been a tragic accident. Yet, you did not see the accident. To be told that K learned that s was F by seeing, hearing, smelling, or tasting is not to be told what K saw, heard, smelled, or tasted.

What, then, determines what it is that we see, hear, taste, smell, and feel? What determines the perceptual object, the object our sensory experience is an experience *of*?

There is a familiar, if not very adequate, reply to this question. The causal theory of perception tells us that we see and hear those objects (or events) which are causally responsible for our perceptual experience. I see the man (not the book he is holding behind him) because the man (not the book) is directly involved in a causal sequence of events (involving the reflection of light rays) which generates in me a visual experience of the appropriate kind. Since the book is not involved in this causal sequence, we do not see the book. And if I mistake Herman for my Uncle Emil, what makes it *Herman* I see (and not my Uncle Emil) is the fact that *Herman* is causally responsible for my sensory experience.[31]

The difficulties with this analysis are well known. *How* must X be "causally involved" in the sequence of events that culminates in the sensory experience in order to qualify as the object of that experience? Suppose Herman hears the doorbell ring and goes to the door to see who is there. For the sake of the illustration we may suppose that Herman knows (at least believes) that someone is at the door. We have the following sequence of events: (1) Someone presses the door button, thereby closing an electric circuit; (2) current flows through the electromagnets of the doorbell; (3) a clapper is pulled against a bell (simultaneously breaking the electric circuit); (4) the resulting vibration of the clapper against the bell sets up an acoustic wave that strikes Herman's eardrums; (5) the pattern of pressure on Herman's eardrums causes a series of electrical pulses to be transmitted to Herman's brain; and finally (6) Herman undergoes an experience that we ordinarily describe by saying that he hears the bell ring.

We say he hears *the bell*, or *the bell ringing*. Why does he not hear the button being depressed? Why does he not hear the membrane vibrating in his ear? Each of these events is causally involved in the process that results in Herman's auditory experience, and each of these events is what H. H. Price calls a *differential condition*.[32] What makes the bell so special that we designate *it* as the thing heard? It is certainly true that if the bell had not rung, Herman would not have had the auditory experience he had, but just as certainly if the button had not been depressed (if the membrane in his ear had not vibrated), he would

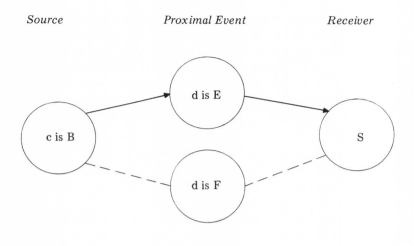

Figure 6.2

not have had that experience. It will not do to say that in such situations the depression of the button is not *audible*. This is doubtless true if we trust our ordinary intuitions about *what can be heard*. But the question we now face is how the audibility and inaudibility of these events can be explained on purely causal grounds.

I do not think that a causal analysis can give a satisfactory account of the objects of our sensory experience. It provides no way of discriminating among the variety of eligible candidates. What is missing, I suggest, is an appreciation of the way the informational relationships operate to determine what it is that we perceive. There are two key facts about the difference between a causal and an informational relationship that are fundamental to a proper understanding of this matter. The first is that (as we saw in Chapter 1) C can cause E without E carrying any significant information about C. Second, E can carry information about some of its causal antecedents in virtue of carrying information about others. These facts, taken together, single out some causal antecedents as unique, and it is these objects (and events), I submit, that constitute the objects of our perceptual states.

Let us first consider, in a highly schematic way, some relevant features of certain (but not all) information-transmission systems. Consider the situation diagrammed in Figure 6.2. A certain state of affairs exists at the source, c's being B, and this causes d to be E. This second event, in turn, produces the state (structure, signal) I have labeled S. The solid lines indicate the route of the causal chain. Sometimes, however, c's being B causes d to be F instead of E. This alternative route has no effect on S; the same state of affairs is produced at the receiver whether or not d is E or F. The broken line indicates an alternative causal sequence, a sequence that is occasionally (say 40 percent of the time) the one that actually occurs.

What is interesting about this diagram (for our purposes) is that it illustrates a pattern of information delivery in which a situation (S) carries information about a distant causal ante-cedent (c's being B) *without* carrying information about the more proximal members of the causal chain (viz., d's being E) *through which* this information (about c) is communicated. S, as it were, skips over (or "sees through") the intermediate links in the causal chain in order to represent (carry information about) its more distant causal antecedents. This is so because the features of S that carry the information that c is B (from which one could learn that something was B) *do not* carry the informa-tion that d is E (one could not learn from them that d was E). Since d is E only 60 percent of the time that S occurs (carrying the information that something is B), S "says" that c is B without "saying" that d is E.

In such situations the state of affairs designated as S carries in-formation about the property B (the information that something—in fact c—is B) without carrying information about the property (viz., E) whose instantiation (by d) is the causal intermediary through which the information about c is transmitted.

This is the first important point of contrast between a causal and an informational relationship. If we confine ourselves to a causal analysis, there is no non-arbitrary way of singling out one of the causal antecedents of S as more special than the others. They are all equally *involved* in the production of the final state (S). Some of these causal antecedents are more remote than others, but this is obviously a matter of degree. Why should some of these (more remote) antecedents be singled out as the object of our sensory states to the exclusion of others. From the point of view of information theory we can begin to see why this should be so. There may be no difference between the way events occurring in our head depend, *causally*, on a number of different antecedent events, but there may be a significant difference in the information these sensory states carry about these causal antecedents.

There is, however, a second fact about information transmission that is relevant to understanding the nature of the perceptual object. Recall our example of the doorbell. It was said that the listener's auditory experience carried information about the bell—information to the effect that it was ringing. But since the ringing bell carries information to the effect that the door button is being depressed (this is why we can know someone is at the door when we hear the bell ring), the auditory experience also carries the information that the door button is depressed. This, it should be noted, is a specific piece of information about a causal antecedent. Yet, as we have seen, the button's being depressed is not the object of our sensory state. We do not hear the button's being depressed. We hear the *bell ringing* (and come to know, thereby, that the button is being depressed—*hear that* someone is at the door). What is the information-theoretical basis for this distinction? Why is one the object and not the other when the auditory experience (by hypothesis) carries specific information about *both*?

The situation may become somewhat clearer if we embellish Figure 6.2 as in Figure 6.3.

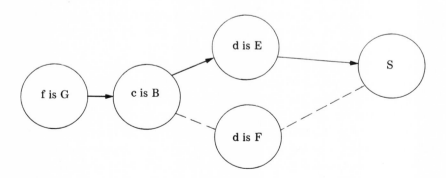

Figure 6.3

Once again, S does not carry the information that d is E (though this is a proximal cause of S). Nonetheless, it carries the information that c (the doorbell) is B (ringing) *and* the information that f (the doorbutton) is G (being depressed). Why is c (the bell) and not f (the button) the perceptual object?

The distinction between c and f is simply that S gives what I shall call *primary representation* to the properties of c but not to the properties of f. S carries information about c (that it is B) and about f (that it is G) but it represents f's properties *by means of* representing c's properties. That is, S's representation of f's being G depends on the informational link between f and c while its representation of c's properties does not depend on it.

> S gives *primary representation* to property B (relative to property G) = S's representation of something's being G depends on the informational relationship between B and G but not *vice versa*.

Our auditory experience represents the bell ringing and it represents the button's being depressed. But only the former is given a primary representation because the information the experience carries about the depression of the button depends on the informational link between the button and the bell while its representation of the bell's ringing does not depend on this relationship. If we short-circuit the doorbell wires (causing the bell to ring periodically when no one is at the door), the informational tie between the bell and the button is broken. When this tie is severed, the auditory experience continues to represent (carry information about) the ringing bell, but it no longer carries information about the depression of the button.

If, contrary to hypothesis, the auditory experience *continued* to represent the button's being depressed (continued to carry the information that the button was depressed) even when its informational link with the ringing bell was broken, *then* we could speak about the button's being depressed as itself receiving primary representation (relative to the bell at least) in the auditory experience of the subject. Its representation would no longer depend on its connection with the ringing bell. But in precisely this situation we would speak of our ability to *hear* the button's being depressed (as well, perhaps, as the bell's ringing). If the button was very rusty, for example, and squeaked loudly whenever it was depressed, we might be able to hear the button being depressed whether or not it was connected to the bell. The explanation for this fact is that, in these altered circumstances, the button's being depressed is no longer being given a *secondary representation* in terms of the bell's ringing.

The signals arriving over a communication system always have their *proper qualities*—the magnitudes to which they give primary representation. Voltmeters, pressure gauges, and speedometers have their proper qualities. By this I mean that whatever information such systems deliver, some properties or magnitudes are, given the nature of the devices, always given primary representation. The voltmeter can tell us about the voltage difference between points A and B (in an external circuit), but it does so by means of registering the current flow (through the instrument itself) that such external voltages generate (when the instrument is properly connected). The flow of electric current constitutes the instrument's proper magnitude. An altimeter can tell us how high we are, but this information about altitude is delivered in terms of pressure. Pressure is the instrument's proper quantity. And (certain) tachometers can tell us how fast our engine is running, but they do so by means of representing the frequency with which the ignition coil is firing. The instrument is sensitive to the *frequency* of these pulses, and it is capable of delivering any information that happens to be embedded in this, its proper, magnitude. If information is to be relayed, transmitted, or carried by such devices, the information must first be transformed into the appropriate magnitude so that the instrument can process it. Voltmeters are used to carry information about a great many things besides voltage differences (temperature, weight, resistance, depth, etc.— anything, in fact, that can be converted into electrical form by a proper transducer), but it can do so only when the information is first translated into the instrument's language, only when it is converted into a *proper* dimension.

Our sensory systems are similar. They have their proper objects, the qualities and quantities to which they give primary representation. If information about temperature is to be coded visually, if we are to be allowed to *see that* the temperature is increasing, the information must be transformed or coded in a way suitable for visual pick-up and processing. Thermometers, of course, effect such a transformation. If the information that it is lunchtime is to be represented auditorily, it must be given an acoustic embodiment. The bell (tone, chimes, buzz, or whatever) does precisely that. Litmus paper is a way of encoding information about acidity into visually processible form, and speech is our main instrument for converting *any* piece of information into auditory form.

Assuming, then, that our sensory experience *does* carry information about our surroundings (assuming, that is, that we can *learn* something about our surroundings by having these experiences), the object of the experience in question (what it is we see, hear, smell and taste) is that object (or set of objects) whose properties the experience represents in a primary way. An experience *need not* (and obviously does not) carry information about *all* the properties of the perceptual object. Nevertheless, of all those properties the experience does carry information about, some comprise the sense modality's proper qualities. The *perceptual object* is the thing that has *these* qualities. The reason we hear the bell, not the button, is because, although our auditory experience carries information about the properties of both the bell (that it is ringing) and the button (that it is depressed), the ringing (of the bell) is represented in a primary way while the depression (of the button) is not.[33]

The distinction between primary and secondary representation serves to explain why we hear the doorbell ringing and not the door button being depressed. But it does *not* help explain why we hear the doorbell ringing and not, say, the vibration of the membranes in our ear. Isn't the ringing of the bell given secondary representation relative to the behavior of the membranes in our ear? Don't we get information about what the bell is doing *in virtue of* (or *by means of*) getting information about what is happening in our ears? If so, we don't (on this account) hear the bell. We hear the (vibration of the) membranes in our ear or, perhaps, the firing of neurons in our brain.

Generally speaking, an organism's way of coding sensory information puts the perceptual object *outside* the perceiving organism. The reason for this should be apparent from Figure 6.2 and the operation of what are called *constancy mechanisms*. Our visual experience, for example, carries highly specific information about the properties of objects (their color, shape, size, movement) without carrying the same kind of specific information about the more proximal events (on the retina, say) on which the delivery of this information depends (causally). Size, shape and color constancy testify to the fact that it is the *properties of objects*, and not (say) the properties of the retinal stimulation (or the firing of neural cells), that is represented by our visual experience under normal viewing conditions. The visual experience that constitutes our sensory encoding of information about ordinary physical objects can, and generally *does*, remain unchanged in response to *quite different proximal stimulation*, and such a pattern of information delivery exemplifies that which is diagrammed in Figure 6.2. Our sensory experience is sensitive to (hence, carries information about), *not* the behavior of our receptors or neural pathways, but the behavior of more distant elements in the causal chain. Since the proximal (peripheral, neural) antecedents of an experience are not (generally speaking) represented in the experience at all, they are not given *primary* representation. They do not, therefore, qualify as the object *of* that experience.

For example, an object (a piece of paper, say) that looks white in daylight continues to look white under drastically diminished illumination even though the intensity of light it reflects is (in near darkness) less than that which a black object reflects in normal daylight. Hence, the experience of whiteness carries information about the reflectance of the paper and not about the intensity of the (local) retinal stimulation reflected *by the paper*. Similarly, objects do not appear to change size and shape as we (or they) move about and change their orientation even though the retinal projection (and, hence, the pattern of neural firings) is constantly changing. The visual representation of a round object (its *looking* round) carries information about the shape *of the object* without carrying information about the shape *of the image* projected on the retina (this can be round or variously elliptical). We experience movement of objects *whether or not* there is any motion of the object's retinal projection. Stationary objects do not appear to move when we change the direction of our gaze (movement of the retinal image), but we experience motion when we "track" a moving object (when there is *no* movement of the retinal image). To experience movement, then, is to receive information, not about what is happening on the retina (there may or may not be movement occurring here) but about what the more distal source is doing.

Woodworth puts the point nicely:

> the retinal image continually changes without much changing the appearance of objects. The apparent size of a person does not change as he moves away from you. A ring turned at various angles to the line of sight, and therefore projected as a varying ellipse on the retina, continues to appear circular. Part of a wall, standing in shadow, is seen as the same in color as the well-lighted portion. Still more radical are the changes in the retinal image that occur when we move about a room and examine its contents from various angles. In spite of the visual flux the objects seem to remain in the same place.[34]

The sensory experience carries information about, and therefore represents, not the proximal events on which it causally depends, but the more distal ancestors in this causal chain. And since the proximal events aren't represented, they are not, a fortiori, represented in any primary way. This, indeed, is why we do not see or hear them. We see (and hear) *through* them.

One plausible explanation of the constancy phenomena is that our sensory systems are sensitive, not to localized stimuli (e.g., the light reflected from object X), but to more global characteristics of the entire stimulus pattern (e.g., the differences between the light reflected from X and the light reflected from X's surroundings).[35] One way of describing this is to say that our perceptual systems are sensitive to "higher order" variables in the stimulus array. The neural circuits in the visual cortex are sensitive, not to local stimulus x (light reaching the retina from X) and local stimulus y (light reaching the retina from Y), but to various *ratios*, *gradients*, and *rates of change* in or among the local (proximal) counterparts of the distal stimuli. So, for example, what accounts for brightness constancy is not (just) the intensity of light coming from X (this can change radically without any apparent change in brightness), but the *ratio* of intensities coming from X and its surroundings (nearby objects). What accounts for size constancy is (among other things) the relative amount of textural details (in the background) occluded by the object. Since there is a gradient in the textural field, the amount of texture occluded will remain constant as the object moves away. Aside from these higher order variables, it also seems clear that our sensory experience is determined, in part at least, by information from other sense modalities.[36] That is, the perceptual system "takes account" of information about the body's tilt (relative to gravity), the position and movement of the eyes, head and trunk, and so on.[37]

Such explanations are plausible enough, and I do not wish to dispute them. These are matters that should be left to the scientific specialists. The only point that concerns me here is that whatever the correct explanation of constancy phenomena may be, they certainly exist. And it is on the existence of such phenomena (not their correct explanation) that the *externality* of the perceptual object depends. It is the *fact* of constancy not the psychological or neurological basis for it, that accounts for the fact that our sensory experience gives primary representation to the properties of distal objects and not to the properties of those more proximal events on which it (causally) depends. It it this fact that explains why we see physical objects and not the effects that these objects have on our perceptual systems.

Whether or not we see ordinary physical objects is (on this account of things) an empirical question—something that must be decided by looking at the kind of information embodied in our sensory experience. There is, as I have tried to indicate, an impressive amount of experimental evidence to support the view that our visual experience (and, to a lesser extent, the other sense modalities) carries highly specific information about the properties of ordinary objects without carrying the same kind of specific information about the intermediate events responsible for the delivery of this information. There is, therefore, an impressive body of evidence to support the commonsense view that we see trees, cats, people and houses and not the neurological events (peripheral or central) that are equally "involved" (causally) in the production of our experience.

This should not be taken to imply that our mode of processing sensory information cannot be changed so as to generate different perceptual objects. The psychologist J.J. Gibson has suggested a distinction between the *visual world* and the *visual field*.[38] According to Gibson the visual world consists of our everyday world of chairs, trees, buildings and people. These are the things we see under normal perceptual conditions. We can, however, get ourselves into a different frame of mind—what is sometimes called a phenomenological frame of mind—or put ourselves under abnormal perceptual conditions (in so-called "perceptual reduction" where much of the information is removed from the stimulus) in which we (according to Gibson) perceive a different constellation of objects. In these altered states we no longer see a stable world of objects but an ensemble of continuously varying entities—things that are continuously changing their brightness and color (as the illumination changes), their size and shape (as we and they move about), their position and orientation. Under such altered (or reduced) perceptual conditions, it is no longer true to say that the subject sees physical objects. One's visual experience still carries information about physical objects, but the properties of these objects is no longer given *primary* representation in the sensory experience. Under such conditions the physical object comes to occupy the status of the depressed button in our doorbell example.

The possibility of confronting a visual field instead of a visual world raises the question of what human infants and animals perceive. They look out on the same world we do, and they doubtless receive much of the same information we do, but how do they perceptually code this information? It *may* be that as we mature we evolve a different way of coding sensory information so that (referring to Figure 6.2) we begin by representing the properties of d (e.g., that it is E) and only later, after sustained interaction with such information bearing signals, begin to give more distal properties (e.g., B) primary representation. That is, our perceptual experience may develop by moving the perceptual object *outward*, away from the perceiving organism. Infants may literally see a different world from adult members of the species.[39]

Paradoxical as this may sound, we can witness something comparable in our auditory processing of information. Listening to an unfamiliar language we hear (as we often express it) *sounds* but not *words*. It will not do to say that since the sounds we hear *are* words, to hear the sounds is to hear the words. Sounds have a certain pitch and loudness; the *word* "bear" has neither of these properties. And the question of whether we hear the *sound* "bear" or the *word* "bear" is a question of whether our auditory experience gives primary representation to the properties of the sound or the properties of the word. Studies suggest that the way we encode information when listening to a familiar language is different from the way we do it when listening to an unfamiliar language. With a familiar language we hear breaks between words even when the *sound* is continuous (no drop in acoustic energy). We hear subtleties associated with the grammatical structure and meaning of the utterance that are totally absent from the pattern of acoustic vibrations reaching the auditory receptors.[40] To learn a language is, to some extent at least, to start hearing properties associated with the words and sentences and to stop hearing acoustic properties.

I do not know whether anything comparable to this occurs when an infant "learns" to see the world. Most of our learning consists of our greater *cognitive* utilization of information already made perceptually available in some determinate sensory representation (e.g., the transition from seeing a daffodil to seeing *that it is* a daffodil). In such learning there is no significant *perceptual* change, no change in what we see. Only a change in what we *know* about what we see. But the possibility exists that normal maturation involves a change, not only in our cognitive resources, but a change in the manner in which things are perceptually represented. Whether this occurs, and, if so, to what extent, is a scientific, not a philosophical, issue.

One point, however, should be stressed before leaving this discussion of the perceptual object. The fact that an animal successfully avoids obstacles and predators, the fact that it efficiently locates food and mates, is a fact that is no certain guide to what it sees, hears, smells and tastes. Success in these practical activities tells us something about the animal's *cognitive* capabilities, but it provides no infallible criterion for determining the way it perceptually represents the elements around it. A rabbit, for example, need not give *primary* visual representation to the fox, need not *see* the fox, in order to get accurate and detailed information concerning the whereabouts, movements, and identity of the fox by visual means. The fact that I answer the door every time someone depresses the door button, the fact that I am so extraordinarily sensitive to the position of the door button, does not mean that I can *hear* (or somehow *sense*) the button being depressed. All it shows is that something I *do* hear carries accurate information about the state of the button. To say that I *know* that the button is being depressed (to specify the object of my *cognitive* state), and that I know this by *auditory* means, is not to say what I hear. As we all know, what I actually hear is the bell. It is this which "tells me" that someone is at the door pressing the button. Practical success in responding to someone's presence on my front porch, even when this success is to be explained in auditory terms, does not imply that I can hear people on my front porch. And, for the same reason, the rabbit's success in evading the fox should not be taken to imply that the rabbit can see, hear or smell the fox. It *may*, of course, but it will take more than facts about the rabbit's cognitive abilities to establish this conclusion.

PART III
MEANING AND BELIEF

Chapter 7
Coding and Content

We have provisionally used the concept of *belief* to distinguish genuine cognitive systems from mere processors of information. A tape recorder receives, processes, and stores information. But unlike a human subject exposed to the same acoustic signal, the electronic instrument is incapable of converting this information into something of cognitive significance. The instrument does not know what we can come to know by using it. The reason the tape recorder does not know is that the information it receives neither generates nor sustains an appropriate belief.

But what is a belief? What makes some systems capable of occupying belief states but not others? Can computers have beliefs? Frogs? Flatworms? We do not speak of a thermostat as having a belief when it "detects" a drop in the room temperature and responds appropriately by sending a signal to the furnace. Yet, if *I* did this, if *I* noticed that it was getting chilly and did something to warm things up a bit, I would be credited with a constellation of beliefs—the belief that it was getting chilly, the belief that a few more logs on the fire would warm things up a bit, and so on. Why? What is the difference?

The information-theoretic account of knowledge remains seriously incomplete as long as it lacks an account of belief. It is not particularly important what we call this special capacity, this capacity that distinguishes genuine cognitive systems from such conduits of information as thermostats, voltmeters, and tape recorders. What is important is that we have a means of distinguishing two types of information-processing system: the type that is capable of converting the information it receives into knowledge and the type that is not. What we want is a way of saying what it is about the first sort of system, but not the second, that qualifies it for cognitive attributes—what it is about us, and perhaps even our cat, that enables us to *know* that it is getting cold in the room while the thermostat, though picking up the same information, knows nothing of the kind. It is not enough to say that we *believe* that it is getting cold in the room while the thermostat does not. That is certainly true, but what, ultimately, does that come down to?

We know from an earlier chapter that *all* information-processing systems occupy intentional states of a certain low order. To describe a physical state as carrying information about a source is to describe it as occupying a certain intentional state relative to that source. If structure S carries the information that t is F, it does not necessarily carry the information that t is G even though nothing is F that is not also G. The information embodied in a structure defines a propositional content with intentional characteristics.

But to qualify for *cognitive* attributes a system must be capable of occupying *higher-order intentional states*. For convenience, and to help clarify this important point, we identify three grades of intentionality:

First Order of Intentionality

(a) All Fs are G
(b) S has the content that t is F
(c) S does not have the content that t is G

When this triad of statements is consistent, I shall say that S (some signal, event, or state) has a content exhibiting the first order of intentionality. So, for example, even though all Elmer's children have the measles, and S carries the information (has the content) that t is one of Elmer's children, S may not carry the information (have the content) that t has the measles. All information-processing systems exhibit this first order of intentionality.

Second Order of Intentionality

 (a) It is a natural law that Fs are G
 (b) S has the content that t is F
 (c) S does *not* have the content that t is G

When this triad is consistent, S's content exhibits the second order of intentionality. For instance, one can believe (know) that the water is freezing without believing (knowing) that the water is expanding even though (let us say) it is nomically impossible for water to freeze without expanding—even though there is a natural law that tells us that water expands when it freezes.

Third Order of Intentionality

 (a) It is analytically[1] necessary that Fs be G
 (b) S has the content that t is F
 (c) S does *not* have the content that t is G

When this triad is consistent, S's content exhibits the third order of intentionality. One might know (believe) that the solution to an equation is 23 without knowing (believing) that the solution is the cube root of 12,167. The fact that it is mathematically (analytically) impossible for 23 to be anything other than the cube root of 12,167 does not make it impossible for one to know (hence to be in a cognitive state having the content) that t = 23 without knowing (being in a cognitive state with the content) that t = the cube root of 12,167.

As the above examples indicate, knowledge and belief have a high order of intentionality. What we believe, and hence the beliefs themselves, must be distinguished even when their contents are interdependent. I will call any propositional content exhibiting the third order of intentionality a *semantic content*.

A signal (structure, state, event) does not possess this higher-order intentionality with respect to its informational content. If the properties F and G are nomically related (there is a natural law to the effect that whenever anything has the property F, it also has the property G), then any structure that carries the information that t is F will also, necessarily, carry the information that t is G.

Indeed, the information that t is G will be *nested* in the situation described by "t is F" in such a way that no signal can carry the one piece of information without carrying the other.

What holds for nomic implications holds, a fortiori, for analytic implications. If "t is F" logically implies "t is G," then it is impossible for any signal or state to carry the information that t is F without, thereby, carrying the information that t is G. Information-processing systems are incapable of separating the information that t is F from the information that is nested in t's being F. It is impossible to design a filter, for example, that will pass the information that t is F while blocking the information that t is G.

A belief, therefore, exhibits a higher-grade intentionality than does a structure with respect to its informational content. Both may be said to have a propositional content, the content, namely, that t is F, but the belief has this as its *exclusive content* (to the exclusion, at least, of nomically and analytically related pieces of information) while the information structure does not. A physical structure cannot have the fact that t is F as its informational content without having *all* the information nested in t's being F as part of its informational content. For this reason a physical structure has no *determinate* or *exclusive* informational content. The pieces of information embodied in a physical structure, although they qualify as propositional contents exhibiting (first-order) intentional characteristics, do not qualify as the kind of *semantic content* characteristic of belief. To occupy a belief state a system must somehow discriminate among the various pieces of information embodied in a physical structure and select *one* of these pieces for special treatment—as *the content* of that higher-order intentional state that is to be identified as the belief.

Earlier in this work (Chapter 2, under The Ordinary Concept of Information) we distinguished the concept of *information* from that of *meaning*. Margaret's utterance, "I am alone" *means* that she is alone (that is what the words she uttered mean) even though her utterance may fail to carry this piece of information (e.g., when she is not alone). And when her utterance *does* carry the information that she is alone, it must also carry the information that she is *not* sipping martinis with Henry Kissinger. Yet, though her utterance necessarily carries the second piece of information whenever it carries the first, her utterance means that she is alone without meaning that she is not sipping martinis with Henry Kissinger. The fact that Henry Kissinger is not comfortably ensconced in her apartment with a drink in his hand is something that is certainly implied by what Margaret said, but it is not itself part of what she said—not part of the meaning of her utterance (though it could be part of what *she meant to be telling us* in saying what she did). Similarly, a signal (e.g., the utterance, "The water is freezing") can *mean* that the water is freezing without meaning that the water is expanding even though it cannot carry the first piece of information without carrying the second. This is simply to say that meaning, like belief (and other cognitive states), exhibits a higher-order intentionality than that associated with a structure's informational content. Since belief and meaning appear to have the same, or at least a similar, level of intentionality, since they both have a *semantic* content, it may not be too unreasonable to expect that a satisfactory account of belief will provide a key to a deeper understanding of meaning.

The first order of business, then, is to understand how higher-order intentional structures can be manufactured out of lower-order intentional states. The task is to describe the way structures having a *semantic content* (third order of intentionality) can be developed out of information-bearing structures.

Once this is done we will be in a position to describe, in the following chapter, the structure of belief. Such an account is needed in order to complete the information-theoretic analysis of knowledge (by supplying an information-theoretic account of belief), to clarify the difference between simple information-processing mechanisms (dictaphones, television sets, voltmeters) and genuine cognitive systems (frogs, humans, and perhaps some computers), and finally to reveal the underlying naturalistic basis of that cluster of mentalistic attributes that assign semantic content to one's internal states.

Suppose structure S constitutes an analog representation of the fact that t is F. To say that S carries this information in analog form is to say (as we saw in Chapter 6) that S carries more specific, more determinate, information about t than, simply, that fact that it is F. It carries the information that t is K where the fact that t is F is nested, either nomically or analytically, in t's being K (but not vice versa). For instance, S might carry the information

KNOWLEDGE AND THE FLOW OF INFORMATION   176

that t is a person in analog form by carrying the information that t is an old lady—the way a picture of t carries the information that t is a person by exhibiting t, say, as an old lady. Not that a picture of a person (who *is* an old lady) must reveal the person to *be* an old lady, but if it is a picture of a person, it must reveal something more specific about the person than that it is a person (posture, size, clothing, orientation, etc.).

If we are seeking to identify (or define) a structure's semantic content, that more or less unique propositional content exhibiting higher-order intentional features, and we are seeking to locate this content among the informational components of the structure, there is little prospect of finding it among the pieces of information that the structure carries in analog form. For insofar as S is an analog representation of t's being F, S must carry more specific pieces of information, pieces of information that are as well, or perhaps even better, qualified to serve as S's semantic content than is the fact that t is F. For if S carries the information that t is F (e.g., that t is a person) in analog form, S must carry information (e.g., that t is an old lady) that is, from the point of view of identifying t as a person, *superfluous*. Yet this superfluous piece of information has as much right to be called S's semantic content as any other piece of information embodied in S. Indeed, it would seem to have a greater right. Its qualifications are more impressive. For if the information that t is a person is nominated for S's semantic content to the exclusion of the information nested in t's being a person (e.g., t's being a mammal, t's being an animal), then why not identify S's semantic content with the fact that t is an old lady to the exclusion of the information nested in *it*—to the exclusion, in particular, of the fact that t is a person?

The point is simply this: if we are seeking to identify a more or less unique informational component of S, something that might plausibly serve as S's semantic content, then any piece of information carried in analog form is immediately disqualified. For if information I is carried in analog form, then I, along with a variety of other information (including all that which is nested in I), is nested, either nomically or analytically, in some further piece of information I'. This is a consequence of the fact that I is being carried in *analog* form. Hence, there is nothing special about I, nothing to set it apart from the other pieces of information nested

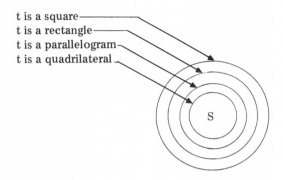

t is a square
t is a rectangle
t is a parallelogram
t is a quadrilateral

S

Figure 7.1

in I', nothing that might qualify it as *the content* (hence the *semantic* content) of S. If we are seeking to identify a *unique* informational component of S, we would be better advised to look at I', that component *in which* all the other information is nested. At least it seems to be unique. It is the *one* piece of information that S carries in *digital* form.

It is this suggestion that I mean to develop in the remainder of this chapter. A structure's *semantic* content is that piece of information that it carries in *digital* form. S carries the information that t is F in digital form if and only if that is the *most specific* piece of information about t that S carries.[2] As I hope to show, in relation to the information it carries in digital form a structure exhibits a higher degree of intentionality than it does with respect to the other information it embodies. Indeed, it exhibits most of the intentional characteristics of a genuine belief.[3] This fact will form the basis of our eventual identification of the belief that t is F with a digitalized representation of this fact (or *putative* fact—see footnote 3). Beliefs are generated by the manner in which information is *encoded* by a system, not by the information so encoded.

As a preliminary attempt, then, an attempt that will eventually have to be modified slightly, let us say that

Structure S has the fact that t is F as its *semantic content* = S carries the information that t is F in digital form

So, for instance, if a signal carries the information that t is a square, but carries no more specific information about t (red square, blue square, big square, little square, etc.), then S carries the information that t is a square in digital form, and therefore has this as its semantic content. Notice that in carrying this piece of information in digital form, S carries a great deal of *other* information in analog form: e.g., the information that t is a parallelogram, that t is a rectangle, that t is a quadrilateral. These are pieces of information that are analytically nested in t's being a square. There is also the possibility, of course, that certain pieces of information are *nomically* nested in t's being a square. The situation is depicted in Figure 7.1. S carries these four pieces of information and, presumably, a great deal else besides. The above proposal suggests that we identify S's semantic content with its *outermost informational shell*, that piece of information *in which* all other information carried by S is nested (either nomically or analytically). This, of course, is merely another way of saying that S's semantic content is to be identified with that piece of information that S carries in digital form. For every *interior* informational shell represents a piece of information that is carried in analog form. So, for instance, S carries the information that t is a parallelogram in analog form since S carries more specific information about the *kind* of parallelogram t is: viz., a rectangle.

It is important to notice that the above definition of "semantic content" supplies us with a notion that possesses higher-order intentional properties. If S carries the information that t is F, and the information that t is G is nested in t's being F, then it follows that S carries the information that t is G. S cannot have the first as part of its *informational* content without having the second as part of its *informational* content. But, and this is the important fact, S has the first as its *semantic content* without having the second as its semantic content, and this because S carries the information that t is F in digital form without carrying the information that t is G in digital form. In this respect S's semantic content is *unique* in the way that its informational content is not. And this uniqueness is generated by the fact that we have identified semantic content with information that is *coded* in a particular way. Niceties aside (for the moment), a structure can have *only one* component of its informational content coded in digital form, *only one* outermost information shell, and this is its *semantic* content.

This suggests that semantic structures, as we have defined them, have the same order of intentionality as beliefs and that, therefore, they are the ideal information-theoretic analogs of belief. Beliefs *are* structures having a semantic content, and this semantic content defines the content of the belief (what is believed). Ultimately, I hope to endorse this equation, or something very close to it, but for the moment the identification is premature. It should be pointed out, for example, that beliefs (most of them, anyway) are the sorts of things that can be *false* (the content of a belief can be false), whereas a semantic structure *cannot* have a false content (since its content is defined in terms of the *information* carried by the structure). There is also the point, so far suppressed, that sometimes the information that t is G is not nested *within* t's being F, nor is the information that t is F nested *within* t's being G, but these pieces of information are (either logically or nomically) *equivalent*. The informational shells coincide. Consider, for example, the information that t is a square and the information that t is a quadrilateral having equal sides and angles. Since, we may suppose, these pieces of information are equivalent, any digital encoding of the one piece of information is automatically a digital encoding of the other piece of information. Therefore, any structure having the one as its semantic content must also have the other as its semantic content. But can we say the same about beliefs? If someone believes that t is a square, *must* he believe that t is a quadrilateral having equal sides and angles? Opinions may differ on this question. Nevertheless, the same problem can be put in terms of nomic (nonanalytic) equivalences. Suppose the properties F and G are related by natural law in such a way that whatever has the one property has the other and vice versa. Then any structure having the semantic content that t is F must also have the semantic content that t is G (and vice versa). Surely, though, one can believe that t is F without believing that t is G. The believer may not realize that they *are* nomically equivalent properties.

I shall return to these important points shortly. For the moment I think it worthwhile to describe, in some greater detail, the special, and very suggestive, properties that semantic structures (= structures conceived of as having a content corresponding to the information they carry in digital form) have.

Notice, first, that semantic structures are sensitive or responsive to a particular piece of information, that piece of information defining their (semantic) content. Let us suppose that a signal arrives bearing the information that t is a red square. Suppose, moreover, that a system processes this information in such a way that some internal state of the system, call it S, constitutes a digital representation of the fact that t is a square. S, then, has the fact that t is a square as its semantic content. Obviously S is not sensitive to those features of the incoming signal that carry the information that t is red. A signal carrying the information that t was a *blue* square will also be able to produce S. If it could not, then S would not, contrary to hypothesis, be a *digital* representation of the fact that t was a square (since S would carry information about the color of t making it, thereby, an analog representation of t's being a square). Those features of the signal (if any) carrying information about t's color are *causally irrelevant* to the production of S. S, as it were, ignores them. It is similarly unresponsive to information about all those aspects of t that are (analytically and nomically) independent of t's being a square (e.g., its size, orientation, location). This in virtue of the fact that S is a *digital* encoding of the information that t is a square.

Furthermore, S is also insensitive to the information nested *in* t's being a square (e.g., the information that t is a parallelogram). Those properties of the signal that are causally responsible for the production of S are *not* those that carry the information that t is a parallelogram. For a signal that carried *this* piece of information but *not* the information that t was a square would be incapable of producing S (if it *did*, or *could*, produce S, then S would not, contrary to hypothesis, carry the information that t was a square). Hence, although any signal carrying the information that t is a square carries the information that t is a parallelogram (a rectangle, a quadrilateral, etc.), it is *only* the former piece of information that is causally responsible for the production of S. Hence, of all the information carried by an incoming signal, a semantic structure is causally sensitive to a unique component of this incoming information. It is sensitive, *selectively sensitive* if you will, to that component of the incoming information that defines the structure's semantic content. It is this selective sensitivity that is of central importance in understanding the nature of semantic structures (and, ultimately, of beliefs).

In virtue of the singular way it codes information, in virtue of its selectivity, a semantic structure may be viewed as a system's *interpretation* of incoming, information-bearing, signals. The structure constitutes an interpretation in the sense that of the many components of information contained in the incoming signals, the semantic structure *features* or *highlights* one of these components at the expense of the others. There is a *resolution* of content, a *focusing* on one thing rather than another. Suppose, for example, that we have a system with the resources of digitalizing different pieces of information and, say, a switching mechanism for determining which piece of information is digitalized when both pieces arrive in the same signal. A signal arrives bearing the information that t is a red square. Let us say that the system generates some internal analog representation of the red square on the basis of the information contained in this signal. This, of course, is meant to correspond to the *perceptual* phase of the total perceptual-cognitive process. The information embodied in this internal (analog) representation can now be digitalized in different ways. Depending on the position of the "internal switch" different semantic structures can be generated. With the switch in one position the system digitalizes the information that t is a square. That is, a structure is produced having this as its semantic content. The system has *extracted* this particular piece of information from the incoming signal and associated internal representation. On the other hand, with the switch in a different position, the perceptual representation gives rise to a semantic structure with the content: t is a rectangle.[4] In this case the system has interpreted the signal as meaning, simply, that t is a rectangle. It has extracted this less specific piece of information. The system has *seen* a red square, but it *knows*, only, that it is a rectangle.

The process just described, the process of generating different semantic structures from one and the same internal analog representation, is meant to correspond to the way the perception of a red square (internal primary representation of the red square) can yield different beliefs about the object (different semantic structures) depending on the background, experience, training, and attention of the subject. The kind of semantic structure evoked by the incoming signal determines *how the system interprets* what it perceives—as a square, as a rectangle, or as something else. The conversion from an analog to a digital representation of the square also reveals (what we saw earlier, in Chapter 6) the sense in which some form of *stimulus generalization* is involved in going from seeing to knowing. In passing from an analog representation of the fact that t is F (a square, say) to a digital representation of this same fact, the system making the conversion necessarily *abstracts* and *generalizes*. It *categorizes* and *classifies*. Indeed, another way of describing what generalization, classification, or abstraction is is to say that each involves the conversion of information from analog to digital form. For if the information that t is F arrives in analog form, then the signal must carry the information that t is K where something's being K implies that it is F *and* G (for some G). To digitalize the information that t is F, the system must *abstract* from the fact that t is G. It must classify this K as an F. It must *generalize* by treating this instance of F as the *same sort of thing* as other instances from which it differs (instances that are *not* K). Until digitalization has occurred, nothing resembling classification or the subsumption under concepts has occurred. The difference between seeing (hearing, smelling, etc.) a t which is F and believing or knowing that t is F is fundamentally the difference between an analog and a digital representation of the fact that it is F.

This is the reason that a television receiver, despite the fact that it receives, processes, and displays enormous amounts of information about the objects and events at the broadcasting studio (and elsewhere), does not know or believe anything. The reason this electronic marvel fails to qualify as a cognitive system is that it is incapable of digitalizing the information passing through it. The information that the weather man is pointing at a map is information that this instrument is certainly capable of picking up, processing, and relaying to the viewer. If the television set could not *transmit* such information, then we, the viewers, could never come to know what was happening at the broadcasting studio by watching it. The crucial difference between the human viewer and the instrument is that the instrument is incapable of digitalizing this piece of information in the way a human viewer is. The television receiver slavishly transforms the information available in the electromagnetic signal into a picture on a screen without ever imposing a cognitive, higher-level intentional structure on any of it. A cognitive system is not one that renders a faithful reproduction of its input in its output. Quite the reverse. If a system is to display genuine cognitive properties, it must assign a *sameness of output* to *differences of input*. In this respect, a genuine cognitive system must represent a *loss of information* between its input and its output.[5] If no information has been lost, than no information has been digitalized. If the same information is available in the output as is available in the input, the system processing this information has not *done* anything with it (besides, perhaps, transforming it into a different physical form), it has not recognized some differences as irrelevant to an essential sameness, it has not categorized or conceptualized the information passing through it.

The process, then, by means of which an information-bearing signal is transformed into something of *semantic significance* (a structure, like belief or knowledge, having a propositional content exhibiting the third order of intentionality) is a process that includes, among other things, a change in the way a piece of information is coded, a conversion from an analog to a digital representation of t's being F. We are all completely familiar with this process on a different level of description. It is (as we saw in Chapter 6) the same difference that is reflected in the contrast between what a person *saw* and what he *learned* (about what he saw).

There is a technical, but nonetheless important, point that should be noted about this characterization of semantic content before we attempt to exploit it (as we will in the next chapter) in the analysis of belief. The fact that structure S carries no more specific information about t than that t is a square does not automatically mean that the information that t is a square constitutes S's *outermost* information ring. It does not mean that there are no larger information shells *in which* this piece of information is nested. All that follows is that there are no larger shells representing more specific information *about t*. It may turn out, for example, that S carries information about some other object r, and the information that t is a square is nested in this other piece of information about r. If this is so, then the information that t is a square, although the most specific piece of information S carries about t, is nevertheless nested in the information S carries about r. And the information about r may be nested in information about u. Schematically, we may have the situation depicted in Figure 7.2.

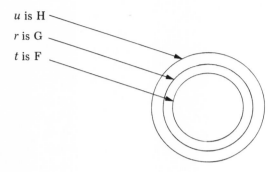

u is H
r is G
t is F

Figure 7.2

If the innermost shell is the most specific piece of information S carries about t, then (in accordance with our definitions) S carries the information that t is F in digital form. Hence, this piece of information qualifies as S's *semantic content.* But if the facts that r is G and u is H happen to be the most specific pieces of information S carries about r and u, then S carries the information that r is G and u is H in digital form also. They also qualify as S's semantic content. Contrary to earlier claims, the semantic content of a structure is not unique.

We can avoid this threatened proliferation, and secure the desired uniqueness of a structure's semantic content, by tightening up our definition. What we need for a structure's semantic content is not the information it carries in digital form (for there may be many such pieces), but its *outermost informational shell,* that piece of information in which *all* other information is nested (either nomically or analytically). Up to this point we have been assuming that the outermost informational shell of a structure was the same as that piece of information it carried in digital form. We now see that this equivalence does not hold. In acknowledgment of this fact we redefine a structure's semantic content as that piece of information it carries in (what I shall call) *completely digitalized form*; i.e.,

Structure S has the fact that t is F as its semantic content =
(a) S carries the information that t is F and
(b) S carries no other piece of information, r is G, which is such that the information that t is F is nested (nomically or analytically) in r's being G.

This definition implies that if S has the fact that t is F as its semantic content, then S carries the information that t is F in digital form. But the reverse implication does not hold. A structure can carry the information that t is F in digital form but not have this fact as its semantic content. In Figure 7.2, if we assume that there are no larger informational shells, S has the fact that u is H as its semantic content. This is the only piece of information that is *completely* digitalized.

To illustrate the importance of this modification of our definition, consider the following sort of case. You read in the newspaper that Elmer died. No further details are given. Let us suppose that this is the most specific piece of information conveyed about Elmer's condition. This piece of information *about Elmer* is nested in the configuration of newsprint that reports his death. That is, it is the appearance of the sentence "Elmer died" in the newspaper that carries the information that Elmer died. If, then, a structure (e.g., the visual experience associated with seeing this sentence in the newspaper) carries the information that the sentence "Elmer died" appears in the newspaper, then it *also* carries the information that Elmer died. This, indeed, is what would allow someone who read that sentence in the newspaper to come to *know* that Elmer died. But we do not want to say that the visual experience associated with seeing the sentence "Elmer died" in the newspaper has, as its *semantic* content, that Elmer died. This, of course, is the most specific piece of information the visual experience carries *about Elmer*, and in this respect it carries this information in digital form, but it does not qualify as the semantic content of the visual experience because this information is not *completely* digitalized by the sensory experience. The semantic content of the sensory experience could only be expressed by a complex sentence describing the detailed appearance of the *newspaper page*. Although the sensory experience associated with *seeing* the newspaper report contains the information that Elmer died (assuming the newspaper report carries this information), the sensory experience has a variety of larger informational shells *within which* this information (about Elmer) is embedded. If we think of Figure 7.2 as a representation of the information carried by the newspaper reader's sensory experience (when he sees, clearly, the words "Elmer died"), the information that Elmer died is one of the *interior* informational shells. The outer shell represents the highly specific and detailed information in the visual experience about the newsprint on the page (including the words "Elmer died"). If we are to have a structure with the *semantic content* that Elmer died, this information must be extracted from the sensory structure and completely digitalized. A new structure must emerge that has the fact that Elmer died as its *outermost* informational shell. This, of course, corresponds to the generation of a *belief* that Elmer died. Only then will the reader have come to the *belief* that Elmer died—or, as we sometimes express it, have seen (by the newspapers) that Elmer died.

Someone who is unable to read, or unable to read English, can *see* the words "Elmer died" on the newspaper page. They can, therefore, *get* the information that Elmer died (this information being nested in a state of affairs they see). What they cannot do is completely digitalize the information that Elmer died when this information is delivered *in this sensory form*. Seeing this pattern of newsprint fails to produce a structure having the fact that Elmer died as its *semantic* content. Illiteracy is not a *perceptual* deficiency. It is, rather, a coding deficiency—an inability to convert information from sensory to cognitive form, an inability to (completely) digitalize the information that is available *in* the sensory experience (in analog form) of the printed newspaper page.

This is why simple mechanical instruments (voltmeters, television receivers, thermostats) do not qualify for semantic structure (third level of intentionality) with respect to the information they transmit about a source. They are always, as it were, reading *reports* about the source. The pointer on a voltmeter, for instance, carries information about the voltage drop across its leads. If we suppose that the most specific information the pointer carries about the voltage is that it is 7 volts, this information is carried in digital form. But it is never *completely* digitalized. This information (about the voltage across the leads) is nested in other, more proximal, structures (e.g., the amount of current flowing through the instrument, the amount of magnetic flux generated around the internal windings, the amount of torque exerted on the mobile armature) which the pointer "reads." The pointer carries information about voltage *in virtue of* carrying accurate and reliable information about these more proximal events (in the same way our sensory experience carries information about Elmer's death by carrying accurate and reliable information about the configuration of ink on a newspaper page). The position of the pointer never has, as its *outermost* informational shell, the fact that the voltage is 7 volts. Given the nature of such instruments, this information about the source is always embedded in larger informational shells depicting the state of those more proximal events on which the delivery of this information depends. This, basically, is why such instruments are incapable of holding *beliefs* concerning the events about which they carry information, incapable of occupying the higher-level intentional states that we (the users of the instrument) can come to occupy by picking up the information they convey. We, but not the instruments, have the capacity to completely digitalize the information that flows *through* the instrument. Structures are aroused in us, but not in the instrument, that have, as their *semantic content*, facts about the remote source.

What endows some systems with the capacity to occupy states which have, as their semantic content, facts about some distant source is the plasticity of the system for extracting information about a source from a variety of physically different signals. The system, as it were, ignores the particular messenger in order to respond to the information delivered by that messenger. If a structure has, as its semantic content, the fact that Elmer died, then even if this particular structure was produced by *seeing* the report, "Elmer died" in the newspaper, even if this was the vehicle by means of which this information arrived, the structure itself carries no information about the means of its production (about the messenger). If it did, then it would not, contrary to hypothesis, be a structure with the *semantic* content that Elmer died (since there would be a larger informational shell, one describing the vehicle of information, within which the information about Elmer was embedded). If the *only* way of producing this structure (the structure having, as its semantic content, the fact that Elmer died) was by means of a visual experience of the sort that (on this occasion) produced it, then the structure would (contrary to hypothesis) carry information about its means of production. It would, in particular, carry the information that the sentence, "Elmer died" appeared in the newspapers. It is, therefore, the fact that this structure can be produced in response to a variety of *different* signals that explains its having this semantic content.

A semantic structure's insensitivity to its particular causal origin, its muteness about the particular manner in which the information (constituting its semantic content) arrived, is merely a reflection of an important fact about beliefs. Our belief states do not themselves testify to their causal origin. The fact that someone *believes* that Elmer died tells us nothing about how he came to believe this, what caused him to believe it. He may have read it in the newspaper or someone may have told him; he may have seen Elmer die, or he may have discovered this in some more indirect way. The fact that a structure has, as its semantic content, its *outermost* informational shell implies that it, like a belief, is silent about its particular causal origin. It carries the information, yes, but it says nothing about how this information arrived.

This plasticity in extracting information from a variety of different signals, a plasticity that accounts for a system's capacity for generating internal states having information about a distant source as their semantic content, is a plasticity that most information-processing systems lack. The voltmeter's pointer carries information about a source (the voltage drop across the instrument's leads), but it does so by means of carrying accurate and detailed information about *the messenger*—the means by which this information is delivered. The *only* way information about voltage differences can reach the pointer is via current flow, induced magnetic field, consequent torque on the armature, and resulting rotation of armature and pointer. Since, given the construction of the instrument, this is the *only* way the pointer's position can register the voltage, the pointer's position carries information about all these intermediate events. Since this is so, the pointer's position does not have, as its *semantic* content, the fact that the voltage is so and so. It cannot completely digitalize this information.[6] This is why voltmeters do not believe anything.

With the idea of a structure's semantic content we are, finally, in a position to give an account of belief. Although we cannot simply identify a belief, the belief (say) that t is F, with a structure having this as its semantic content, we are but a short way from our objective. We already have, in the idea of a semantic structure, something with the appropriate level of intentionality. What remains to be done is to show how such structures can evolve into something possessing the full range of properties we associate with beliefs. This is the task of the following chapter.

Chapter 8
The Structure of Belief

A structure's semantic content has been identified with the information it carries in completely digitalized form. Since the information a structure carries cannot be false, a structure's semantic content cannot be false. But we can certainly have false beliefs. Therefore, beliefs are not semantic structures—not, at least, if this requires identifying the content of the belief (*what* is believed) with the structure's semantic content.

There may, of course, be *some* self-certifying beliefs, beliefs which, given the nature of their content, cannot be false, but we certainly do not want an account of belief which makes it impossible for *any* belief to be false. We want to make room for both the belief that we have beliefs *and* the belief that it will be sunny for tomorrow's picnic. For this reason the information-theoretic analog of a belief must be capable of having a false content. It must be capable of *misrepresenting* how things stand with respect to the matters whereof it speaks.

It may be useful to consider such artifacts as maps, diagrams, and charts. How is it possible for the colored lines, dots, and areas on the paper to *misrepresent* certain features of an area's geography? What enables the map to say, truly or falsely as the case may be, that there is a park here, a lake there? It seems reasonably clear that the power of these cartographical symbols to represent, and misrepresent, the geography of an area depends, fundamentally, on their information-carrying role. These symbols are used to convey information about the location of streets, parks, and points of interest in the city. What makes the map a conventional device is that the symbols are more or less arbitrary (bodies of water could be represented by areas of red ink rather than blue ink); hence their information-carrying capacity must be *underwritten* by the intentions, integrity, and executive fidelity of the people who make the maps. A crucial link in the flow of information (from the physical terrain to the arrangement of marks on paper) is the map maker himself. He constitutes a link in the communication chain in which information can be lost through ignorance, carelessness, or deceit. Unless this link is firm, unless it is a link *through which* information about the geography of an area *can* pass (and normally *does* pass), the map will neither represent nor misrepresent the location and orientation of streets, parks, and so on. Unless we assume that the configuration of marks on paper is, under optimal conditions at least, a *purveyor of information* about an area's geography, the resultant map is powerless to either represent or misrepresent how things stand. It cannot say what is false, let alone what is true, because it cannot *say* anything at all.

If two decks of playing cards are independently shuffled, the placement of cards in the first deck neither represents nor misrepresents the placement of cards in the second deck. Even if the king of clubs appears (quite by chance) at the top of both decks, its appearance at the top of the first deck does not represent anything about its placement in the second. It does not "say" that the king of clubs is at the top of the second. If, however, we supposed a mechanism existed for bringing the king of clubs to the top of the second deck whenever (say) a black card appeared at the top of the first, then a black card at the top of the first would *say* something. It would say that the king of clubs was at the top of the second even if a fault in the mechanism resulted in the jack of hearts being there.

Similarly, if the appearance of the various lines, dots, and colored areas on a map stood to the geography of a city in the way one well-shuffled deck of playing cards stood to another, then however accurately the "map" might correspond (given standard cartographical conventions) to the placement of the city streets and parks, it would neither represent nor misrepresent their location. The map could not "say" there was a lake in the park, let alone say it truly, because there would be no mechanism for embedding this information in the pattern of marks on paper. The expressive resources of our first deck of playing cards are limited by the kind of information it can carry about the arrangement of cards in the first. Similarly, the expressive power of a map, and hence its ability to *misrepresent* how things stand, is circumscribed by the sorts of information that, under normal conditions, it carries about the terrain it is designed to represent. This is why a *blue* wiggly line on a map does not *misrepresent* the color of the water. Under normal map-making conventions this is not the kind of information the color of the line is designed to carry.

What, then, can we learn from this brief digression on the representational power of maps? Does it help us to understand the way a semantic structure might come to *misrepresent* a state of affairs?

Recall, a map can misrepresent the geography of an area only insofar as its elements (the variously colored marks) are understood to have *a meaning* independent of their success in carrying information on any *given* occasion. A particular configuration of marks can *say* (mean) that there is a lake in the park without there actually being a lake in the park (without actually carrying this piece of information) because this particular configuration of marks is an instance (token) of a general type of configuration which *does* have this information-carrying function. The symbol token inherits its meaning from the symbol type of which it is a token; and the symbol type has an information-carrying role independent of the success (if any) of its tokens in carrying this information. In the case of a cartographical symbol (and other conventional vehicles of communication) this information-carrying role is normally *assigned* to the symbol type by those who produce the map. The map is provided with a key which constitutes the assignment of information-carrying roles to the various symbol types, and this is compatible with particular tokens of those types failing to play their assigned role—failing, that is, to carry the information which it is their function to carry. This is what makes it possible for a map to misrepresent things: a symbol token fails to carry the information that, in virtue of the type of which it is a token, it is its job to carry.

But what functions as *the key* with respect to those neurological structures we mean to identify with the beliefs of living organisms? Who or what assigns meanings, or information-carrying roles, to these structures?

Suppose that during the period L a system is exposed to a variety of signals, some of which contain the information that certain things are F, others of which contain the information that other things are not F. The system is capable of picking up and coding this information in analog form (i.e., giving it a perceptual representation) but, at the onset of L, is incapable of digitalizing this information. Suppose, furthermore, that during L the system develops a way of digitalizing the information that something is F: a certain type of internal state evolves which is selectively sensitive to the information that s is F. This semantic structure develops during L in response to the array of information-bearing signals (assisted, presumably, by some form of training or feedback). Once this structure is developed, it acquires a life of its own, so to speak, and is capable of conferring on its subsequent tokens (particular instances of that structure type) *its* semantic content (the content it acquired during L) *whether or not these subsequent tokens actually have this as their informational content.* In short, the structure type acquires its meaning from the sort of information that led to its development as a cognitive structure.[1] Subsequent tokens of this structure type inherit their meaning from the type of which they are tokens. What this means, of course, is that subsequent tokens of this structure type can *mean* that s is F, can have this propositional content, despite the fact that they fail to carry this information, despite the fact that the s (which triggers their occurrence) is not F. The meaning of a structure derives from the *informational* origins of that structure, but a structure *type* can have its origins in information about the F-ness of things without *every* (indeed, without any) subsequent token of that type having this information as its origin.[2]

What I have just described, in information-theoretic terms, is a simple case of concept formation.[3] Typically, one learns the concept F, learns what an F is, by being exposed (in the *learning* situation: L) to a variety of things, some of which are F and some of which are not F. Not only is one exposed to Fs and non-Fs, but the fact that the Fs *are* F and the non-Fs are *not* F is made perceptually *obvious* or *evident*. In other words the learning situation is one in which the *information* that something is F (or not F as the case may be) is made available to the subject for the purpose of shaping his discriminatory and identificatory responses. What is fashioned when one learns what an F is, at least in the simple ostensive cases now in question, is an internal structure selectively sensitive to information about the F-ness of things. To develop such an internal semantic structure is to acquire a simple concept— a concept corresponding to the semantic content of the structure so developed.

In teaching someone the concept *red*, we show the pupil variously colored objects at reasonably close range and under normal illumination. That is, we exhibit the colored objects under conditions in which *information* about their color is transmitted, received, and (hopefully) perceptually encoded. This is why we cannot teach someone the colors if we put the objects 400 yards away; even if the subject can *see* the colored objects, information about their color is not (or may not) be available. This is why this method will not work with the color-blind; we cannot get the information *in*. This is why we do not carry out such training in the dark or under abnormal illumination. (I discuss the possibility of teaching someone color concepts under abnormal lighting conditions in the next chapter.) If the subject is to acquire the concept *red*, he or she must not only be shown red things (and, presumably, nonred things), they must be allowed to receive the information that they are red (and not red). The reason for this should be clear: it is the information that the object is red that is needed to shape the internal structure that will eventually qualify as the subject's concept *red*. We need information to manufacture meaning (the concept) because information is required to crystallize a type of structure with the appropriate semantic content.

In the learning situation special care is taken to see that incoming signals have an intensity, a strength, sufficient unto delivering the required piece of information *to* the learning subject. If the lights are too dim, they are turned up. If the objects (those that are F and those that are not F) are too far away, they are brought closer. If the subject needs his glasses, they are provided.

Such precautions are taken in the learning situation (during L) in order to ensure that an internal structure is developed with the appropriate semantic content, an internal structure that constitutes a (complete) digitalization of the information that s is F. If the information that s is F is missing, then, obviously, no internal structure with the appropriate semantic content (that x is F) can evolve.

But once we have meaning, once the subject has articulated a structure that is selectively sensitive to information about the F-ness of things, instances of this structure, tokens of this type, can be triggered by signals that *lack* the appropriate piece of information. When this occurs, the subject *believes* that s is F but, because this token of the structure type was not produced by the information that s is F, the subject does not *know* that s is F. And if, in fact, s is not F, the subject falsely believes that s is F. We have a case of misrepresentation—a token of a structure with a false content. We have, in a word, meaning without truth.

We can see this process at work in simple cases of concept acquisition. During learning the subject develops a selective sensitivity to certain kinds of information. Until the pupil is able to exhibit a pattern of discriminatory responses symptomatic of the appropriate level of digitalization, we refuse to credit him or her with mastery of the concept. And *what concept* we credit the subject with is a function of *what information* we believe was instrumental in the formation of the relevant internal structure (what *semantic structure* was actually developed). Consider, for example, a child being taught to recognize and identify birds. The child is shown a number of robins at close range and in such a way that their distinctive markings and silhouette are clearly visible. A few bluejays are thrown in for contrast. The child is encouraged to say "robin" in reference to the robins and "not robin" for all the others (the bluejays). After a satisfactory training period the child spots a sparrow in a nearby tree, points at it excitedly, and says "robin." What the child says is false, of course. The bird is *not* a robin. But we are not now interested in assessing the truth or falsity of what the child *says*, but rather the truth or falsity of what the child *believes*. To determine this we have to know what the child believes, and it is not at all clear that the child is accurately expressing what she believes with the word "robin."

Does the child believe the bird (the sparrow) to be a robin? Or does she, perhaps, simply believe it to be a brown bird of some sort (a nonblue bird)? Given the rather limited range of contrasts to which the child was exposed during training (only bluejays), it is not clear what information she was responding to when she succeeded in identifying all the robins in the sample class. Hence it is unclear what *concept* the child is expressing with the word "robin," what *belief* the child has when it points at the sparrow and says "robin." If, contrary to expectations (given the restricted learning conditions), the child actually developed an internal structure with the semantic content: x is a robin,[4] if it was this piece of information to which she became selectively sensitive during the training period (and which explained her initial success in distinguishing the robins from the bluejays in the sample class), then the belief she is expressing when she points at the sparrow and says "robin" is a *false* belief. For the child believes that the bird is a robin, the present stimulus is producing an instance (tokening) of a structure type with the semantic content "x is a robin" with respect to an s (the sparrow) that is not a robin, and this belief is false. If, on the other hand, the child was (during training) merely responding to the color of the birds, calling those "robin" that were not blue, then the child's belief when it says "robin" while pointing at the sparrow is true. For what it believes is that the bird is not blue, and this is true.

What this example is intended to illustrate is the way concepts, beliefs, and semantic structures are related. More will be said in the next chapter about the nature of concepts. For the present it suffices to note that we now have, in the idea of a semantic structure, and in the distinction between a structure type and a structure token, the information-theoretic resources for analyzing beliefs and their associated concepts. As we have seen (Chapter 7), a semantic structure has a more or less unique content, a content with a degree of intentionality comparable to that of a belief. If, then, we identify beliefs with the *particular instances* (tokens) of these abstract semantic structures, we solve the problem with which this chapter began, the problem of how (in terms of informational structures) to account for the possible falsity of beliefs, the problem of *mis*representation. The way this problem is resolved is by realizing that a *type* of structure (a concept) may have informational origins (in the sense that that type of structure *developed* as a system's way of coding certain sorts of information) without (subsequent) instances of that structure having similar informational origins.

There is, however, another dimension to beliefs—one that is distinct from, but nonetheless related to, their intentional structure. D.M. Armstrong, following F.P. Ramsey, takes belief to be a kind of (internal) map by means of which we steer.[5] This, of course, is nothing but a suggestive metaphor, but it does reflect two properties that are commonly taken to be essential to the idea of a belief: (1) the idea of structure with some representational powers (hence a map), and (2) the idea of a structure that has some *control* over the output of the system of which it is a part (hence something by means of which *we steer*). Up to this point we have concentrated exclusively on the first aspect of belief. The idea of a semantic structure, I submit, captures all that is worth capturing in the metaphorical equation of a belief with a map. Just as a map represents certain geographical features of an area, a particular instance of a semantic structure represents (or misrepresents, as the case may be) the way things stand with respect to a given source. But we must also take note of the second property of beliefs, the fact that these structures, in order to qualify as beliefs, must shape or be capable of shaping the behavior of the system of which they are a part.

Consider, for example, an ordinary home thermostat. This device has an internal bimetal strip that registers room temperature by its degree of curvature. The physical state of this component has a role to play in the performance of the system as a whole. What the *thermostat* does is dependent, in part at least, on what this component does. When the bimetal strip bends enough to touch an adjustable contact (adjustable to correspond with desired room temperature), an electric circuit is closed and a signal is sent to the furnace. In information-theoretic terms the bimetal strip is a temperature detector: its curvature depends on, and carries information about, the ambient temperature. The thermostat's responses (sending a signal to the furnace) are controlled by this detector. If, however, we should mechanically remove the adjustable contact so that no electrical contact could be made no matter how much the bimetal strip bent in response to the temperature, the thermostat itself would grow lifeless. No signal would ever be sent to the furnace. In such a case the information about room temperature is still reaching the thermostat. The thermostat is still "sensing" the drop in room temperature (its component temperature detector still carries this information). Nevertheless, this informational state has lost its functional significance for the system as a whole. The information embodied in the curvature of the bimetal strip is now powerless to affect the output of the thermostat itself. We still have an internal "map," but it no longer has its hand on the steering wheel.

A belief is like the configuration of a bimetal strip in a properly functioning thermostat: it is an internal state that not only represents its surroundings but functions as a determinant of the system's response to those surroundings.[6] Beliefs *are* semantic structures, but that is not *all* they are. They are semantic structures that occupy an *executive* office in a system's functional organization. Until a structure occupies this executive office, it fails to qualify as a belief. Hereafter, those semantic structures that have an executive function, that help to shape a system's output, shall be called *cognitive structures* for the system in which they occur.

This is not to say that a cognitive structure must actually be determining some concurrent piece of behavior. It does not even mean that the cognitive structure must *sometime* determine *some* piece of behavior. The information (or putative information) comprising the semantic content of a structure may simply be filed away for future use—stored in some accessible form for future determination of output. This, of course, is memory—a very large topic about which I will have very little to say. I hope, though, that what I do say about the cognitive structures underlying knowledge and belief will lend itself, rather naturally, to an account of memory in similar terms.

When I speak of a semantic structure determining output, I mean that the information (our putative information[7]) constituting the semantic content of that structure is a causal determinant of output. I have already (Chapter 4) explained what is meant by the information in a structure or signal causing something to happen: viz., information (in signal or structure S) causes E insofar as the properties of S that carry this information are those the possession of which (by S) makes it the cause of E. So, for example, if S

carries the information that *s* is *F*, and this information is carried by means of *S*'s having the property *G*, then we may say that if *S*'s being *G* causes *E*, the information that *s* is *F* causes *E*. If a structure has the semantic content *m*, then *m* causes *E* insofar as the properties of *S* which give it this content are those which are responsible for *S*'s causing *E*.

This point is important because it is the *content* of our beliefs, *what* we believe, that shapes our behavior (what we do), and we want this fact reflected in the causal efficacy of semantic structures. A semantic structure qualifies as a *cognitive* structure (and therefore, we shall argue, as a belief) insofar as its *semantic content* is a causal determinant of output in the system in which it occurs. It is possible, of course, for a structure to be causally efficacious in virtue of having properties that are quite unrelated to its having the particular semantic content it does. If, for example, I tell you (by a prearranged hand signal) that I am ready to go, my gesture causes you to believe that I am ready to go. It may also frighten away a fly. It is, presumably, the information that I am ready to go that causes you to believe what you do, but it is not this information that frightens the fly. The *gesture* is the cause in both cases, but it is different features of the gesture that are causally efficacious. Scratching my nose would have frightened away the fly, but it would not have told you I was ready to go. Whether or not it was the information that I was ready to go that caused you to believe that I was ready to go depends on whether those properties of the gesture that carried this information were the ones that were instrumental in your coming to believe.

To qualify as a cognitive structure, therefore, an internal state must not only *have* a semantic content, it must *be* this content that defines the structure's causal influence on output. Only then can we say that the system does *A* because it occupies an internal state with the content that *s* is *F*—*because* (in other words) it believes (or knows) that *s* is *F*.

This point is also important for understanding why certain semantic structures, although (in a way) causally efficacious in the control of output, do not themselves qualify as *beliefs*. They do not qualify as beliefs, as structures with *cognitive* content, because it is not *their* semantic content that determines output. For example, one hears certain neural cells (or networks of cells) described as edge detectors, movement detectors, or ratio (gradient) detectors. The word "detector" in this context may suggest that these cells or networks themselves qualify as cognitive structures (proto-beliefs) with a content corresponding to the feature detected (e.g., *s* is an edge, *s* is moving). On this view the subject (consciously) believes only that a truck is passing by, but his nervous system is infested with a host of simpler beliefs out of which is manufactured this higher-level belief about the truck. The entire process begins to look like, and is often described as, a complex *inductive inference* in which the final, consciously held belief is the culmination of a computational process (involving hypothesis formation and testing) that begins with simple beliefs about lines, colors, movements, textures, and angles.[8]

I think this is a mistake—a mistake that is fostered by a confusion of information-carrying structures on the one hand and genuine cognitive structures on the other. Even if we grant that the output of these preliminary neural processes has a semantic content, this does not, by itself, qualify them for *cognitive* status. For unless these preliminary semantic structures have a hand on the steering wheel, unless *their* semantic content is a determinant of system output (in which case, of course, the system would qualify for beliefs to the effect that there was an edge here, an angle there, a brightness gradient on the left, etc.), they do not themselves have cognitive content. Information about angles, lines, and gradients is obviously *used* in the production of a perceptual belief (e.g., a truck is passing by), but this information is (or may be) systematically eliminated in the digitalization process by means of which a final semantic structure is synthesized. A structure having the semantic content "*s* is a truck" cannot carry information about the neural processes that led (causally) to its formation. If it did, then (contrary to hypothesis) it would not constitute a complete digitalization of the information that *s* was a truck. It would not, therefore, be a structure with this semantic content. Since, therefore, the information from these preliminary processes may not be available in the final, output-determining, structure, the semantic content of these preliminary processes may exercise no control over output. In such cases they have no cognitive status. They do not qualify as *beliefs*.

Compare a pattern-recognition device capable of recognizing

patterns of type T in *any* orientation. Such a device may *use* information about *this particular* pattern's orientation in arriving at its identification of it as a pattern of type T (by, say, some distinctive output label). But the output label will *not* carry information about the particular orientation of the pattern being recognized. If it did, then the device (contrary to hypothesis) would be incapable of recognizing the *same* pattern in *different* orientations (since the same output would not be produced by differently oriented patterns of type T). Information about orientation may be used in achieving an identification, but information (about orientation) may not be available in the state that constitutes the system's identification.

This is also the reason our sensory experience, the experience associated (say) with *seeing* a truck passing by, does not qualify as a cognitive structure. It has a semantic content (expressible by a complex sentence describing all the information carried in the visual experience), but *this* semantic content exercises no control over output. What determines output is some structure having as its outermost informational shell (semantic content) a piece of information that the sensory experience carries in analog form (as an interior informational shell). Until digitalization has occurred, nothing of cognitive significance has appeared; and once digitalization has occurred, the semantic content of the (causally) antecedent states (including the sensory experience) has disappeared.

This account of belief, though still skeletal,[9] has an etiological cast. That is to say, a certain type of structure acquires its content, the sort of content we associate with belief, by its informational origins. An internal structure develops (during learning) as a system's way of completely digitalizing information about, say, the F-ness of things. This way of encoding information (as the semantic content of an output-determining structure) makes the information so encoded relevant to explaining the system's behavior. It is this origin that defines the content or meaning of the internal structures. It defines *what* a system believes when one of these structures is later instantiated with respect to some perceptual object. *That* a system believes something depends, partially, on the *effects* (on system output) of these internal states, since to qualify for cognitive content an internal structure must have executive responsibilities. But the content is determined solely by the structure's origin—by its information heritage.

This is not to say that output can be ignored. Quite the contrary. For *epistemological* purposes the character of the output (its appropriateness, directedness, and purposefulness) is evidence, and often the only available evidence, for determining what is believed. If we are dealing with a creature that can be presumed to have normal desires, purposes, and needs, certain patterns of behavior will *evince* beliefs of a certain sort, and we use this behavior as a basis from which to infer the content of these beliefs. But although we, often enough, determine what a creature believes by examining its behavior, the beliefs themselves are not determined by this behavior. What is believed is determined by the etiology of those structures that are manifested in behavior.

Contrasted with this etiological account of belief, or belief *content*, is an effect-oriented approach to the same problem. According to the latter view, those internal structures that mediate input and output, those internal states that are to be identified with a system's beliefs, derive their content, not from their causal origin but from their *effects* on output. This seems to be an especially attractive approach in connection with language-using animals because the output, or some of the output, of such systems already has a *semantic* dimension, a *meaning*, that neatly parallels the kind of content we want to attribute to the internal states (thoughts, beliefs) that produce it. The idea, roughly, is that if k utters the words, "The sun is shining" (or is disposed to utter these words under certain circumstances), and if his utterance of these words is brought about in some suitable way by a central nervous state, then the central state has the content, "The sun is shining" and may thus be identified with k's belief that the sun is shining. [10] The meaning of our verbal output is primary. The meaning or intentional structure of our cognitive states is secondary—a mere reflection of the semantic properties of the verbal behavior these internal states (tend to) produce. I will call this view consequentialism. It is, I believe, a version of behaviorism. Internal states derive what meaning they have from their effects on behavior.

This approach to the problem of intentionality loses some of its plausibility, of course, when we turn to organisms that do not possess language. Nevertheless, the same basic idea is often applied in a slightly modified form.[11] Some behavior is appropriate to food. Other behavior is appropriate to danger. Normally, food is eaten and danger avoided. It is the *appropriateness* of these responses to one thing rather than another, just as it is (given the ordinary *meanings* of the words) the appropriateness of the utterance, "The sun is shining" to one state of affairs (a shining sun) rather than another, that confers on the internal source of that behavior a propositional content (of sorts). Roughly speaking, if the dog eats it, he must *think* it is food. Thinking it is food, however, is simply being in a state that prompts or disposes the dog to exhibit behavior appropriate to food—e.g., salivation, chewing, swallowing, etc. The internal states acquire their semantic properties only by grace of issuing in a sort of behavior that has a meaning or significance independent of its source. The intentional properties of our internal states are a reflection, but *only* a reflection, of the intentional properties of the behavior they induce. To say that the dog knows or believes that s is food is to say, *only*, that the dog is in a state that disposes it to behave toward s in a way appropriate to food. If that *same* neural state disposed the dog to run from s, then it would have a different content—e.g., s is dangerous, a predator, or harmful.

The consequentialist's approach to the analysis of the so-called propositional attitudes (those, like knowledge and belief, having a propositional content) has a certain degree of plausibility. Nevertheless, it always flounders on the circularity inherent in analyzing the content of our internal states in terms of something (output, response, behavior) that either *lacks* the requisite intentional structure (has no meaning of the requisite kind) or derives what meaning it has from the meaning of its internal cause (the beliefs, intentions, and purposes that produce it). In the first case the behavior has no meaning to give. In the second case it has a meaning, but a meaning that it borrows from its internal source. In either case it is wholly unequipped to serve as the primary locus of meaning or content.

This circularity is most obvious when the attempt is made to understand the intentional structure of our cognitive attitudes (belief and knowledge) in terms of our *verbal* behavior. For it is clear, I think, that what is relevant about our verbal behavior is not the frequency, amplitude, or duration of the acoustic patterns we manage to produce when we speak but, rather, what we manage to *say* in producing such patterns. That is, it is the *meaning* of our utterances that is relevant to the content of those internal states that are causally responsible for such utterances. The only way the intentional structure of belief could be analyzed in terms of the intentional structure of our verbal behavior is if this verbal behavior *already* had a semantic content of the requisite order of intentionality, already had a meaning whose analysis did not depend on intentions and beliefs. But it seems most natural to say (following Paul Grice[12]) that the intentionality of our symbolic behavior, the fact that certain utterances, gestures, and signs have what Grice calls a nonnatural meaning (something with *semantic* content) derives from the semantic structure of those internal states (in particular, the intentions and beliefs) that give rise to that behavior. If this approach is even roughly correct, as I believe it is, then to suppose that our internal states derive their content from the behavior they produce is to put things exactly backward. It is, instead, that our verbal behavior *means* something (in Grice's nonnatural sense of "meaning") because it is an established way of satisfying certain communicative intentions by agents with certain beliefs.

It is for precisely this reason that it would be silly to attribute beliefs to a machine (e.g., a digital computer) simply because its output consisted of meaningful symbols. This would be silly *even if* the meaning of the output symbols corresponded to the information being processed by the machine. For the question must always be: whence comes the meaning (the *semantic* significance) of these symbols? I can replace a doorbell with a tape recorder that emits the sounds, "Someone is at the door" when, and only when, someone pushes the door button, but this does not mean that the system is now manifesting a *belief* to the effect that someone is at the door. The *information* that someone is at the door is being picked up and processed. It is being delivered in an acoustic form (viz., the sounds, "Someone is at the door") that may be said to mean that someone is at the door. But this is a meaning the acoustic pattern has *for us*, not for the system which has this as its output. From the point of view of the system itself, this output has no more meaning (*semantic* content) than does the *ringing* of a normal doorbell when someone presses the button.

The output may be said to mean that someone is at the door in Grice's *natural* sense of "meaning," but this is simply to say that it (like the ringing of an ordinary bell) carries the information that someone is at the door. The output (in whatever form) does not have a semantic content. It does not exhibit the third level of intentionality characteristic of linguistic meaning. This is why it does not qualify as *verbal* behavior.

We cannot take an intentional property of the output (the meaning or semantic content of the symbols produced by a system) and assign it to the cause of that output because, until the cause has an independent semantic content, the output does not qualify for the relevant semantic properties. It does not have the requisite kind of meaning (linguistic or nonnatural meaning). If a computer is to believe something, it must have internal structures with the relevant semantic content. If it has these, then it has beliefs whatever may be the conventional meaning (if any) of its output. If it does not, then the output (whatever its conventional meaning *to us*) is irrelevant to the assignment of cognitive attributes.

Even if we set aside our verbal behavior (or at least that aspect of it concerned with the conventional meaning of the sounds and marks we make), the consequentialist is confronted by the same problem in a slightly different form. The appropriateness of our behavior is not something to which we can reduce the meaning or content of the internal states that produce it. For until the internal states that produce that behavior already have a meaning *independent* of the behavior they produce, the behavior can be deemed neither appropriate nor inappropriate. If I *want* to mislead my blind associate about the time of day, there is certainly nothing inappropriate about my saying, "The sun is shining" when I know (or believe) that it is midnight. At least there is nothing inappropriate about it in any sense of "appropriate" that tells you anything about what I know or believe. The hen runs from the fox unless it wants to protect its chicks. In this case it might engage in behavior which we might deem more appropriate to a playful encounter. If a man wants to die, his eating what he believes to be poisonous mushrooms may be the appropriate thing to do. If he wants to live, this is not an appropriate thing to do. Until we know what a man wants to do, what his intentions, purposes, and beliefs are, his behavior can be deemed neither appropriate nor inappropriate. The appropriateness of behavior is a property of behavior that betrays the telltale traces of its intentional source. As such, this property cannot be used to analyze the intentional structure of those internal states that give rise to behavior. For until the internal states already have a semantic content of the sort we are trying to understand, the behavior does not have this property. Once again, this is putting things exactly backward.

What, after all, is the behavior appropriate to the belief that s is a daisy, a tree, a dog, a stone, water, liver, the postman, or the sun? What response is appropriate to these beliefs depends, not only on what your intentions and purposes are, but on what *else* you believe. One animal sniffs the daisy and forthwith eats it; another sniffs and walks away; a third merely gives it a casual glance. The gentleman clips the flower and puts it in his lapel, the youngster tramples it, and the gardener pours water on it. Sorting out which of these responses is appropriate (aside from the presumed beliefs and intentions of the agents) is a fool's errand. Even if I *want* to destroy all daisies, and *believe* that this is a daisy, there is nothing inappropriate about my pouring water on it. Not if I believe (mistakenly) that water will kill it.

There are some words we use to describe beliefs that *suggest* how the agent having the belief is likely to respond. Terms such as predator, food, dangerous, obstacles, harmful, unsafe, shelter, useful, threatening, sexy, and friendly are examples. To be told that the animal believes s is dangerous is to be told something about how the animal is likely to respond to s. To be told that it believes s is food is to be told something about how the animal (if hungry) is likely to behave with respect to s. But this is nothing more than a *suggestion*. The suggestion arises from the fact that these concepts are more or less directly related to an animal's normal needs and purposes. And *if* we are dealing with an animal whose needs and purposes can be *assumed* to be normal, we can reasonably expect certain distinctive patterns of behavior. Dennett describes a dog who, when shown a beefsteak, makes a nest for it, places the steak in the nest, and sits on it.[13] Does the dog think the steak is an egg (and itself a chicken)? Or does it believe that it is a beefsteak (or food) and want to confuse observers? If this sounds too bizarre, assume that the dog has been trained to treat beefsteaks in this unusual way. In this case the dog's behavior is perfectly appropriate, but it should also be clear that we are now explicitly using the term "appropriate" to describe the dog's behavior *relative* to its unusual desires acquired during training. Dogs (*normal* dogs) not only eat food, they also hide it, bury it, and urinate on it. The only reason I can see why all this behavior is appropriate to food is because of (concealed) assumptions about what the dog is *trying* to do—what its intentions, purposes, and other beliefs are. That is, the behavior is classifiable as appropriate or inappropriate in relation to the presumed content of those internal states that bring it about. It is therefore altogether circular to suggest, as the consequentialist does suggest, that the content of the dog's internal states is analyzable in terms of the appropriateness of the behavior they produce.

What we do is relative, not only to what we believe and intend, but also to a great many incidental circumstances that bear upon the successful completion of those things we *try* to do. After all, we do not always succeed in doing what we attempt to do. The fact that I splash water in my face instead of drinking it, smash the vase instead of putting it on the shelf (as I intended), may indicate nothing about either my beliefs or my intentions. It may indicate something about my coordination. As an extreme example of this, consider the case of the unfortunate salamanders whose right and left forelimbs are interchanged so that each "faces backward." Salamanders have sufficient regenerative capacity that the interchanged limbs heal into their new positions and are innervated by nerves from the spinal cord. What is found is that the surgically altered animals execute forelimb movements that push the animal away from food and toward noxious stimuli.[14] Are the salamander's responses appropriate or inappropriate? Well, in one sense they are inappropriate. The tail and hindlimbs work against the forelimbs and the animal swings back and forth without ever moving from the spot. What does such behavior tell us about the animal's beliefs? Little or nothing. If the creature has beliefs at all, we can easily suppose that it believes of the food that it is food, and of the noxious stimulus that it *is* noxious, even though such beliefs never get translated into appropriate responses. Even if the creature suffered this debilitating lack of motor coordination from birth, we could still suppose, despite the fact that its responses were *never* (not even originally) appropriate, that it *recognized* food and noxious stimuli.[15] For what gives the internal states the content: *this is food* and *this is noxious* (the kind of content implied by attributing *recognition* of the food as food and the noxious stimulus *as* noxious to the animal) is not the appropriateness of the behavior these states inspire, but the kind of *incoming information* to which these internal states are sensitive. Since the salamanders described above are obviously *encoding* information in the normal way, their internal states have a content corresponding to this information, *however* inappropriate may be the behavior these states determine.

The significance of this interference with the normal input-output relations may be made even more pointed by comparing the sort of case just described with that of experiments involving the rotation of an animal's eyes. R. W. Sperry reports the following experiment:[16]

> Our first experiment was to turn the eye of the newt upside down—to find out whether this rotation of the eyeball would produce upside-down vision, and if so, whether the inverted vision could be corrected by experience and training. We cut the eyeball free of the eyelids and muscles, leaving the optic nerve and main blood vessels intact, then turned the eyeball by 180 degrees. The tissues rapidly healed and the eyeball stayed fixed in the new position.
>
> The vision of animals operated on this way was then tested. Their responses showed very clearly that their vision was reversed. When a piece of bait was held above the newt's head it would begin digging into the pebbles and sand on the bottom of the aquarium. When the lure was presented in front of its head, it would turn around and start searching in the rear.
>
> . . .The operated newts never relearned to see normally during the experiment. Some were kept with their eyes inverted for as long as two years, but showed no significant improvement.

Once again we have the animal persisting in a form of inappropriate behavior, but unlike the case of the salamander, we take *this* case to be a result of *different beliefs* on the part of the animal. The salamander knew where the food was but could not get to it. The newt is perfectly coordinated, he can get to the food, but he does not know where it is. It seems natural to say that the newt has false beliefs (but not the salamander) because, although the newt's responses are as inappropriate as those of the salamander, we have, in the case of the newt, reason to believe that these responses are being produced by an internal structure that misrepresents the location of things, an internal structure with a false content. That is, signals bearing the information that *the bait is in front*, signals that were formerly (before eye rotation) coded in one way, are now (after rotation) being coded in a structure designed to carry the information that *the bait is in back*. The information that the bait is in front is now (as the result of eye rotation) producing a semantic structure having the content: the bait is in back. The information about the location of the bait is being coded in a completely different structure—a structure which has a false content and which (in virtue of old, established efferent connections) continues to produce inappropriate behavior.

What such considerations show, I submit, is that a system's internal states derive their content, not from the appropriateness or inappropriateness of their effects on the system's output but from their information-carrying role—from the sort of situation they were developed (or prewired[17]) to represent. With normally functioning animals we may use their responses as a basis for making inferences about what they believe (want and intend), but one should not mistake this epistemological relationship (determination of cause by effect) for anything more substantial— as, for instance, the *ontological* determination of cause (belief) by effect (behavior). Internal states derive their content (in the first instance at least) from their informational origin, not from their effects, although (from an evolutionary standpoint) it is hard to see why or how structures of this type could develop unless they had some beneficial (and therefore appropriate) effect on behavior.

There is an understandable reluctance on the part of some philosophers to assign beliefs to animals that lack language. I think such caution is well advised. We either do not know what the semantic content of their internal state is or we suspect that, if they have a content, it may not be expressible in *our* language. It sounds a little strange (to my ear at least) to describe the cat as believing that *s* is liver, a little more natural to describe it as believing that *s* is food (or something to eat). I may hesitate to describe my dog as believing that *s* is the postman, much less reluctant to describe him as believing that *s* is an intruder or a stranger. The words "food," "intruder," and "stranger" are more closely allied to distinctive patterns of behavior (in animals with normal needs, desires, and purposes), and I can therefore more confidently attribute beliefs with these terms than with others. Still, this reluctance on *our* part to assign a more determinate content to a creature's internal states does not imply the absence of more specific beliefs. The cat *may* believe that *s* is liver. The dog may believe that *s* is the postman. Everything depends on whether the state determining their response (or disposition to respond) to *s* has this, or something else (or nothing at all), as its semantic content. If the cat will eat *only* liver, if the dog barks and chases only the postman (not *this* postman, but whoever delivers the mail), there is some evidence to suggest that the cat recognizes this food *as* liver (believes it to be liver) and the dog recognizes the intruder *as* the postman (believes him to be the postman). For these distinctive responses indicate that the animals are responding to particular pieces of information—the information, namely, that *s* is liver (not just food) and *s* is the postman (not just any stranger). The responses, it should be noticed, are not particularly appropriate (not, at least, in a way that helps to define the content of belief). If the cat *refused to eat* only liver, and the dog *wagged his tail* in the presence of (and only in the presence of) the postman, we could make similar inferences about what they believed. The key to what they believe is the *meaning* of those structures determining their response (*whatever* this response) to *s*, and the meaning of these structures is their semantic content: the kind of information they were developed to carry in completely digital form.

It may be objected that our hypothetical dog and cat deserve less credit. Their discriminating responses (to liver and the postman) show only that they recognize liver *as* food and the postman *as* an intruder. Furthermore (for whatever reason) they recognize *only* liver as food and only the postman as an intruder. Hence, they do not believe that *s* is liver and *s* is the postman. At best they believe *of* liver (and *only* liver) that it is food and of the postman (and only the postman) that he is an intruder. And since the contents of *these* beliefs (having to do with food and intruders) derive from the appropriateness of the behavior they inspire, we are, once again, back to the consequentialist's account of belief.[18]

This description of the situation may, of course, be the correct description. But then again it may not. It all depends on the cat and the dog. Suppose the cat *does* recognize other food (e.g., chicken and fish) *as* food but dislikes them. If you starve it long enough, it will eat fish but only under duress. Suppose the dog *does* recognize other intruders *as* intruders (barking and chasing them) but shows a particularly violent and distinctive response to postmen. How shall we account for the cat's *special* response to liver and the dog's *special* response to postmen? We cannot do it simply by saying that the cat believes the liver is food, because this is not the cat's normal response to food. It does not eat most of what it recognizes *as* food. We cannot account for the dog's frenzied reaction to the postman simply by saying that the dog believes the postman to be an intruder, since this is not the dog's typical reaction to intruders. We must, of course, assign more specific beliefs to the animals in order to account for these specialized patterns of response. And what better beliefs are available than that *s* is liver (to the cat) and than that *s* is the postman (to the dog)? These may not be accurate expressions of the information to which these animals are responding. Perhaps the dog should only be described as believing *of* the postman that he carries a large leather bag and makes noise at the mailbox. Perhaps the cat should only be described as believing *of* the liver that it looks and smells a special way (the way only liver looks and smells). The point to notice, however, is that if we are going to give an explanation of the animals' discriminatory responses in *cognitive* terms, in terms (partly at least) of what it thinks or knows, then we must assign *some* more specific content to their internal states than can be expressed by such terms as "food" and "intruder."[19] And until we are supplied with a more complete description of these animals, including a description of their past training and experience (and hence what kind of cognitive structures they may have developed), the belief that *this* is liver and the belief that *that* is the postman seem to do as well as any other in explaining why our cat eats *this* and why our dog gets so excited about *that*.

The etiological account of belief (or belief content) supplied in this and the last chapter is much too crude to handle many beliefs. The most that has been given is an account of a system's capacity for acquiring and holding certain *de re* beliefs of a rather simple kind: beliefs of the form "This is *F*" where *this* is the perceptual object (*what* is seen, heard, tasted, etc.) and *F* is an expression of some ostensively learned simple concept. I have said nothing about how one might acquire the capacity to hold beliefs of the form, "My grandmother is dead" (i.e., certain *de dicto* beliefs) where the reference, what one has the belief *about*, is fixed in other than perceptual ways. Neither have I said anything about beliefs involving concepts about whose instances one has never received information—either because the concept in question has no instances (e.g., ghost, miracle, unicorn) or because, though having instances, the believer has never been exposed to them. How can an organism develop an appropriate *semantic* structure, something that *means* that x is F, if he or she has never received the information that something was F?

Although we have not yet said anything about these matters and, to this extent, our analysis remains incomplete, I think enough has been said about the information-theoretic approach to cognitive structure and meaning to reveal its promise in successfully coping with these problems. What we have so far given is an analysis of simple *de re* beliefs involving primitive concepts.[20] We have therefore provided a *semantics* for the internal language of thought and belief by assigning a meaning, a semantic content of the requisite order of intentionality, to the internal states of an information-processing system. What we have not yet described is the *syntax* of this internal language, the combinatorial and transformational mechanisms that are available, or may develop, for enriching the expressive resources of these internal morphemes. We shall say something about these matters in the final chapter. But for the moment we must content ourselves with the observation that the semantics provided, the meaning or content assigned to these internal structures, is something that our theory of information was capable of supplying. This, in turn, implies that the problem of meaning, insofar as this refers to the propositional content of our cognitive attitudes, is something that can be understood using *only* the resources available to *physical* theory. Beliefs (and therefore knowledge) have been identified with physical states or structures. A belief is realized *by* or *in* a physical structure. The *content* of the belief, however, is something quite distinct from the physical structure in which it is realized. Just as the information contained *in* a vibrating diaphragm must be distinguished from the vibrating diaphragm itself (since the same information can be found elsewhere—in *different* physical structures), so must a belief be distinguished from its particular realization in the hardware of a system. A belief is a physical structure having both representational and functional properties in the system of which it is a part. If another system has an internal structure with the same *representational* properties (and some, perhaps different, functional properties), then it has a belief with the same content. Since the two structures are numerically distinct, there is a sense in which physically distinct, and physically (not to mention functionally) quite different, structures can be the same belief while remaining distinct beliefs. They are distinct beliefs in the sense that Jack's beliefs and Jill's beliefs are different (if Jack dies, Jill still has *her* beliefs), but the same belief in that *what they believe* (e.g., that the hill is steep) is the same.[21]

Chapter 9
Concepts and Meaning

A concept is a *type* of internal structure: one whose semantic content, when instantiated, exercises control over system output. When this type of structure (having a content expressible as "*x* is *F*") is instantiated relative to some perceptual object *s*, we have a (*de re*) belief with the (propositional) content: *s* is *F*. Beliefs, therefore, require concepts, and concepts imply the capacity for holding beliefs. If concepts are understood to be the structures that *have* meaning, then concepts are "in the head." This should not be taken to imply, however, that *meanings* are in the head.

A system *has* concepts insofar as its internal states constitute an alignment, some degree of coordination, between input and output. But the fact that there exists this kind of coordination between input and output does not determine *what concepts* a system has. What concepts a system has depends on what kind of information it is *to which* the coordination has been made.

A semantic structure does not qualify as a concept until there has been an alignment of its representational and functional roles (until, that is, it has become a *cognitive* structure), but *what concept* it qualifies as is determined by its representational (semantic) properties. In this respect a concept is a two-faced structure: one face looks backward to informational origins; the other

214

face looks ahead to effects and consequences. No structure qualifies as a concept unless it has both the backward-looking, informational aspect and the forward-looking, functional aspect, but what gives the structure its conceptual identity, what makes it *this* concept rather than *that* concept, is its etiological specificity.

SIMPLE AND COMPLEX CONCEPTS

I have so far suppressed an important feature of semantic structures, a feature that would appear to be an embarrassment for this account of beliefs and their associated concepts. Consider two properties that are equivalent—either nomically (it is a law that F if and only if G) or analytically ("F" means the same as "G"). If F and G are thus equivalent, then any signal carrying the information that s is F also carries the information that s is G and vice versa. The two pieces of information are, as it were, inseparable. Hence, if a structure constitutes a complete digitalization of the one piece of information, it also constitutes a complete digitalization of the other. Any structure having the semantic content: x is F will also have the semantic content: x is G. But, given the analysis of concepts (and belief) in terms of a structure's semantic content, this has the consequence that it is impossible for anyone to believe that s is F without believing that s is G and vice versa. The concepts F and G turn out to be the *same* concept. But surely, it will be argued, these concepts must be distinguished. We distinguish the belief that s is F from the belief that s is G even when the properties F-ness and G-ness are nomically equivalent—even (sometimes) when the expressions "F" and "G" are synonymous.

The solution to this difficulty lies in recognizing the restricted scope of the analysis so far provided. We have been chiefly concerned with simple, primitive concepts—concepts that are not themselves decomposable into more elementary cognitive structures. If we are dealing with primitive concepts, the above remarks are perfectly valid, but they no longer constitute an objection. For the only way a system can have distinct concepts F and G, when these concepts are equivalent in one of the described ways, is if at least one of them is complex, if one of them is built up out of conceptual elements that the other is not. So, for example, if s's being F is (analytically or nomically) equivalent to s's being G, but something's being G *consists* of its being H and K (for the system in question), then, despite the *semantic* equivalence of the two cognitive structures (they have the same *semantic* content), they remain distinct *cognitive* structures. They remain distinct cognitive structures because of their compositional differences. A cognitive structure with the content *s is G* is a composite structure each component of which is itself a determinant of output. Hence, these semantically equivalent structures influence behavior in different ways. It may be difficult to tell from output alone whether the belief being manifested is a belief involving a simple concept (i.e., *s is F*) or a complex concept (*s is G*), since these two structures (the one conceptually simple, the other complex) may in fact issue in the *same* behavior. Nevertheless, just as we can distinguish between the effect of *joint* forces and the effect of a *single* force that constitutes their vector sum by altering conditions in some suitable way (e.g., selective shielding), so can we detect the compositional differences of semantically equivalent beliefs. Two different individuals may both respond to a square by behavior that indicates they believe it to be a square (e.g., they both say, "That is a square"). Nevertheless, one may be giving expression to a complex belief, a belief that embodies the idea of *four-sidedness*, while the other is giving expression to a (conceptually) simple belief. The latter may not even *have* the concept of *four-sidedness*. The individual in question must obviously rely on the information that *s* has four sides in recognizing *s* as a square, but if it lacks this concept it will have no cognitive structure with *four-sidedness* as its semantic content. It will therefore lack the capacity to recognize squares, rectangles, and parallelograms as the *same kind of figure*. This may be the situation of a pigeon or a monkey that has been trained to peck at (push) only square targets. There is no reason to think that these animals have the concept of a quadrilateral just because we choose to think of a square as a *complex* idea embodying the notion of four-sidedness. For them the concept square may be primitive, something having no conceptual parts. The same might be said of a two-year-old child—one who had not yet learned to count.

What is impossible on the present account of things is to have *two primitive* concepts that are equivalent. If they are equivalent, the cognitive structures with which they are being identified have exactly the same semantic content. And if they are both primitive, this unarticulated content is, in both cases, what controls output. This is a distinction without a difference. To be both primitive and (semantically) equivalent is to be *identical*.[1]

This, I think, is as it should be. We are trying to give an account of the intentionality of belief. We have succeeded in showing how the belief that *s* is *F* might differ from the belief that *s* is *G*, how (therefore) the concepts *F* and *G* might differ, despite the semantic equivalence of the corresponding structures. This gives us the level of intentionality that we desire. To try to go farther, to try to separate or distinguish primitive equivalent concepts, would be to pursue a level of intentionality *beyond that* to be found in cognitive structures as ordinarily understood. For we do not distinguish beliefs involving semantically equivalent concepts unless at least one of these concepts is complex, unless we can distinguish the beliefs (and concepts) in terms of their *compositional* structure. We can, for instance, distinguish the belief that *s* is a square from the belief that *s* is a right-angled equilateral as long as we can treat the concept *square* as a simple (primitive) concept for the subject in question—or, at least, as a concept having a different (conceptual) resolution than that of being a right-angled equilateral. For as long as we can treat the concept *square* as simple, the belief that *s* is a right-angled equilateral commits the believer to something that the belief that *s* is a square does not—viz., the belief that *s* is equilateral. And with this difference in belief goes a corresponding difference in behavior (or disposition to behave) with regard to *s* and other figures.

Consider the theoretical identification of light with electromagnetic waves, sound with vibrations of the air (or medium), heat with the motion of molecules, and water with H_2O. Even if we should suppose that being H_2O is an *essential* (and the *only* essential) property of water, even if we suppose, therefore, that there is no *informational* distinction between something's being water and its being H_2O (every structure or signal that carries the one piece of information necessarily carries the other), we can still make out a clear difference between a cognitive structure with the content that *x* is water and a cognitive structure with the content that *x* is H_2O. These cognitive structures can differ so long as we regard the one as being compositionally distinct (and therefore functionally distinguishable) from the other. Having identical semantic contents is not enough to make two structures the same *cognitive* structure. They must, in addition, be *functionally* indistinguishable for the system of which they are a part. And if the one structure is a composite structure, having parts that are themselves cognitive structures, and the other is not (or is built up out of simpler cognitive structures in a different way), then the two structures constitute different concepts despite their *semantic* equivalence. It is this fact that makes it possible to distinguish, on purely information-theoretic grounds, between the *belief* that s is water and the *belief* that s is H_2O despite the fact that the information that s is water cannot be distinguished from the *information* that s is H_2O.[2]

It is this that makes possible a nontrivial belief to the effect that water is composed of H_2O molecules despite the fact that what is believed, the content of the belief, has an informational measure of *zero*. For although there is no information associated with water's being H_2O (or, indeed, any necessary truth), the belief that water is H_2O constitutes an assimilation of two *different* cognitive structures in terms of their *sameness* of content. If we looked *only* at the contents of the structures representing water and H_2O, it would be difficult to see how the belief that water was H_2O could differ from the belief, say, that water was water. For the structures corresponding to the two concepts in this belief (water and H_2O) have identical semantic contents. Nevertheless, these structures are *compositionally distinct* in a way that makes them *functionally* distinguishable. Their functional difference resides in the fact that the two structures are composed of functionally different units (cognitive structures). To believe that water is H_2O is to achieve a convergence in the functional properties of structures that are already equivalent in terms of their content.

It is for this reason that the knowledge of a necessary truth, though requiring no information for its realization (since what is known has an informational measure of zero), is not the trivial, effortless thing it might otherwise appear to be. Even if we suppose that robins are *necessarily* birds, that being a bird is an *essential* property of robins, the discovery that robins are birds may constitute a significant cognitive achievement. One does not need information to make this discovery, but insofar as discovery implies knowledge, and knowledge implies belief, one *does* need the belief that robins are birds. And, as we have just seen, the acquisition of this belief is no trivial matter. It requires a realignment in the functional properties of various structures, and an investigation may be required in order to effect this change. The investigation may be necessary, *not* in order to acquire information in excess of what one has when one has the information that the objects under observation are robins (for one cannot *get* the information that s is a robin *without* getting the information that s is a bird), but in order to bring about a consolidation of one's representational structures. The investigation may be necessary, that is, in order to solve what is basically a *coding* problem: the problem, namely of determining which cognitive structures (if any) encode information that is already encoded, either in whole or in part, by other cognitive structures.[3]

We have said that concepts are acquired under an optimum set of conditions—optimum, at least, from an informational point of view. One learns what an F is (acquires the concept F) by being exposed to various things that are F and (normally) things that are not F, the exposure taking place under conditions in which the information that s is F, and the information that t is not F, is made available to the learner. The internal structure that is to represent something's being F, that is to have this semantic content, is then articulated in response to messages about the F-ness of things. What confers upon these internal structures an appropriate content is their sensitivity (developed during learning) to a particular component of information. A structure's selective sensitivity to the information that s is F is just another way of describing the fact that this structure develops as a digital representation of the F-ness of things in the kind of circumstances characteristic of the learning situation. Once the structure has been formed, subsequent tokens of it *mean* that s is F whether or not the occasioning stimulus bears this information about s.

In the last chapter this process of acquiring a primitive concept was illustrated by describing some hypothetical subject learning what a robin was. This is not an altogether realistic example, since most people learning to identify birds are already quite sophisticated, conceptually, when they undertake this task. They know what birds are and what it means to be able to fly. Hence, they can exploit these previously acquired concepts in learning what a robin is. For example, they can look at *pictures* of robins or examine *stuffed* robins. If they already know what a thrush is, they can be told that a robin is an orange-breasted thrush. In acquiring the concept in these more or less indirect ways, one is not, of course, receiving information to the effect that *s* is a robin. But if one already knows what a bird and a picture are, one can, as it were, manufacture the concept *robin* out of these previously acquired conceptual resources and the presently available information. A robin is *a bird* with the distinctive markings and silhouette *illustrated in this picture.* In such a case the concept is acquired in the absence of the appropriate piece of information (viz., *s* is a robin), but just as clearly, I think, this is not an instance of someone acquiring a *primitive* concept. For a person learning what a robin is in the indirect way described above, the concept of a robin would be a complex concept, one that had the concept *bird* as one of its ingredients.

Suppose, however, that we are teaching a completely naïve subject what a robin is. We start from scratch. Our pupil has neither the concept *robin* nor the concept *bird*. If we suppose that robins are distinctive-looking birds, sufficiently so that they can be recognized on the basis of their silhouette and markings alone, then it should be possible to teach our naïve subject what a robin is *without letting her know that robins are birds.* I say this should be possible because if *s* can be known to be a robin (recognized as a robin) on the basis of silhouette and markings alone, then it should be possible to condition the subject to the information that *s* is a robin *without* conditioning her to the information that *s* is a bird. That is, we should be able to develop a semantic structure with the content: *x* is a robin, without building up a structure with the content: *x* is a bird. Even though the information that *s* is a bird is *nested within* the information that *s* is a robin (assuming it to be an essential property of robins that they are birds), so that we cannot communicate the latter piece of information without communicating the former piece of information, we can nevertheless build up a structure that *digitally* encodes the latter piece of information without building up any structures that *digitally* encode the former piece of information. Although our subject is (necessarily) receiving the information that *s* is a bird as she acquires the concept robin (in virtue of its being *nested within* the piece of information that *s* is a robin), she does not *digitalize* this information. Through a careful program of reinforcement she succeeds in digitalizing only the more specific piece of information. As a result, she acquires the concept *robin* without acquiring the concept *bird*. Should this occur, the subject will be able to believe of particular birds that they are robins without believing, without even being *able* to believe (since lacking the relevant concept), that they are birds.

This particular consequence of the information-theoretic characterization of concepts (and the associated beliefs) may strike some readers as paradoxical. The consequence is not only *not* paradoxical, it illuminates an important fact about the nature of concepts, a feature of concepts (or meaning) that has recently become clearer through the work of Saul Kripke, Hilary Putnam, and others.[4] One can have the concept F, or (if one does not like to talk of concepts) one can have beliefs to the effect that this is F, without knowing *all*, without knowing *any*, of the essential properties of Fs. One can have the concept robin, hence believe that the creature perched on yonder branch is a robin, without knowing what is essential to something's being a robin, without knowing that robins can fly or that robins are birds. Indeed, this is what makes it possible to believe that something is a robin and yet require an *empirical* investigation to discover what robins are. One does not have to know everything, or anything, that is essential to something's being gold to believe that one has struck gold. If this were required (assuming that the only plausible candidate for an essential property of gold is its atomic constitution), then the California prospectors of an earlier generation not only did not know they had struck gold, they did not even believe it.

The possession of a concept is something quite different from the knowledge of those conditions that may be regarded as necessary to, and jointly sufficient for, the application of the concept. One can have a concept and still have much to learn about the things to which it applies, much to learn about what is necessary for a thing's being an instance of that concept. We can no longer continue with the traditional idea that it is the task of science to discover the accidental properties of things while it is the task of linguistic or conceptual analysis to reveal the essential properties of things. What we have found is something quite different. In analyzing a particular system's concept of C we may find no cognitive representation of C's essential properties. The distinction between what can be known a priori (by some form of conceptual analysis) about a type of thing and what is *necessary* (essential) to a thing's being of that type is a distinction that has been made most credibly by Saul Kripke in his lectures on naming and necessity (see note 4). The originality (if any) of the present analysis lies, *not* in this distinction between an F's essential properties and what can be known in some a priori way (via conceptual analysis) about Fs, but in the idea that the difference registered by this distinction is a difference that has its source in the information-theoretic nature of meaning (concepts).

THE INFORMATIONAL ORIGIN OF CONCEPTS

I have argued that it is necessary to the formation of a primitive concept that the system (for which the concept is primitive) be capable of receiving, and in fact *has* received (during learning), the requisite kind of information. This was alleged to be necessary for the development of the appropriate semantic structure. I postponed several objections to this thesis in order to paint a fuller picture of, and to give the reader a better feel for, the framework being developed. It is time we confronted these difficulties. I cannot hope to ward off every pertinent objection. There are wrinkles here that just will not go away. Nevertheless, by discussing what I see to be the major problems to this approach, I hope to clarify just how far one can go in clarifying the nature of concepts and the associated phenomenon of meaning.

Before we begin, it should be remembered that we are dealing, for the moment at least, only with *primitive* concepts. A primitive concept requires the system possessing it to have the capacity for receiving, and in fact to have received, information corresponding to the meaning of that concept (its *semantic* content). This, of course, is not true for complex concepts. It is obvious enough that someone can believe that *s* is a ghost, a miracle, or a unicorn without ever having received the information that something *was* a ghost, a miracle, or a unicorn. If such things do not (and never did) exist, no one ever received these pieces of information. Nevertheless, such concepts, I submit, are always complex. They are built up out of more elementary cognitive structures.[5] Since I am not going to argue for this claim, I hope it is sufficiently plausible not to *need* argument. Since I assume that there must be *some* primitive concepts (and concepts with null extension are not among them), I will restrict attention to concepts that might plausibly be taken to be primitive for *some* organism at *some* time.[6] The thesis about the necessity of informational antecedents is a thesis about *these* concepts.

Aside, then, from a covert appeal to complex concepts, there is a type of learning situation in which it may be thought that an organism could acquire a primitive concept without the requisite sort of information. The idea is this. Teach someone the concept *red* by showing him white objects under red light.[7] Or teach someone what a robin is by showing him clever mechanical replicas that chirp and fly just like real robins. Since the subject will not be shown anything that *is* red (anything that *is* a robin), he will not be receiving, nor will he develop a selective response to, the information that something is red (or a robin). Hence, no structure can develop with the semantic content "*x* is red" or "*x* is a robin." Nevertheless, it may be argued, one could acquire the concept *red* or *robin* in this unorthodox way. Once the training period is over, the abnormal circumstances will be removed and our subject will blend in with the rest of us. If he has learned his lesson well, he will (under normal illumination) describe red objects as being red and will withhold this description from differently colored objects. Or, if the subject happened to be a pigeon, the bird will (under normal illumination) peck at the red chips and refuse to peck at the chips of other colors. Even under abnormal circumstances, the kind of circumstances that characterized the learning situation for our unusually trained subject, no differences will be apparent. For, assuming that no one is made aware of the abnormal circumstances, both the normally trained subject and our unusually trained subject will describe white objects (under red light) as red. It seems, therefore, that if normally trained subjects are to be credited with the concept *red*, so must our unusually trained subject. This, though, violates the thesis presently being defended: our subject did *not* acquire his concept in response to information about the color of objects. He did it in response to *mis*information.

The first point to be noted about this example is that it makes no difference what word our subject is trained to use in response to red-looking things. What word is used to express what one believes is irrelevant to assessing what, in fact, someone believes (although in normal situations it is certainly a relevant piece of evidence). We are not now asking what the word "red" means. We are asking what concept or belief our unusually trained subject is using this word to express. We could have trained him to say "hexagonal." This would not show that he believed red (looking) objects were hexagonal when he described them as "hexagonal."

One thing seems clear: the concept our subject does have (after this sort of training) cannot be the concept *red* if it *correctly* applies to nonred things. Since this is so, we can show that our subject does not have the concept *red* if we can show that the concept he does have correctly applies to the white objects on which he was trained.

Let R stand for the concept that the subject has actually acquired during the training period described above, the concept he now uses the word "red" to express. The question, then, is whether the white objects (under red light) that he was shown during training are really R.

When the subject responds "red" to these white objects—something he is *trained* to do—his response is obviously incorrect in the sense that this response involves the use of a word that, given its meaning in the public language of which it is a part, fails to apply to the objects to which he is applying it. But in assessing the correctness or incorrectness of the response, we are not allowed to use this fact. For we are now trying to determine what concept *the subject* is using this word to express, what *he* means by "red," and we cannot assume that this is the concept *red* without begging the question.

What, then, could it mean to say that the white training objects (under red light) were not R? This could only make sense if we assumed that there were criteria for the correct application of R that were independent of what the subject was trained to use— only, that is, if we assume that the response (or the internal state that gives rise to it) has a meaning *independent* of what it acquires in the learning situation. But, if we set aside the conventional meaning of the word "red," this is precisely what does not make sense. It is the information to which the subject is made responsive in the learning situation that *defines* what constitutes a correct response, not, of course, for the *words* the subject is trained to utter (for these are part of a public language with independent criteria of application), but for the *concepts* (if any) which he uses these words to express. *Until* the subject has acquired the concept *R*, no response constitutes an *incorrect* application of that concept, since no response constitutes an *application* of that concept. And once the subject has acquired the concept, the question of *what concept* he has acquired, and therefore the question of what constitutes a correct application of that concept, is determined by what properties it was developed to represent. Hence, it makes no sense to suppose that when the subject is trained to respond "red" to red-looking white objects, he is being trained to *incorrectly* apply some concept to these objects. What he is being incorrectly trained to do is to use the word "red" to express the concept he is applying.

I should want to say, then, that our unusually trained subject does not have the concept *red*. At best he has the concept *looks red* or, perhaps, some concept that applies, indifferently, to both red things and things that look red (assuming the concept applies, if it applies at all, to the perceptual object *s*). The fact that he expresses this concept with the word "red" and the fact that he will normally be operating in standard conditions of illumination (in which white objects do not look red) accounts for the difficulty in detecting his eccentric concept and corresponding beliefs. But the difficulty in discovering this conceptual anomaly should not be confused with the quite different possibility of there *being* such a conceptual anomaly.

The point can be made more dramatically by using an example of Hilary Putnam's.[8] Suppose there is a place (call it Twin Earth) in which there are two substances XYZ and H_2O, chemically quite different but both having the superficial properties of water. By "superficial" properties I mean the properties we ordinarily rely on (outside the laboratory) to identify something as water. Some of the lakes and rivers on Twin Earth are filled with H_2O; others are filled with XYZ. Some houses have H_2O running out of their taps; others have XYZ. It rains H_2O in some parts of the country, XYZ in other parts. In some places there is a mixture. Both substances are called "water" by the Twin Earthlings since they are (apart from elaborate chemical analysis) indistinguishable. Both substances quench thirst, taste the same, boil and freeze at (almost) the same temperature, and so on.

Consider, now, some Twin Earthling (call him Tommy) being taught what water is on a part of Twin Earth in which both H_2O and XYZ are available. As it turns out (quite by accident), he is taught to identify water (or what the Twin Earthlings call "water") by being exposed to only H_2O. After learning what water is (to the complete satisfaction of his teachers), he emigrates to a part of Twin Earth where there is to be found *only* H_2O. Or (to make the point in even clearer terms) we may suppose that Tommy is miraculously transported to Earth, where there is to be found only H_2O. Since there are no other significant differences between Twin Earth and Earth, Tommy blends in without any trouble. Everything Tommy says about water (using the word "water") will correspond with what his new-found friends say and believe about water (also using the word "water").

The question, of course, is not what Tommy says, but what Tommy *believes*. Tommy does not have the same *concept* as his Earthling associates. What Tommy believes when he says, "This is water" is not what his Earthling friends believe when they say, "This is water." What Tommy means by "water" is *either* H_2O or XYZ. This, of course, is how *we* (knowing all the facts of the case) would describe it, not Tommy. If asked, Tommy will say that he means *water* by "water," and he surely does mean this. But the point is that *more things* qualify as water for Tommy than for his Earthling friends. If we should imagine that some XYZ was also suddenly transported to Earth, Tommy's belief of this substance that it was water would be *true* while his Earthling friend's belief that it was water would be *false*.

The information-theoretic explanation of this difference is to be found in the difference in the *kind of information* to which Tommy and his Earthling friends were made responsive during their respective learning periods. Even though it turns out (quite by accident) that Tommy and his Earthling friends were exposed to the same substance throughout the training period (viz., H_2O), the information that it was H_2O was made available to the Earthlings but not to Tommy.[9] On Twin Earth this information was not available because on Twin Earth (but not on Earth) signals carried the information, not that s was H_2O, but that s *was either H_2O or XYZ*. It was this latter, essentially disjunctive, piece of information to which Tommy became selectively responsive during

training. Since XYZ is not to be found on Earth (and, we are supposing, cannot be brought to Earth by anything short of a miracle),
Earthlings acquired a different concept because their discriminatory
responses were shaped by a different piece of information—the
information, namely, that this was H_2O. Since the regularities pre-
vailing in these two worlds are different, the kind of information
to be found in physically indistinguishable signals is different.
Hence, the *semantic content* of structures developed in response
to these signals is also different. This is why Tommy's concept,
though developed in response to the same sort of physical stimuli
(the sort associated with seeing, tasting, and feeling water), though
(in fact) developed in association with the same substance (H_2O),
is quite different from the Earthling concept. They both use the
same word to express what they mean, but they mean something
different. At least they have concepts with *different extensions*.
There is no way of discovering this difference by looking "inside
their heads"—by examining the physical properties of their internal states. For the different extensions (hence different concepts)
are a result of the different sort of information to which they were
exposed during learning, and this difference is a difference, not
of what is in their head, but of the informationally related regularities that dominated the environment in which they learned.[10]

Putnam's example may be deemed excessively fanciful. I have
heard it dismissed as having little or nothing to do with the way
we form concepts or with the application of the concepts we have.
This is a mistake. The example has an unfortunate science-fiction
flavor, but the lesson it carries is practical enough. It tells us that
one cannot acquire the concept F by exposure to signals that carry
only the information that things are F or G. Or, to put the same
point in information-theoretic terms, the (primitive) concepts one
acquires are limited by the kind of information available in the signals to which one develops a selective response, and the concepts
so acquired have their identity (meaning) determined by this information. If there are no other birds that look and sound exactly like
robins, *then* I can learn what a robin is by looking and listening to
robins. This, presumably, is the way our world is. But if there were
other birds (or mechanical replicas) that were, under normal viewing and listening conditions, indistinguishable from genuine robins,
then what I acquired by watching and listening to robins would

not be the concept *robin*. It would be a more inclusive concept—something that contained these other birds (or mechanical replicas) in its extension. And this conceptual difference is a result of the informational difference between these worlds: in the latter world (but, presumably, not in our world) one would not get the information that yonder bird was a robin by casual looking and listening.

Tommy's situation on Earth is identical to that of our hypothetical subject (trained to respond "red" to red-looking white objects) once he emerges from the artificially contrived learning environment. He does not have the concept *red*. What he has is a concept that applies to those white objects on which he was trained. Tommy's concept, the one he expresses with the word "water," applies to things that are not water (i.e., not H_2O, not what *we* mean by water); and our subject's concept, the one he expresses with the word "red," applies to things that are not red. The fact that his verbal responses to red objects under normal illumination will be as accurate and as discriminating as that of normally trained subjects says absolutely nothing about what concept it is that he is applying when he says of an object that it is "red." All it shows (as in the case of Tommy) is that he happens to be operating in an environment, or under conditions, in which the concept he *does* have is coextensive with the concept his associates have.

This discussion should not be taken to imply that one cannot acquire the concept *red* as a primitive concept by being exposed to variously colored objects in the way that most children are taught their color words. It does *not* mean that we cannot, so to speak, *use* the fact that things *look* red to teach someone what it means to be red. What it *does* mean is that to acquire the concept *red* as a primitive concept one must operate in more or less normal circumstances, circumstances in which *s*'s looking red carries the information that *s* is red. In order to develop the requisite semantic structure, one having a content expressible as "*x is* red" (in contrast to "*x looks* red"), it will be necessary, of course, to make the subject responsive to information about the color things *are* and not just the color they appear to be. This will doubtless require training under a variety of lighting conditions (e.g., sunlight, dusk, artificial light) and a variety of contexts (e.g., differently colored backgrounds). The fact that such a (normally trained) subject can later be fooled into thinking something is red that is only made to look red (by selective illumination with red light) does not show that he really has the concept *looks red* instead of the concept *red*. One could as well argue that someone did not have the concept *robin* because he could be fooled by a clever mechanical replica or that a child did not have the concept of *distance* because she thought the moon quite near.[11]

A consequence of this analysis (one noted earlier) is that when C is a primitive concept, it cannot have an empty extension. It must apply (or have applied) to something—if only those objects available during the time when the concept was being acquired. Furthermore, if C is primitive for K, K must have received information to the effect that something was C. This much is implied by our characterization of how one acquires a primitive concept.[12] This has a rather surprising epistemological consequence. If C is a primitive concept, one cannot *believe* that s is C unless one is (or was) equipped to *know* that things were C. For one cannot believe that s is C unless one has the concept C. One cannot acquire this concept unless one received, processed, and encoded information about the C-ness of things—unless, that is, one developed a means of digitally encoding information about the C-ness of things. Since knowledge has been identified with information-produced belief, any organism capable of believing that something is C must have (or have had) the information-processing resources for knowing that things are (or were) C. Without this capability an organism could never have developed the concept C, could never (therefore) have beliefs to the effect that something was C.

The classical formula (knowledge = justified true belief) assures us that knowledge requires belief. It now seems, however, that some beliefs (those involving primitive concepts) require, if not knowledge, then the *possibility of knowledge* on the part of the system holding the beliefs. How damaging this consequence is to the traditional skeptical thesis will depend, of course, on just how widespread are one's beliefs involving primitive concepts. But this much, surely, can be said: the view that nothing *can* be known is demonstrably false. Its demonstration requires (besides acceptance of the present view of belief and knowledge) only the premise that we *have* beliefs. As far as I know, most skeptics have not challenged this premise.

Presumably, most of the concepts we deploy in our description of our surroundings are complex concepts, structures that are built up in various ways out of more primitive elements. If C_1 is a primitive structure having the content *red* and C_2 is a primitive structure having the content *square*, the concept of a red square can be thought of as a composite structure having C_1 and C_2 as components. The rules determining the formation of complex concepts, the syntax of this internal language, cannot, of course, be the simple sort of thing suggested by this example. The concepts: (1) red and square, (2) red or square, (3) red only if square, and (4) red but not square are all different concepts, but they all have *red* and *square* as constituents. They are, as it were, manufactured from the same (semantic) ingredients in accordance with different (syntactic) recipes. The syntax of this internal language, the sort of compositional mechanisms responsible for the formation of complex concepts, must be extremely sophisticated if it is to account for the variety and subtlety we find in a system of mature concepts. This is especially true, of course, when we look at language-using organisms. Indeed, it seems hardly a metaphor to speak of the internal compositional mechanisms responsible for the generation of complex concepts as themselves a language—the language of thought.[13] But this, in turn, may only be a reflection of the fact that the internal conceptual mechanisms are, in part at least, an internalization of the compositional and projectional devices inherent in the public language we learn. We learn more subtle recipes for the construction of complex concepts as we learn language because (perhaps) the recipes for manufacturing these complex concepts are provided by the increasingly rich and differentiated network of responses (and discriminations) involved in the acquisition of language. In acquiring a language, we provide ourselves with a richer system of representationally distinguishable internal states, and this, as we have seen, is the essence of conceptual development.[14]

These matters are too technical to be discussed here. They are, at least, beyond my technical competence. Questions having to do with concept formation, especially as this bears on the way language users are capable of generating more complex concepts out of some preexisting stock, are best left to the specialists equipped to study them. For my limited purposes it suffices to note that a language has both a syntax and a semantics. And whatever the syntax of this internal language may be, it has been the purpose of this chapter (and the last) to supply a rough account of how this internal language (set of meaningful internal structures) acquires its *meaning* or *interpretation*—how it obtains its *semantics*. What I have argued is that our internal states acquire their meaning in terms of the information to which their original formation into functional units was a response. It is the information embodied in these original, formative, stimuli that supplies the content to those internal structures—a content that these structures retain even when they are subsequently aroused by stimuli that lack the relevant information.

INNATE CONCEPTS

I have placed considerable stress on the learning situation because, generally speaking, it is here that the alignment, the coordination, between information and function takes place that is characteristic of concepts. Typically, it is during the learning situation that organisms develop internal states with a distinctive semantic content. Despite this emphasis, the possibility exists that an organism may come into this world already "tuned" to certain pieces of information. No learning is necessary. The organism comes, hard-wired as it were, with a set of internal states that are both selectively responsive to certain pieces of perceptually received information and instrumental in shaping output. The exigencies of survival have led to the selection of individuals with the *cognitive* wherewithal to respond, selectively, to certain vital pieces of environmentally obtained information. Some information is automatically digitalized for the determination of important responses (avoidance, flight, pursuit, concealment, etc.). In virtue of this inherited alignment or coordination between functionally significant structures and their informational sensitivity, such structures have a meaning or content *prior* to any actual exposure to signals bearing the relevant information. What we are talking about, of course, are *innate concepts*: functionally significant internal structures that, prior to learning, prior to exposure to signals bearing the information that s is C, constitute the system's way of digitally representing the fact that something is C.

Whether an organism has any innate concepts and, if so, whether they can be identified with the concepts it possesses in its fully mature state, are empirical questions. The issues here are those that have long separated the nativists and the empiricists in developmental psychology. I have no wish to take sides in this controversy. But as an illustration of how this traditional issue appears when transformed into the information-theoretic idiom of the present work, we may note one of the more striking recent studies on depth perception. Gibson and Walk's experiments with the visual cliff suggest that a variety of animals (including human beings) have a concept of *depth* that manifests itself very early.[15] When exposed to a visual cliff (information about a rapid increase in distance downward) chicks, turtles, rats, lambs, kids, pigs, kittens, and dogs display a remarkably similar reaction. "At the age of less than 24 hours the chick can be tested on the visual cliff. It *never* [my emphasis] makes a "mistake" and always hops off the board on the shallow side."[16] Furthermore:

> Kids and lambs, like chicks, can be tested on the visual cliff as soon as they can stand. The response of these animals is easily predictable. No goat or lamb ever stepped on the glass of the deep side, even at one day of age. When one of these animals was placed upon the glass of the deep side, it displayed characteristic stereotyped behavior. It would refuse to put its feet down and would back up into a posture of defense, its front legs rigid and its hind legs limp.[17]

Such experiments suggest that a variety of animals are capable of recognizing something as deep *before* learning has taken place, *before* their responses have been shaped (by various feedback processes—e.g., falling *off* the cliff) to signals containing information about depth. They come into this world with a guidance system already selectively sensitive to information about depth.

Different animals display this reaction at characteristically different ages. The age at which an animal displays this reaction is related to its life history:

> The survival of a species requires that its members develop discrimination of depth by the time they take up independent locomotion, whether at one day (the chick and the goat), three to four weeks (the rat and the cat) to six to 10 months (the

human infant). That such a vital capacity (recognition of depth) does not depend on possibly fatal accidents of learning in the lives of individuals is consistent with evolutionary theory.[18]

To qualify as an innate concept, therefore, it is not necessary that the functionally relevant semantic structure be operative *at birth*. The crucial question is whether the structure emerges during normal maturation independently of trial-and-error learning. "The simple fact that a behavior appears later than infancy does not necessarily mean that it is learned. It may represent the natural unfolding of innate processes occurring along with the individual's physiological development. We call this process maturation, and we may classify it as a special kind of innate behavior."[19] And, likewise, we may call that internal structure that selectively codes the relevant information, and is (in part at least) responsible for this special kind of innate behavior, an *innate concept*.

One must not, of course, confuse the innate concept with the behavior that manifests this concept. It may turn out, for example, that an organism has an innate concept of depth, a functionally relevant structure that is selectively sensitive to information about the depth of things, but because of motor disabilities, retarded development, or simple immaturity is unable to successfully convert these beliefs into *appropriate* behavior. Recall, if you will, the discussion of the salamander with the interchanged forelimbs: it *believes* that there is food in front of it, but (for perfectly understandable reasons) its behavior is quite inappropriate to such a belief. Or consider the following sort of plausible explanation for why infants typically *misreach* for nearby objects:

> The fact that infants will initially misreach has often been taken to show that they cannot perceive depth. If they can in fact perceive depth, the misreaching remains to be explained. A clue to an explanation is given by the fact that the most obvious change in an infant as he develops is a change in size. It seems likely that an infant who misreaches does so not because of poor depth perception but because he simply does not know how long his arm is. Since arm length is going to change drastically during development, it would be uneconomical—indeed, positively maladaptive—if the perceptual-motor system were geared at birth for a particular arm length.[20]

And Gibson and Walk caution that infants should not be left close to a brink no matter how well they may discriminate depth because it is clear that their perception of depth matures more rapidly than their locomotor abilities.[21] In their awkward maneuverings to reach the shallow side of the apparatus, the infants frequently backed onto the deep side. Without the protective glass, they would have experienced a painful fall.

We have argued that *what* concept an individual possesses is determined by the kind of information to which the (functionally relevant) internal states are selectively sensitive. In the case of acquired (learned) primitive concepts the identity of the concept (*what* concept the individual has) is completely determined by the sort of information available to him during the learning process. Since innate concepts are not fashioned in response to information-bearing signals during the life history of the individual, it is not possible to identify the concept by identifying the kind of information to which *the individual* was sensitized during learning. The identification of innate concepts (i.e., *what* concept a particular animal has) must necessarily take account of the manner in which that structure developed *in the species* of which the animal is a member. For innate concepts the question becomes: what information did the process of natural selection design that structure to carry in completely digital form? What is the semantic content of those cognitive structures that were, because of their adaptive significance, developed, preserved, and genetically transmitted? It is the informational heritage of both acquired and innate structures that determines their conceptual identity. In the case of acquired concepts, the relevant informational antecedents are to be found in the learning period during which the individual acquired the concept. In the case of innate concepts, the informational antecedents are those that operated in the evolutionary development of the inherited cognitive structures.

Since a structure owes its evolutionary development to its adaptive utility, and its adaptive utility to the appropriateness of the responses it provokes, the *meaning* of an innate structure is, to this extent, directly related to its effects on output. Nevertheless, even here, it is *not* the kind of output these structures produce that determines their meaning or content. Both acquired and innate cognitive structures derive their meaning from their informational origin. Informationally sensitive internal structures could hardly survive and flourish if they had no adaptively useful function—unless, that is, they issued in some kind of *appropriate* behavior—but it is not the appropriateness of response from which a structure derives its content. Appropriate responses, like good government, merely make possible the survival and development of something that draws its meaning from elsewhere.

Notes

1. I shall always mean by "the mathematical theory of information" (or, when there is a need to distinguish it from the *semantic* theory of information developed in Chapter 3, "communication theory") the theory associated with Claude Shannon's "The Mathematical Theory of Communication," *Bell System Technical Journal*, July and October 1948 (reprinted with the same title, and an introductory essay by Warren Weaver, by the University of Illinois Press, 1949). As Yehoshua Bar-Hillel points out ["An Examination of Information Theory," *Philosophy of Science*, vol. 22 (1955), pp. 86–105], at some time between 1928 and 1948 American engineers and mathematicians began to talk about "theory of information" and "information theory," understanding by these terms approximately and vaguely a theory for which Hartley's "amount of information" is a basic concept [see R.V.L. Hartley, "Transmission of Information," *Bell System Technical Journal*, vol. 7 (1928), pp. 535–563]. Hartley was a precursor to Shannon, and his "amount of information" is, in less developed form, the same as Shannon's. As Bar-Hillel further notes, by the mid-forties Norbert Wiener and Shannon were also using this terminology, although in Great Britain things developed in a different direction; whereas the term "theory of information" came to be used in the United States, at least as from 1948 (probably because of the impact of Wiener's *Cybernetics*, New York, 1948), as a certain not too well defined subscience of communication theory, the British usage of this term moved away from communication and brought it into close contact with general scientific methodology.

There are, of course, many names associated with the development of these ideas, and I do not mean to slight these other contributions by using the name of Shannon as a peg on which to hang the theory. Aside from Hartley and Wiener, one could mention Boltzmann, Szilard, Nyquist, and others. For a brief history, see E. C. Cherry, "A History of the Theory of Information," *Proceedings of the Institute of Electrical Engineers*, vol. 98 (III) (1951), pp. 383–393; reprinted with minor changes as "The Communication of Information" in *American Scientist*, vol. 40 (1952), pp. 640–664.

2. See Shannon's discussion of the reasons for selecting a logarithmic function, and in particular the logarithm to the base 2, as the measure of information: p. 32 of *The Mathematical Theory of Information*.

3. See Fred Attneave, *Applications of Information Theory to Psychology:*

A Summary of Basic Concepts, Methods and Results, Henry Holt and Company, New York, 1959, p. 6. The coin-flipping example is taken from Attneave.

4. When the probability of each alternative is the same, the use of formula (1.1) gives both the surprisal value associated with the occurrence of each individual event *and* the average information generated at the source (the entropy), since each surprisal is the same. When everyone is the same height, their average height equals the height of every individual. Hereafter, when referring to the average information associated with a process, I will use the symbol $I(s)$; when referring to the information associated with the occurrence of some particular event, I will use subscripts, as in formula (1.2)— e.g., $I(s_2)$.

5. George A. Miller, "What Is Information Measurement?" *The American Psychologist*, vol. 8 (January 1953), p. 2.

6. Yehoshua Bar-Hillel, *Language and Information*, Reading, Mass., 1964, p. 295.

7. Warren Weaver, "Recent Contributions to the Mathematical Theory of Communication" appearing as the introductory essay in Shannon and Weaver's *The Mathematical Theory of Communication*, University of Illinois Press, Urbana, Ill., 1949, p. 14.

8. In the original case we are supposing an optimal set of circumstances— optimal, at least, from the point of view of communication theory. For example, the employees have no deceitful intentions (the name they inscribe on the memo is always an accurate indication of their nominee), the messenger is perfectly reliable, and so on. For more about the circumstances defining the *channel* of communication, see Chapter 5.

9. Noise is always relative to some specific source. So, for example, the "crackle" on your radio is noise relative to the auditory events occurring at the broadcasting studio (since the origin of this sound is independent of what the announcer is saying), but it is not noise relative to what is occurring in your neighbor's bathroom (it carries information about whether or not he is using his new electric shaver). Generally speaking, I will not bother to make this point explicitly. As long as the source is understood, a reference to *noise* should always be understood as *noise relative to that source*.

10. The diagrams are adapted from the one given by Miller in "What Is Information Measurement?" Also see Attneave's diagrams for three variables on pages 56 and 58 of *Applications of Information Theory to Psychology*.

11. It is important to understanding this example properly that the note to the employer (with some employee's name on it) not itself be taken as a kind of performative act *constituting* the employees' *choice* of the person named in the note. Rather, the note is intended to convey information about a prior, independent choice—i.e., who lost the coin-flipping game. Understood as a performative act, the message to the employer is neither accurate nor inaccurate; rather, the appearance of the name "Herman" on the note constitutes the employees' selection of Herman. Understood, however, as a communication about who lost the coin-flipping game, the message can

be correct or incorrect depending on whether the name on the memo corresponds with who was selected by flipping coins. The situation should be understood in the latter way, since only in this case does the memo contain information about some independent state of affairs.

12. Generally speaking, I follow Wendell R. Garner's development of these ideas (though I use a different notation); see his *Uncertainty and Structure as Psychological Concepts*, New York, 1962.

13. It should be noted here that my discussion of "noise" and "equivocation" is unorthodox from a technical standpoint. Within communication theory these quantities are always numerically the same because $I(s)$ and $I(r)$ are the same. Hence, any increase in noise is automatically an increase in equivocation, and a noiseless channel *is* an equivocation-free channel.

The equivalence of noise and equivocation is a result of selecting the set of possibilities at the source and receiver so as to make $I(s) = I(r)$. What I have done in the text is to envisage changes in the output ensemble [the set of possibilities defining $I(r)$] without corresponding changes in the input ensemble [those possibilities defining $I(s)$] and vice versa. If this is allowed, there is no necesssary equivalence between noise and equivocation.

14. A negative sign appears in front of Formula (1.6) because the logarithm of a probability is generally negative (since the logarithm of a fraction less than 1 is negative and the probabilities in question are generally less than 1). Since $\ln 1/x = -\ln x$, we could rewrite the formula without the minus sign by taking the logarithm of the reciprocal probability [i.e., $1/P(r_7/s_i)$], but this would merely make the notation more cumbersome than it already is.

15. Intuitively, this corresponds to the fact that in the first case (Figure 1.6) the signal r_2 "tells" the receiver what happened at s (viz., s_2), while in the second case it does not. In the second case the signal only "tells" the receiver that *either s_1 or s_2 or s_3* occurred, and this represents much less information. We might express this by saying that the first signal carries the information *that* s_2 occurred (2 bits) while the second signal carries only the information *that* either s_1 or s_2 or s_3 occurred (.4 bits). This, however, is premature. We have not yet identified anything that might be called the *informational content* of a signal or state of affairs. We are presently dealing exclusively with quantitative matters—*how much* information a signal carries, not *what* information.

16. There is an enormous literature on the dispute about the deterministic implications, or lack of them, of quantum theory. A well-known proponent of the "hidden variable" view is David Bohm; see his *Quantum Theory* (Prentice-Hall, Englewood Cliffs, N.J., 1951) and, for a more polemical stance, his *Causality and Chance in Modern Physics* (London, 1957). Also see Norwood Hanson's *The Concept of the Positron* (Cambridge University Press, 1963) and the exchange between Paul Feyerabend and Hanson in *Current Issues in the Philosophy of Science*, Herbert Feigl and Grover Maxwell (eds.), Holt, Rinehart and Winston, New York, 1961. For a scholarly review of the background of this problem, see *The Conceptual Development*

of Quantum Mechanics by Max Jammer (McGraw-Hill, New York, 1966), especially chaps. 7 and 9.

17. This is an orthodox empiricist view of causality. Its most illustrious ancestor is, of course, David Hume, but one need not accept Hume's view that causation is *only* a matter of regular succession to endorse the idea, expressed by the above principle, that causation at least *involves* regular succession. For a useful collection of articles, including ones expounding the regularity doctrine, see Tom L. Beauchamp (ed.), *Philosophical Problems of Causation*, Dickenson Publishing Co., Encino, Calif., 1974.

18. Such an analysis is considered in "Causal Irregularity" *Philosophy of Science*, March 1972, and "Causal Sufficiency: A Reply to Beauchamp," *Philosophy of Science*, June 1973, authored by myself and Aaron Snyder.

19. For a recent attempt see J. L. Mackie, *The Cement of the Universe: A Study of Causation*, Clarendon Press, Oxford, 1974.

20. "Such a fiber responds best when a dark object, smaller than a receptive field, enters that field, stops, and moves about intermittently thereafter. The response is not affected if the lighting changes or if the background (say a picture of grass and flowers) is moving, and is not there if only the background, moving or still, is in the field. Could one better describe a system for detecting an accessible bug?" J. Y. Lettvin, H. Maturana, W. S. McCulloch, and W. H. Pitts, "What the Frog's Eye Tells the Frog's Brain," *Proceedings of the IRE*, vol. 47, p. 1951.

21. "Vision in Frogs," *Scientific American*, March 1964; reprinted in *Perception: Mechanisms and Models*, with introductions by Richard Held and Whitman Richards, W. H. Freeman and Company, San Francisco, 1971, pp. 157–164.

22. *Ibid.*, p. 160.

23. This is not an unrealistic figure. "The smallest number of light quanta required for vision however is not large. A few quanta acting upon the human retina are capable of giving a sensation of light to a human observer. By activating one molecule of visual pigment, one single quantum may cause the excitation of a dark-adapted rod cell in the retina. And one quantum is of course the smallest quantity of light which may be emitted or absorbed by matter." M. H. Pirenne and F.H.C. Marriott, "The Quantum Theory of Light and the Psycho-Physiology of Vision," in *Psychology: The Study of a Science*, Sigmund Koch (ed.), New York, 1959.

24. The assumption is not very plausible, since when operating at threshold levels the spontaneous activity of the receptor cells ("dark light") will occasionally generate a response that is indistinguishable from that generated by the low-intensity test stimulus. That is, even when the light is off, thermal sources in the eye and the activity in the blood vessels will occasionally fire enough receptor cells to simulate the absorption of four photons by the visual pigment. Since this is so, it is an exaggeration to say that the sensation, when it occurs, carries a *full* 1 bit of information about the test light. There is *some* equivocation—the amount of equivocation depending on how close to threshold one is operating. For a fuller discussion of these matters, see

David E. Rumelhart's *Introduction to Human Information Processing*, John Wiley & Sons, New York, 1977, chap. 1.

25. Henry Quastler, "Information Theory Terms and Their Psychological Correlates," in *Information Theory in Psychology: Problems and Methods*, Henry Quastler (ed.), Free Press, Glencoe, Ill., 1955, p. 152.

26. I have in mind Alvin Goldman's well-known article, "A Causal Theory of Knowing," *Journal of Philosophy*, vol. 64, 12 (June 22, 1967), 355-372.

27. This is Goldman's *Pattern 2* type of causal connection illustrated in Figure 3 of "A Causal Theory of Knowing."

Chapter 2

1. Bar-Hillel and Rudolf Carnap are, perhaps, the best-known (to philosophers) critics of the statistical theory of information as an adequate tool for semantic studies. Their attempt to develop a genuine semantic theory of information is found in their "An Outline of a Theory of Semantic Information," Technical Report 247 of the Research Laboratory of Electronics, Massachusetts Institute of Technology, 1952; reprinted as Chapter 15 in Bar-Hillel's *Language and Information*. See, also, Bar-Hillel's papers, "An Examination of Information Theory" and "Semantic Information and Its Measures," reprinted as Chapters 16 and 17 in *Language and Information*, Reading, Mass., 1964. Also see Warren Weaver's introductory essay in Shannon and Weaver, *The Mathematical Theory of Communication*; Colin Cherry, *On Human Communication*, Massachusetts Institute of Technology, 1957, p. 50; Jaakko Hintikka, "On Semantic Information" in *Information and Inference*, J. Hintikka and P. Suppes (eds.), D. Reidel Publishing Company, Dordrecht, 1970; and Max Black, "How Do Pictures Represent?" in *Art, Perception and Reality* by E. H. Gombrich, Julian Hochberg, and Max Black, Baltimore, Md., 1972.

2. *The Mathematical Theory of Communication*, p. 31.

3. *Ibid.*, p. 8. Kenneth Sayre makes the same point, I believe, when he notes that although the communication of semantic content may not be necessary for the communication of information in the information-theoretic sense of this term, the latter may be necessary for the former: "Despite the fact that such information may have no semantic content, some information of this sort must be communicated as a necessary condition for the communication of information of any other sort whatsoever. If a communication system could not transmit specific sequences of symbols in an unambiguous, reproducible way, it would for that reason be incapable of reliably transmitting messages with semantic significance." *Recognition: A Study in the Philosophy of Artificial Intelligence*, University of Notre Dame Press, 1965, p. 229.

4. *Ibid.*, p. 8.

5. Wendell R. Garner, *Uncertainty and Structure as Psychological Concepts*, pp. 2-3.

6. Cherry, *On Human Communication*, p. 9.

7. Lejaren Hiller and Leonard Isaacson, "Experimental Music" in *The*

Modeling of Mind: Computers and Intelligence, Kenneth M. Sayre and Frederick J. Crosson (eds.), New York, 1963, p. 54; reprinted from *Experimental Music* by L. Hiller and L. Isaacson, McGraw-Hill, 1959.

8. "A History of the Theory of Information," *Proceedings of the Institute of Electrical Engineers*, vol. 98 (III) (1951), p. 383.

9. Norbert Wiener, *The Human Use of Human Beings*, Houghton Mifflin Company, Boston, 1950, p. 8 (as quoted by Bar-Hillel in "An Examination of Information Theory," p. 288).

10. There is, of course, a use of the term "meaning" that is close (if not equivalent) to the ordinary sense of "information." When we say, for example, that a blown fuse *means* the circuit has been overloaded, a sputtering engine *means* we are out of gas, and George's fingerprints on the glass *mean* that he was at the scene, we are using "meaning" in what Paul Grice calls its *natural* sense. When I say that information must be distinguished from meaning, I have in mind Grice's *nonnatural meaning*, the sense of meaning that is relevant to language and semantic studies. The way in which spots mean measles (natural meaning) is quite different from the way in which "I have the measles" means he (the speaker) has the measles (nonnatural meaning), and it is the latter sort of meaning that I intend to be distinguishing from information. See Grice's "Meaning," *Philosophical Review*, vol. 66 (1957), pp. 377–388.

11. "Philosophy and Cybernetics," in *Philosophy and Cybernetics*, Kenneth Sayre and Frederick J. Crosson (eds.), New York, 1967, p. 11.

12. *The Mathematical Theory of Communication*, p. 59. When C is the channel capacity (in bits per second) and H is the amount of information being generated at the source (in bits per second), this theorem says that by devising proper coding procedures it is possible to transmit symbols over the channel at an average rate which is nearly C/H but which, no matter how clever the coding, can never be made to exceed C/H. To put the point even less technically, when the rate at which information is generated is less than the channel capacity, it is possible to code it in such a way that it will reach the receiver with arbitrarily high fidelity. For this "informal" expression of the theorem, see J. L. Massey, "Information, Machines and Men," p. 50 in *Philosophy and Cybernetics*.

13. Unless one keeps in mind the divergent interests of communication theorists, some of their claims will appear extravagant or absurd. For instance, in many discussions of information theory one finds calculations of how much information is contained in a sample text of the English language. These calculations are carried out in terms of 27 possibilities (26 letters and the space). Discounting for the different probabilities of each letter (i.e., i is more probable than x) and a high degree of redundancy (a string of letters narrows the possibilities, and changes the probabilities, for the next letter), it is estimated that each letter in written English text has an average informational measure of approximately 1 bit. Hence, each 5-letter word has an average informational measure of 5 bits. See Shannon's original estimate (2 bits per symbol) in *The Mathematical Theory of Communication*, p. 56, and

his lowered estimate (1 bit per symbol) in "Prediction and Entropy of Printed English," *Bell System Technical Journal*, vol. 30 (1951), pp. 50-64. For a nontechnical exposition, see J. R. Pierce, *Symbols, Signals and Noise*, New York, 1961, chap. 5.

There are two respects in which these estimates are irrelevant to information as ordinarily understood: (1) they are concerned with averages; and (2) they are concerned, not with the information a token sentence *carries about* some other situation, but with the information *generated by* the occurrence of that particular sequence of letters on the page. In terms of our original example, the memo with the name "Herman" on it would (according to the communication theorist) embody roughly 6 bits of information (since it was composed of 6 letters). This estimate is obviously made in total disregard for what we ordinarily think of as the information carried by this name on the memo. In our original example the appearance of the name "Herman" on the memo carried 3 bits of information *about which employee was selected*. From an ordinary point of view, *this* is the important quantity. The engineer's interest in the information *generated by* a sequence of letters has merely inspired the view (derogatory in spirit) that communication theory is concerned with genuine information in only a *syntactical* sense.

14. At least there is a reasonable approximation to the conditions governing the theory's application. In telecommunications one is dealing (or, at least, assumes that one is dealing) with stochastic processes in which events occur with certain determinate probabilities. Assumptions are also (more or less reasonably) made about the character of these stochastic processes—e.g., that they are ergodic or "statistically homogeneous." Events are deemed "possible" that occur with some frequency (however small) in the process under consideration. For a discussion of the restrictions on the theory's application see Shannon, *The Mathematical Theory of Communication*, pp. 45-56.

15. This is not to deny that in some experimental situations it may be more convenient to define information in terms of what the subject *believes* about the number of possible different stimuli and his estimates of their relative probabilities. Harold W. Hake describes two ways of measuring information: "Where the human observer is the receiver of a message, however, we must be aware of two domains of information measurement. There is, first, the measurement based upon the actual probability of occurrence of the message. There is, second, the information measurement which is based upon the subjective notions of the receiver about the likelihood of occurrence of each of the possible messages in the set, as he sees them." "The Perception of Frequency of Occurrence and the Development of 'Expectancy' in Human Experimental Subject," *Information Theory in Psychology: Problems and Methods*, Henry Quastler (ed.), Free Press, Glencoe, Ill., 1955, p. 19.

Although we shall (Chapter 3) relativize information to what the subject already *knows* about the various possibilities at the source, the set of conditional probabilities defining equivocation are independent of what the subject knows or believes about them.

16. *An Enquiry Concerning the Human Understanding* (The Open Court Publishing Co., LaSalle, Ill., 1955), Section XII, p. 171.

17. "Information Theory and Phenomenology," *Philosophy and Cybernetics*, p. 121.

18. One cannot use the concept of information in the analysis of such epistemic concepts as *knowledge, recognition*, and *memory* if one turns around and uses epistemic concepts (such as *learn, identify*, or *correctly interpret*) in the analysis of information. This makes the entire program circular.

Kenneth Sayre's early effort to apply information theory to the analysis of recognition suffers from this defect (*Recognition*, Chapter 11). In attempting to distinguish between recognition and perception-without-recognition (e.g., seeing the letter W without recognizing it) Sayre claims that recognition requires the subject to gain information about the perceived entity. This sounds plausible. It would even be illuminating if there was some *independent* specification of what information was. Yet, although he uses the technical resources of information theory (suggesting thereby that he is using the information-theoretic concept), Sayre trivializes his thesis by insisting that the amount of information contained in a signal depends on the receiver's *correct identification* or *interpretation* of that signal (pp. 240–241). This not only makes information something that radios do not receive, it transforms the thesis that recognition involves a gain in information into the obvious truth that recognition requires correct identification. This is not a very novel conclusion, and it certainly is not something that one needs information theory to reach.

19. "Suppose that in telegraphy we let a positive pulse represent a dot and a negative pulse represent a dash. Suppose that some practical joker reverses connections so that when a positive pulse is transmitted a negative pulse is received and when a negative pulse is transmitted a positive pulse is received. Because no uncertainty has been introduced [i.e., the equivocation remains the same], information theory says that the rate of transmission of information is just the same as before." J. R. Pierce, *Symbols, Signals and Noise*, p. 274.

20. This point has an obvious relevance to the "inverted spectrum" problem in the philosophy of perception. A person for whom all red things look blue (and vice versa) is a person who is getting the *same information* as normal observers about the color of objects. The information is merely being coded in an unusual way. If the inversion is imagined to be congenital, however, the subject should experience no more difficulty in "cracking" this code (thereby extracting the relevant information) than do normal observers.

21. This example is merely an expression of a familiar epistemological point—the point, namely, that one can learn that P from someone who says that P only if that person's saying that P is an expression of what he knows (not simply of what he truly believes). From the point of view of the xerox principle, the requirement that your informant *know* that P is merely the

requirement that his beliefs carry *information* about the matters whereof he speaks. More of this later.

22. As an example of how the losses can be made to add up, suppose there are eight possibilities at the three stations A, B, and C. Each of the eight possibilities at each station is equally likely. c_2 occurs at C, generating 3 bits of information. The conditional probabilities between B and C are such that b_2's occurrence at B raises the probability that c_2 occurred to .9 and lowers the probability that each of the other possibilities occurred to .014. Calculating the equivocation between b_2 and C in accordance with (1.8) reveals that $E(b_2)$ = .22 bits (approximately). Hence b_2 carries approximately 2.78 bits of information about what occurred at C. Suppose, moreover, that the channel joining A with B is identical: a_2 occurs, thereby raising the probability that b_2 occurred to .9 and lowering the probability of all the other possibilities at B to .014. Hence a_2 carries 2.78 bits of information about what occurred at B. If, however, we calculate the equivocation between A and C, we find that $E(a_2)$ = 1.3 bits (approximately). a_2 carries only 1.7 bits of information about what happened at C.

If one supposes that a 3-bit message can be transmitted in the face of positive equivocation (equivocation less than, say, .25 bits), then we reach the paradoxical result that b_2 tells us what happened at C (carries the information that c_2 occurred), and a_2 tells us what happened at B (viz., that b_2 occurred), but a_2 cannot tell us what happened at C. This contradicts the xerox principle. A similar paradox can be constructed *no matter how low* one puts the equivocation (as long as it is greater than zero) that can be tolerated in the transmission of informational content (the message).

23. Similarly, a visual signal may carry enough information (quantitatively) to have the content that *s is a person* but not enough to qualify for the content that *s is a woman*. Relative to the description "*s* is a woman," therefore, the signal has positive equivocation. Relative to the description "*s* is a person," it has zero equivocation. Getting a closer look, turning up the lights, or whatever, is a way of increasing the *amount* of information one receives about *s* so that one can *see whether s* is a woman or a man (i.e., get the information *that s* is a woman).

Chapter 3

1. In saying that the conditional probability (given r) of s's being F is 1, I mean to be saying that there is a nomic (lawful) regularity between these event types, a regularity which *nomically precludes r*'s occurrence when s is not F. There are interpretations of probability (the frequency interpretation) in which an event can fail to occur when it has a probability of 1 (or occur when it has a probability of 0), but this is *not* the way I mean to be using probability in this definition. A conditional probability of 1 between r and s is a way of describing a lawful (exceptionless) dependence between events of this sort, and it is for this reason that I say (in the text) that if the conditional probability of s's being F (given r) is 1, then s *is F*. I shall have more to say about these nomic regularities later in this chapter.

2. Whenever the conditional probability of s's being F (given r) is less than 1, the conditional probability of the alternatives to this state of affairs is greater than 0. Hence the equivocation is positive. As a result [formula (1.5)], $I_s(r)$ is *less than* $I(s)$.

3. Generally speaking, I follow Tyler Burge's excellent account of the distinction between *de re* and *de dicto* contents in his "Belief *De Re*," *The Journal of Philosophy*, vol. 74, 6 (June 1977), pp. 338–362. Burge argues that the customary way of drawing the *de re/de dicto* distinction (in terms of the substitutivity criterion) does not adequately capture the intuitive distinction between these two sorts of beliefs. There is, however, clearly a close relationship between a *de re* content (whether this be thought of as the content of a belief or as the informational content of a signal) and freedom of substitution (of coextensive expressions) for the subject term. I shall have more to say, later in this chapter, about the opacity/transparency issue as it applies to informational contents.

4. This is not to say, of course, that the signals that carry these two pieces of information must somehow carry the information that they are different pieces of information—the information, namely, that *this* ≠ *that*.

5. The sorts of problems avoided by concentrating exclusively on *de re* contents are not only the problems associated with articulating a general theory of reference but also problems having to do with presupposition and (what I have elsewhere called) contrastive focusing. So, for example, we might want to distinguish the contents, *"My cousin* ate the cherries" (understood as conveying information about *who* ate the cherries) from "My cousin ate *the cherries"* (understood as conveying information about *what* my cousin *ate*) despite their identical verbal expression. The semantic focusing (indicated by the italicized words and usually signaled in speech by emphasis or different intonation) has the effect of shifting presuppositions, changing the referential character of certain phrases, and in general, altering the *assertive content* of the whole expression. For this reason one might wish to distinguish the above two expressions, despite their identical lexical constituents, as representing different pieces of information and, hence, possibly different objects of belief and knowledge. I have tried to deal with some of these matters in "Contrastive Statements," *Philosophical Review*, October 1972, and "The Content of Knowledge," *Forms of Representation*, Bruce Freed *et al.* (eds.), North Holland, Amsterdam, 1975.

6. The intentional, or semantic, aspect of information is typically masked or suppressed in technological applications of communication theory by the fact that statistical data are used to determine the relevant probabilities and possibilities. So, for example, if F and G are perfectly correlated, the probability of G, given F, is set equal to 1. This practice collapses the distinction between a mere (chance) correlation between F and G and a lawful or nomic dependence and creates the impression that this distinction is irrelevant to the flow of information, irrelevant to the determination of those conditional probabilities defining E (equivocation), N (noise), and $I_s(r)$ (amount of transmitted information).

That this impression is mistaken should be obvious. Correlations are relevant to the determination of informational relationships *only insofar* as these correlations are manifestations of underlying lawful regularities. In most applications of communication theory (e.g., telecommunications) this is usually the case. Indeed, there is normally an elaborate body of theory that stands behind the attributions of probability. Correlations are used to define the relevant conditional probabilities *because* these correlations are taken to be indicative of nomic dependencies. It is important to realize, however, that it is not the correlations that are significant to, or responsible for, the flow of information. It is the underlying lawful regularities presumably manifested by these correlations that are significant to the communication of information. As soon as one looks at cases in which there is no underlying *lawful* regularity, this becomes apparent. The example in the text (two independent systems of communication, *A–B* and *C–D*) is a case in point.

Genuine communication occurs only when the statistical correlations are symptoms of underlying *lawful* processes, processes that have the *modal* authority to sanction attributions of possibility and probability. Only by ignoring these facts about the assumptions implicit in actual applications of communication theory can it be made to appear as though communication theory was free from the intentional features of genuine information.

7. I have attempted an analysis in "The Laws of Nature," *Philosophy of Science*, vol. 44, no. 2 (June 1977).

8. For the purposes of this example it is being assumed that there is one and only one peanut under the shells, and this is known by all relevant parties. If there were other possibilities (e.g., no peanut under the shells), then there would be a positive amount of information associated with the fact there was a peanut under one of the shells. In this case a peanut's being under shell 4 would have an informational measure *greater* than 2 bits (since there were more than four equally probable alternatives) and a peanut's not being under shell 1 would have an informational measure of *less* than that alleged in the example (since the probability of the shell's being empty would be greater than .25). These altered values accurately reflect the fact that under these changed circumstances one cannot learn where the peanut is (e.g., that it is under shell 4) by finding three of the shells empty.

9. D. C. Dennett, *Content and Consciousness*, Routledge & Kegan Paul, London, 1969, p. 187.

10. In commenting on the relative character of information, Donald M. MacKay observes: "This does not of course make the concept any less objective in principle, since one can always postulate a 'standard receiver,' and this is in effect what is done in communication theory; but it does prevent the magnitude associated with it from having a unique value. The same item can have quite different information-contents for different receivers." See MacKay's *Information, Mechanism and Meaning*, The M.I.T. Press, Cambridge, Mass., 1969, p. 96 (footnote).

11. In suggesting that information qualifies as a *semantic* idea in virtue

of its intentional character, I do not mean to imply that the semantic properties of information are the same, say, as the semantic properties of meaning.
As we shall see in Part III, the concept of meaning has a higher-order intentionality than does the concept of information, and this higher-order intentionality confers upon it a different set of semantic properties. Although we
will continue to insist on the distinction between the concept of *meaning* and
the concept of *information*, we will later argue that the idea of information
is more fundamental. Meaning is generated by the way information is *coded.*

Chapter 4

1. The concept of *justification* (or some related epistemic notion) is
often taken to be primitive. Other concepts (including knowledge) are then
defined on this primitive basis. Since one is given little or no guidance in
determining whether or not the primitive term applies to a situation, one
is, perforce, left to consult one's intuitions about when, and whether, someone is justified *enough* to know something. The result, of course, is that one
relies on one's firmer intuitions about when, and whether, someone knows
something to determine when, and whether, someone has a satisfactory
level of justification. See, for example, Chisholm's treatment in *Theory of
Knowledge*, second edition, Englewood Cliffs, N.J., 1977; also Marshall
Swain, "An Alternative Analysis of Knowing," *Synthese*, vol. 23 (1972),
pp. 423-442.

2. The restriction to situations with which there is associated a positive
amount of information is a way of restricting the analysis to what might be
called *empirical knowledge*, knowledge of states of affairs which *could* have
been otherwise (to which there are possible alternatives). I shall have more
to say later about our knowledge of necessary truths.

3. Notice, even though the information that s is G is nested (nomically
or analytically) in s's being F (the way that the information that someone
has arrived is nested in the information that the courier has arrived), it does
not follow that if the information that s is F causes E, then the information
that s is G also causes E. For the feature of the signal carrying the information that the courier (in particular) has arrived may cause E without that
feature of the signal carrying the (less specific) information that someone
has arrived causing E. This is merely to say that something's being square,
say, can produce a particular effect without its being true to say that its
being rectangular had that effect.

4. Since the same information can be carried in a large variety of physically different signals, the possibility exists of there being no readily available causal explanation of a signal's effect in terms of its *physical* properties
(the properties that *carry* the information). One may have to appeal to the
information contained *in* the signal to explain its effects. For example, even
though it is a signal's having physical property P (carrying the information
that s is F) that causes E, a signal's having Q, R, or S (carrying the *same*
information) might also have this same effect. If, then, we want to say what
it is about these physically different signals (one visual, one acoustic, one

tactile) that explains their common effect (e.g., the belief that *s* is *F*), we may have no choice but to describe their *common informational content*.

As we examine information-processing systems of increasing complexity, systems with the resources for extracting the *same* information out of a wide variety of physical stimuli, it becomes more and more natural to describe effects in terms of the *information* to which they are a response. The physical properties of the signal, those properties that carry the information, drop out of the picture. These possibilities are examined in greater detail in Part III.

5. For some ingenious examples illustrating the technical difficulties in formulating a generally satisfactory definition of a sustaining cause, see Keith Lehrer's *Knowledge*, Clarendon Press, Oxford, 1974, pp. 122–126. For an attempt to overcome some of these difficulties, see Marshall Swain, "Reasons, Causes and Knowledge," *The Journal of Philosophy*, vol. 75, no. 5 (May 1978), p. 242. My own account resembles D. M. Armstrong's in *Belief, Truth and Knowledge*, Cambridge, 1973, pp. 164ff.

6. I take this to be one of the defects in Armstrong's regularity analysis of knowledge. The fact that *K* knows that *s* is a dog does not mean that we can learn from *K* that *s* is a dog. For if *K* mistakenly thinks wolves are dogs (and, hence, would believe that *s* was a dog *if* it was a wolf), then *K*'s knowledge that *s* (an easily recognizable dachshund) is a dog is not something he can communicate to us by telling us that *s* is a dog. His belief that *s* is a dog does not carry the information that *s* is a dog. See Armstrong's analysis in *Belief, Truth and Knowledge*, Part III. I borrow the wolf-dachshund example from Alvin Goldman, "Discrimination and Perceptual Knowledge," *The Journal of Philosophy*, vol. 73.20 (1976).

7. The thermodynamic counterpart to "*s* is hot" is not intended to be equivalent in *meaning* to the original. Rather, it represents an attempt to say, in terms of precise but comparatively unfamiliar concepts, what is in fact true of an object when (as we ordinarily say) it is hot. The information-theoretic analysis of knowledge should be judged in the same terms. The only relevant question is whether the right-hand side of the theoretical equation is true when, and only when (barring exceptions that can be explained away) the left-hand side is true (and, of course, whether there are grounds for thinking that this equivalence is no accident).

8. My own informal, and highly unscientific, poll among nonphilosophers indicates the common opinion to be that one does *not* know that the ball is pink if there are *any* nonpink balls in the urn from which the selection is made. This is my own, theoretically prejudiced, view of the matter. Other philosophers, with different theoretical prejudices, have judged these cases differently.

9. "Is Justified True Belief Knowledge?" *Analysis*, vol. 23 (1963), pp. 121–123.

10. This "principle" is a modification of the one Gettier states and uses in the construction of his counterexamples. His own version is: "for any proposition *P*, if *S* is justified in believing *P*, and *P* entails *Q*, and *S* deduces

Q from P and accepts Q as a result of this deduction, then S is justified in believing Q." I have criticized the *general* validity of this principle ["Epistemic Operators," *The Journal of Philosophy*, vol. 67, no. 24 (Dec. 24, 1970)], but the problems associated with its general validity do not affect the sort of case being discussed in the text.

11. In considering such examples as this, William Rozeboom concludes, correctly I think, that "when a person's justified true belief p is accompanied by a justified false belief q, it may well prove troublesome to decide whether or not this belief in p is related to his belief in q in such fashion that the falsity of the latter should disqualify the former as knowledge." See his "Why I Know So Much More than You Do," *American Philosophical Quarterly*, vol. 4, no. 4 (1967); reprinted in *Knowing*, Michael D. Roth and Leon Galis (eds.), New York, 1970, p. 135.

12. For an early discussion of the "lottery paradox" and its bearing on inductive logic, see H. H. Kyburg, "Probability, Rationality and the Rule of Detachment," *Proceedings of the 1964 International Congress for Logic, Methodology, and Philosophy of Science*, Y. Bar-Hillel (ed.), North Holland, 1965. Also see Herbert Heidelberger's "Knowledge, Certainty and Probability," *Inquiry*, vol. 6 (1963). For a more recent discussion of this paradox as it relates to epistemological issues, see D. M. Armstrong, *Belief, Truth and Knowledge*, Cambridge University Press, 1973, pp. 185ff.

13. Although nobody *knows* he is going to lose, people sometimes *say* they know they are going to lose. This is little more than an expression of resignation, an attempt to suppress unreasonable expectations. If people really knew they were going to lose, their purchase of a lottery ticket would be inexplicable. Why bet one dollar on P when you know that not-P?

14. Norman Malcolm comes close to endorsing this strange view in "Knowledge and Belief" (*Knowledge and Certainty*, Englewood Cliffs, N.J., 1963) when he asserts: "As philosophers we may be surprised to observe that it *can* be that the knowledge that P is true should differ from the belief that P is true only in the respect that in one case P is true and in the other false. But that is the fact." (p. 60) Although I say Malcolm "comes close" to endorsing this strange view, it is fairly clear that, in this passage at least, he does not actually accept it. He says that the knowledge that P can differ from the belief that P only with respect to the truth of "*P*." He does not say that it *always* does or that it does in situations such as that described in the lottery examples.

15. Brian Skyrms considers the conjunction principle and concludes that unless one requires evidence of (probability) 1, the principle does not hold. He suggests that this supports the skeptic *or* shows that knowledge does not satisfy this principle. See his "The Explication of 'X knows that p'" in *The Journal of Philosophy*, vol. 64, no. 12 (June 22, 1967); reprinted in *Knowing*, Roth and Galis (eds.), pp. 109–110. Since I require a probability of 1 (zero equivocation), I conclude that the principle *does* hold. I attempt to show in the following chapter why this does *not* support skepticism.

16. Or he is the sort of fellow described in note 6—the sort who, though he

knows that *s* is *F*, cannot be *trusted* about whether or not something is *F*.

17. For example, Professor Jay Rosenberg has suggested to me that knowledge may be related to information (measured in bits) as wealth is related to capital assets (measured in number of pennies). Just as we can fritter away our wealth, penny by penny, without being able to say just when or where we ceased to be wealthy, so it may be that we can fritter away knowledge, bit by bit, without being able to say just where (in the communication chain) knowledge ceases.

Attractive as this suggestion may be, it founders on the fact that the concept of knowledge (insofar as we understand it to be a knowledge of *facts*, not *things*), unlike the concept of wealth, is not a *comparative* concept. One person can be *wealthier* than another even though they are both wealthy, but one person cannot know *that it is raining* (say) more than, or better than, another. More of this in the next chapter.

Chapter 5

1. William Rozeboom's reaction is typical. He doubts whether our de facto world contains any nomic regularities perfect enough to vouchsafe any belief beyond all possibility of error. Expressed in information-theoretic terms, Rozeboom doubts whether the conditional probabilities (defining equivocation) are ever zero. Rozeboom draws skeptical conclusions from this fact; see his "Why I Know So Much More than You Do," in *Knowing*, Michael Roth and Leon Galis (eds.), New York, 1970, p. 149.

2. William Epstein describes the prevalent view in psychology as follows: "Agreement is widespread regarding the relationship between distal and proximal stimuli. The conventional view . . . is that the distal-proximal relationship is intractably equivocal. . . .Indeed the claim that proximal stimulation cannot specify the properties of the distal situation is an assumption held by almost all twentieth century theoreticians, regardless of their differences." *Stability and Constancy in Visual Perception*, William Epstein (ed.), New York, 1977, p. 3.

Egon Brunswik expressed this point by saying that the ecological and functional validities are always less than unity. Ecological validity refers to the level of correlation between the distal and proximal stimulus (e.g., distant object and retinal projection). Functional validity refers to the level of correlation between distal variable and perceptual response. See Leo Postman and Edward D. Tolman, "Brunswik's Probabilistic Functionalism" in *Psychology: A Study of a Science*, vol. 1, Sigmund Koch (ed.), New York, 1959, pp. 502–562. Expressed in information-theoretic terms, Brunswik's view could be described by saying that the amount of information contained in a sensory signal is always *less* than the amount of information generated at the source by the occurrence of some event. Hence, the proximal stimulus (or the perceptual response) never contains the information that the distal event has occurred. According to this view of things, then, it is impossible to *know* anything about the distal stimulus if knowledge requires the receipt of information (i.e., zero equivocation). Either skepticism is true or the present account of knowledge is wrong.

The transactionalists made the same point by talking about "equivalent configurations," the family of physical arrangements at the source for which the signal is invariant (and, thus, equivocal). See Ittleson, *Visual Space Perception*, New York, 1960, Chap. 4. James J. Gibson's work is, of course, a prominent exception to this traditional line of thought: e.g., *The Senses Considered as Perceptual Systems*, Boston, 1966.

3. Peter Unger, "A Defense of Skepticism," *The Philosophical Review*, vol. 80, no. 2 (April 1971) and, more recently, *Ignorance*, Oxford, 1975.

4. Unger traces the absoluteness of knowledge to the notion of certainty. On this point, then, we are in disagreement.

5. As John Austin would say, "flat" is a substantive-hungry word: a flat X may not be a flat Y just as a real X may not be a real Y. *Sense and Sensibilia*, Oxford, 1962, p. 69.

6. For epistemic purposes there is always a discrete, finite set of voltages at R. One learns (comes to know) that the voltage at R is 7 *rather than* 6, 8, or some other value appreciably different from 7. If one's claim to know that the voltage is 7 implies, or is taken to imply, that the voltage is not 7.001 or 6.999, then, of course, the instrument must deliver a correspondingly greater amount of information in order for one to know, since the number of alternative possibilities eliminated is greater. Generally speaking, the number of digits used to express what is known will correspond with the implied level of precision. In a sense, it helps to indicate *what* is known. For this reason it takes more information (hence a more sensitive instrument) to know that the voltage is 7.000 than it does to know that it is 7.

7. If a condition is known to obtain on independent grounds (one has, for example, just checked the elasticity of the restraining spring), then the conditional probabilities defining transmitted information are computed relative to the known value of the condition in question. These conditions are merely those denoted by k in our definition of a signal's information content (see Chapter 3).

8. During calibration (using the instrument to measure *known* values of a quantity) the pointer may carry information about the state of the spring. But in normal operation it does not. More of this in a moment.

9. Strictly speaking this is not true. Since resistance depends on temperature, and the temperature may vary during the time the instrument is being used, the resistance will vary slightly. For ordinary purposes, however, these slight variations can be ignored, since they produce no equivocation. The changes induced occur well below the level of precision at which the instrument operates.

10. The appearance of a *familiar* person (wife, husband, etc.) in an Ames room (distorted room made to appear normal from the viewer's restricted vantage point) illustrates the way our perceptual systems operate, almost automatically, in accordance with these principles. Instead of the familiar person appearing excessively large or small (as do objects or persons whose size is unknown), the *room* appears distorted. From an information-theoretic point of view this may be described by saying that the perceptual system

takes the familiar person's size as a *fixed* reference point (channel condition) for purposes of assessing the configuration of surrounding material. For this series of interesting experiments, see *Human Behavior from the Transactional Point of View*, Franklin P. Kilpatrick (ed.), Department of the Navy, Washington, D.C., 1952.

As further examples of channel conditions for our sensory systems one might mention the distance between the eyes (for stereoscopic information about depth), the distance between the ears (for accurate information about direction), and the fact that normal outdoor lighting comes from above (for getting information from shadows about depressions and protrusions).

11. Not to mention *self-defeating*, since such precautions are possible only by deploying *other* channels of communication (whose reliability goes unchecked) in the form of instruments used to check one's instruments.

12. See Irvin Rock, *An Introduction to Perception*, Macmillan, New York, 1975, chap. 5; also R. L. Gregory, *Eye and Brain*, McGraw-Hill, New York, 1966, chap. 7.

13. "These examples suggest the surprising conclusion that the intention or 'command' to move the eyes is recorded centrally in the brain and treated as information that the eyes *have* moved. . . .The evidence, therefore, supports the conclusion that the crucial information is not afferent (proprioceptive) but a copy or record of *efferent* or outflowing signals *to* the muscles." Irvin Rock, *op. cit.*, p. 187.

14. This example resembles those given by Gilbert Harman to illustrate a different (indeed, an *opposite*) point: viz., that knowledge depends on the proximity (or general availability) of information (evidence) one does not possess; *Thought*, Princeton University Press, 1973, chap. 9. I have used a different example because I have doubts about exactly what Harman's particular examples show. For example, it does not seem to me that if you saw Donald off at the airport one month ago (headed for Italy), you now know he is in Italy (one month later) with no additional information. Nevertheless, intuitions seem to differ widely on these cases (see William G. Lycan's "Evidence One Does Not Possess," *Australasian Journal of Philosophy*, vol. 55.2 (August 1977), pp. 114–126), and I will return to this point shortly.

15. "Discrimination and Perceptual Knowledge," *The Journal of Philosophy*, vol. 73, no. 20 (1976).

16. This example is taken, with minor modifications, from my "Epistemic Operators," *The Journal of Philosophy*, Dec. 24, 1974.

17. Unless, of course, circumstances have changed, or one is operating within a more restricted context in which a signal that is otherwise equivocal becomes reliable. In *Seeing and Knowing* (Chicago, 1969) I illustrated this effect by describing an assembly-line worker who could recognize resistors when they appeared on the assembly line but whose cognitive abilities were sharply curtailed outside the factory. His ability to recognize resistors inside the factory is to be explained by the fact that *in that factory, on that assembly line*, nothing is allowed to appear that he might confuse with a resistor (inside the factory there is no equivocation). Nevertheless, since he does not

know the difference between a resistor and a capacitor, and since some capacitors look very much like resistors, he cannot (outside the factory) recognize a resistor (even those he correctly calls resistors). If, then, we include *his being in the factory* as one of the channel conditions (something we might explicitly do by saying "*In the factory* he can tell"), as something we tacitly *hold fixed* in reckoning equivocation, there is nothing to prevent us from saying that (in the factory) he *is* getting the information that *s* is a resistor. We often (explicitly or implicitly) make similar provisos about an organism's *natural habitat* in characterizing its cognitive capacities.

18. Besides myself and Goldman, Ernest Sosa in "How Do You Know?" *The American Philosophical Quarterly*, vol. 11.2 (1974), Gilbert Harman in *Thought*, D. M. Armstrong in *Belief, Truth and Knowledge*, Cambridge, 1973, chap. 12, and many others. Many so-called "defeasibility" analyses of knowledge concern themselves (in different terminology) with the same sort of issues—see, e.g., Marshall Swain's "Epistemic Defeasibility" in *The American Philosophical Quarterly*, vol. 11.1 (1974) for a review of such efforts and a useful bibliography.

19. I am grateful to Fred Adams for refusing to be satisfied with a version of the present chapter that was even less adequate than the present one.

Chapter 6

1. The following is typical: "Sensation, perception, memory and thought must be considered on a continuum of cognitive activity. They are mutually interdependent and cannot be separated except by arbitrary rules and momentary expediency." R. N. Haber, "Introduction" in *Information Processing Approaches to Visual Perception*, R. N. Haber (ed.), New York, 1969.

2. The parenthetical "about *s*" is necessary at this point since, as we shall see (Chapter 7), information *about s* that is coded in digital form may nonetheless be nested in information about some other item.

3. See Leonard Uhr, *Pattern Recognition, Learning, and Thought*, Englewood Cliffs, N.J., 1973, chap. 2.

4. It is not *merely* the conversion of information from analog to digital form that qualifies a system as a perceptual-cognitive system. The speedometer-buzzer system described above neither *sees* nor *knows* that the vehicle is going between 25 and 49 mph when the third tone is activated. To qualify as a genuine perceptual system, it is necessary that there *be* a digital-conversion unit in which the information can be given a cognitive embodiment, but the cognitive embodiment of information is not *simply* a matter of digitalization. What additional conditions must be satisfied to qualify a structure as a *cognitive* structure (besides digitalization) will be discussed in Part III.

5. It has also been called the *Precategorical Acoustic Store* [by R. G. Crowder and J. Morton, "Precategorical Acoustic Storage (PAS)," *Perception and Psychophysics*, vol. 5 (1969), pp. 365–373. Roberta Klatzky (*Human Memory*, San Francisco, 1975) notes that the term precategorical is important "because it implies that information held in the registers is not held there as recognized, categorized, items, but in raw, sensory form. . . .That the

sensory registers are precategorical deserves emphasis here, because a central problem in research relating to the registers is the separation of true effects of sensory storage from possible effects of recognized information," pp. 39–40.

6. Karl H. Pribram, *Languages of the Brain*, Englewood Cliffs, N.J., 1971, p. 136.

7. See John R. Anderson and Gordon H. Bower, *Human Associative Memory*, Washington, D.C., 1973, p. 453.

8. In commenting on the SIS (sensory information storage), Lindsay and Norman (*Human Information Processing*, New York, 1972, p. 329) note that this "discrepancy between the amount of information held in the sensory system and the amount that can be used by later stages of analysis is very important. It implies some sort of limit on the capacity of later stages, a limit that is not shared by the sensory stages themselves."

9. T. G. R. Bower, "The Visual World of Infants," in *Perception: Mechanisms and Models*, San Francisco, 1972, p. 357. Ulric Neisser also notes that the progressive deletion of microtexture at an edge yields a compelling perception of one surface going behind another and that this kind of information comes into existence only when something moves (it does not exist in the frozen array), "Gibson's Ecological Optics: Consequences of a Different Stimulus Description," in *Journal for the Theory of Social Behavior*, vol. 7, no. 1 (April 1977), p. 22.

In a summary of kinetic-size constancy Gunnar Johansson concludes that even under extremely impoverished stimulus conditions the sensory system is capable of extracting sufficient information (for the constancy effect) from *changing* patterns; p. 382 in "Spatial Constancy and Motion in Visual Perception," in *Stability and Constancy in Visual Perception*, William Epstein (ed.), New York, 1977.

10. See Gibson's *The Senses Considered as Perceptual Systems*, London, 1966, and the earlier *The Perception of the Visual World*, Boston, 1950. There may be some question of whether Gibson's notion of information is the same as that with which we are operating in this work. In a conference on philosophy and psychology (Cornell University, April 2–4, 1976), Ulric Neisser claimed that Gibson's concept of information could be identified with Shannon's. David Hamlyn denied this, and if I understood him correctly, so did Gibson. Yet, the following passage is revealing:

Let us begin by noting that *information about* something means only *specificity to* something. Hence, when we say that information is conveyed by light, or by sound, odor, or mechanical energy, we do not mean that the source is literally conveyed as a copy or replica. The sound of a bell is not the bell and the odor of cheese is not the cheese. Similarly the perspective projection of the faces of an object (by the reverberating flux of reflected light in a medium) is not the object itself. Nevertheless, in all these cases a property of the stimulus is univocally related to a property of the object by virtue of physical laws. This is what I mean by the conveying of environmental information. (p. 187, *The Senses Considered as Perceptual Systems*.)

This, it seems to me, fully justifies Neisser's judgment. It is, moreover, in reasonably close agreement with the concept of information developed in Chapter 3 of the present work. See Ulric Neisser, "Gibson's Ecological Optics: Consequences of a Different Stimulus Description" and D. W. Hamlyn, "The Concept of Information in Gibson's Theory of Perception" in the *Journal for the Theory of Social Behavior*, vol. 7, no. 1 (April 1977).

11. The underlying sensory mechanisms may even involve what some investigators (following Helmholtz) are pleased to describe as *computational* or *inferential* processes. Although I see nothing wrong with using this terminology to describe sensory processes, I think it a mistake to be (mis)led by it into assigning *cognitive* structure to such processes. We may describe sensory phenomena in informational terms, in terms that involve (to this extent at least) a structure's having a *propositional content*, but a structure's having a propositional content should not be confused with its having the sort of content we associate with knowledge, belief, and judgment. I return to this point in Chapter 7.

12. R. M. Warren, "Perceptual Restoration of Missing Speech Sounds," *Science* (1970), p. 167.

13. Which is not to say that peripherally seen things will *look* colorless. This may be viewed as a case of perceptual restoration. The point is, however, that this restoration does not carry *information* about the color of the objects seen, since it does not depend in the requisite way on the color of the objects. Similarly, there is a spot on the retina (the blind spot) where the optic nerve leaves the eye which is incapable of picking up information from the stimulus. Nevertheless, if a homogeneous field (e.g., a sheet of white paper) is fixated (with one eye), we do not see a black spot. One should not suppose, however, that this sensory "interpolation" carries information about the stimulus. For, obviously, if there happened to be a black spot at this point in the field, then (under rigorously constricted viewing conditions) we would not see it. This information would be lost.

14. See, for example, Ulric Neisser, *Cognitive Psychology*, New York, 1967, pp. 94–104. Also see D. O. Hebb, "Summation and Learning in Perception": "The primitive unity of a figure is defined here as referring to that unity and segregation from the background which seems to be a direct product of the pattern of sensory excitation and the inherited characteristics of the nervous system on which it acts. The unity and distinctiveness of such figures from their background, then, are independent of experience, or "primitive," pp. 140–141 in Peter A. Fried (ed.), *Readings in Perception*, Lexington, Mass., 1974.

15. George A. Miller, "The Magical Number Seven, Plus or Minus Two: Some Limits on Our Capacity for Processing Information," *The Psychological Review*, vol. 63 (March 1956). The number seven is an index to our capacity for making accurate absolute judgments of unidimensional stimuli. Our common ability to accurately identify any one of several hundred faces, any one of several thousand words, etc., should not be taken as an exception to this "rule." For faces, words, and objects are *multidimensional* stimuli.

16. J. R. Pierce, *Symbols, Signals and Noise*, New York, 1961, pp. 248–249.

17. G. Sperling, "The Information Available in Brief Visual Presentations," *Psychological Monographs*, vol. 74, no. 11 (1960). Also Averbach and Coriell, "Short-Term Memory in Vision," *Bell System Technical Journal*, vol. 40, no. 196, and "Short-Term Storage of Information in Vision," *Information Theory: Proceedings of the Fourth London Symposium*, C. Cherry (ed.), London, 1961.

18. Ulric Neisser, *Cognitive Psychology*, chap. 2.

19. "It appears as if all of the information in the retinal projection is available in this iconic storage, since the perceiver can extract whichever part is asked for." Ralph Norman Haber and Maurice Hershenson, *The Psychology of Visual Perception*, New York, 1973, p. 169.

20. Irvin Rock interprets these experiments as suggesting that "in some sense of the term perception, all items in the array are perceived. Some sensory representation of each item endures for a fraction of a second. Perception during that brief period is based on the persistence in the visual system of the neural discharging triggered by the retinal image of the letters even after the letter display is turned off. Unless the items are further processed, however, these sensory representations will quickly fade away." *An Introduction to Perception*, New York, 1975, p. 359. For the sense of the term "perception" in which all items are perceived, see below under The Objects of Perception.

21. *Principles of Perceptual Learning and Development*, New York, 1969, p. 284.

22. But how then explain the different responses? "If experience is to have an effect, there nevertheless must first be a perception of the pattern that is itself *not* a function of experience, and through that perception the relevant memory traces can be activated on the basis of similarity," Irvin Rock, *op. cit.*, p. 361.

23. William Epstein, *Varieties of Perceptual Learning*, New York, 1967.

24. See, for example, George J. Steinfeld, "Concepts of Set and Availability and Their Relation to the Reorganization of Ambiguous Pictorial Stimuli," *Psychological Review*, vol. 74, no. 6 (1967), pp. 505–522. Also Irvin Rock, "But there is a genuine perceptual change when in viewing potentially familiar figures one goes from an initial "nonsense" organization to a subsequent "meaningful" organization. The figure looks different when it is recognized." *op. cit.*, p. 348.

25. Eleanor Gibson, *op. cit.*, p. 292.

26. In his excellent introductory text, Irvin Rock, *op. cit.*, is careful throughout to distinguish perceptual and cognitive issues. As a case in point: "learning a discrimination entails more than just perception; cognitive factors are also involved. An animal might perceptually distinguish a triangle and circle from the start, but nevertheless requires training to learn that response to one stimulus is followed by reward whereas response to the other stimulus is not. A human subject might require several trials before realizing that a

triangle is always rewarded and a circle is not. *But no one would argue from this fact that on these first few trials the subject did not perceive the forms veridically* (my emphasis)," p. 369.

27. I put the word "recognition" in scare quotes because this is *not* a genuine cognitive achievement. No *beliefs* are produced by this simple mechanical system—nothing having the intentional structure of *knowledge*. For more about what constitutes the distinguishing features of a belief state, see Part III.

28. The word "perception" is often reserved for those sensory transactions in which there is some cognitive uptake (identification, recognition, etc.). The sense of the term I allude to here is the sense in which we can see, hear, and smell objects or events (be aware or conscious *of* them) without necessarily categorizing them in any way. This point is more fully discussed below (footnote 29 and the following section of this chapter).

29. In *Seeing and Knowing* (Chicago, 1969) I argued that seeing *s* (a dog, a tree, a person) was essentially nonepistemic: no *beliefs* were essential to the seeing. Although we (adults) typically acquire a variety of beliefs about the things we see, seeing a dog, a tree, or a person is itself a relationship that is independent of such beliefs—one *can* see *s* without believing that it is *F* (for any value of *F*). My present way of expressing this point is different, but the point remains the same. The only modification consists in the requirement that in order to qualify as a perceptual state (seeing *s*) a structure must be *coupled* to a cognitive mechanism capable of exploiting the information held in the sensory representation. In this respect my present view is somewhat closer to Frank Sibley's in his "Analyzing Seeing," in *Perception* (London, Methuen, 1971), edited by F. Sibley. I am indebted to David Ring for helpful discussion and clarification on this point.

30. The circumstances I have in mind are circumstances in which one sees Herman in a crowd of people but, looking frantically for one's lost child, fails to notice him or pay any particular attention to him.

31. For a careful exposition of this theory see H. P. Grice, "The Causal Theory of Perception," *Aristotelian Society Proceedings*, Supplementary Volume 35 (1961).

32. H. H. Price, *Perception*, London, 1932, p. 70.

33. If we have two bells that produce indistinguishable sounds, it may appear as though my account of the perceptual object implies that one cannot hear the bell that is actually ringing since the auditory signal does not carry information about *which* bell is ringing. This is a mistaken reading of my view. If Tom and Bill are twins (visually indistinguishable), this does not (on my account) prevent one from seeing Tom. One does not have to get the information *that it is Tom* in order to see Tom. Rather, the information one is getting must be information *about* Tom (that he is wearing a red shirt, scratching his head, etc.). That is, the properties being given primary representation must be properties *of* Tom. Similarly, in the case of the bells, to hear bell *A* it is not necessary to get information sufficient unto distinguishing bell *A* from bell *B*. All that is necessary is that the information

being received *be* information about *A* (e.g., that it is ringing, that it has a certain pitch).

34. R. Woodworth, *Experimental Psychology*, London, Methuen, 1938, p. 595.

35. See Edwin H. Land's excellent illustration of this point in "The Retinex Theory of Color Vision" in *Scientific American*, vol. 237, no. 6 (Dec. 1977), pp. 108–128.

36. For example, "In constancies for gravitationally oriented targets the visual input must be processed jointly with body tilt information, for in the absence of the latter visual input is totally insufficient to convey information about gravitational orientation." Sheldon M. Ebenholtz, "The Constancies in Object Orientation: An Algorithm Processing Approach," in *Stability and Constancy in Visual Perception*, William Epstein (ed.), New York, 1977, p. 82.

37. See William Epstein's "The Process of 'Taking-into-Account' in Visual Perception," *Perception*, vol. 2 (1973), pp. 267–285.

38. James J. Gibson, *The Perception of the Visual World*, Boston, 1950, chap. 3. Irvin Rock, following Arien Mack, refers to these two aspects of perceptual experience as the *constancy mode* and the *proximal mode*. He points out that in the case of size we perceive in the proximal as well as in the constancy mode and that under reduction conditions the proximal mode of perception moves into the center of the stage—"There is no longer a dominant objective percept that supersedes it." (p. 346). See Rock's "In Defense of Unconscious Inference," in *Stability and Constancy in Visual Perception*, William Epstein (ed.), New York, 1977, pp. 339, 342.

39. Although perceptual experience may evolve in this way, there is a growing body of evidence to suggest that it does not. T. G. R. Bower's experiments with infants reveal that it was not retinal similarity, but (distal) object similarity that generated the most responses. "Rather than being the most primitive kind of perceptual ability, it would seem the ability to register the information in a retinal image may be a highly sophisticated attainment and may indeed have to be learned." See Bower's "The Visual World of Infants," *Scientific American* (December 1966) reprinted in *Perception: Mechanisms and Models*, San Francisco, 1972, p. 357.

40. See J. A. Fodor and T. G. Bever, "The Psychological Reality of Linguistic Segments," *Journal of Verbal Learning and Verbal Behavior*, vol. 4 (1965), pp. 414–420 and M. Garrett, T. Bever, and J. Fodor, "The Active Use of Grammar in Speech Perception," *Perception and Psychophysics*, vol. 1 (1966), pp. 30–32. Fodor puts the point this way: "One might put it that one does not hear the formant relations in utterances of sentences even though one does hear the linguistic relations and the formant structure (*inter alia*) causally determines which linguistic relations one hears," *The Language of Thought*, New York, 1975, p. 50.

Chapter 7

1. If the reader has Quinean objections to the idea of analyticity, the

distinction between the second and third orders of intentionality may be regarded as simply a matter of *degree* and not of *kind*. I have no desire to defend the analytic-synthetic distinction, nor do I think that anything I have to say in this essay depends on it, but I do find "analytic" a useful term to suggest a range of cases that have interested philosophers, and I use it here to indicate such cases.

2. More technically, S carries the information that t is F in digital form if and only if (1) S carries the information that t is F, and (2) there is no other piece of information, t is K, which is such that the information that t is F is nested in t's being K, but not vice versa.

3. *Most* of the intentional characteristics of a belief but perhaps not *all*. This will depend on what one takes to be included in the idea of intentionality. It should be noted, for example, that beliefs can be false (have false contents) but the information a structure carries in digital form *cannot* be false (because it is *information*). Hence, the definition of semantic content supplied below, a definition that identifies a structure's semantic content with the information it carries in digital form, gives us a propositional content exhibiting the third order of intentionality (I shall argue), but not yet with a content that can qualify as the content of a belief. If the possible falsity of a structure's content is taken to be part of what is meant by intentionality, then semantic structures do not exhibit *all* the intentional characteristics of belief.

4. Or the content: t is red. There are obviously a large number of possibilities (e.g., t is a red parallelogram, t is a figure of some sort), any one of which, or any combination of which, might (depending on the switching mechanism) be realized on a given occasion. The point to keep in mind, however, is that each of these (different) semantic contents would have to be embodied in a different physical structure, since a structure's semantic content is the information it carries in *digital* form and these different pieces of information cannot be digitalized by the *same* structure in one and the same system.

5. Conversion of information from analog to digital form *always* involves the loss of some information, but not every loss of information represents a process of digitalization. A radio receiver, for instance, loses a significant portion of the information contained in the arriving electromagnetic wave (how much will depend on the "fidelity" of the receiver), but this loss is indiscriminate and unselective with respect to the information contained in the arriving signal.

6. Such simple information-processing instruments as those described (voltmeters, thermostats, television receivers) not only fail to completely digitalize information about the source (by "source" I mean here the state of affairs that we, the users of the instrument, typically use the instrument to get information about), they also fail to completely digitalize *any* information. The information-carrying structures of such instruments fail to have a semantic content because, normally, they have no *outermost* informational shell. These structures carry information about antecedent states of affairs,

but every piece of information the structure carries is nested, chinese-box fashion, in yet a larger informational shell. The arrangement of informational shells is something like the set of real numbers *less than* 1. For every number less than 1 there is always a larger that is still less than 1. For any state of affairs distinct from the structure itself, the structure will carry information about that state of affairs only insofar as it carries accurate information about some intermediate state of affairs. This, of course, is merely a reflection of the fact that such information is communicated by causal means, and there is no way of stopping (short of the effect) and specifying the nearest, or most proximal, causal antecedent. Genuine cognitive systems have the same continuity in the causal processes by means of which a semantic structure is produced, but (as we saw in Chapter 6—especially Figure 6.2) the structures so produced carry no information about their immediate causal predecessors. They represent the source without representing the more proximal events by means of which information about the source is delivered.

Chapter 8

1. Roughly, a cognitive structure is a semantic structure whose (semantic) content exercises some control over output. I return to this point below.

2. Hereafter, the content of a structure type will be expressed with an open sentence (e.g., "x is F") and the content of its tokens by a closed sentence in which a constant (s, suggesting source and designating the perceptual object) replaces the variable x. This reflects the fact that although both structure types and structure tokens have *meaning*, only the tokens have a truth value. This is the difference between the concept F and a (*de re*) belief that something is F.

3. This is not intended to be a general account of (concept) learning. What is now being described is the acquisition of a simple concept in some straightforward ostensive way. More about simple vs. complex and innate vs. acquired concepts in Chapter 9.

4. At this stage of the process it would, perhaps, be premature to credit the child with the concept *robin*. We might prefer to say that she has a *visual concept* of a robin. This way of expressing the child's conceptual achievement is a way of acknowledging the information-theoretic fact that as yet (given the restricted learning conditions) no structure has evolved with the semantic content "x is a robin." Rather, some structure has developed which is (at best) selectively sensitive to the information that s is a robin *when this information is delivered in visual form*. Hence, the resulting structure carries *some* information about the means by which the information (that s *is* a robin) was delivered and, therefore, does not constitute a *complete* digitalization of the information that s is a robin.

5. D. M. Armstrong, *Belief, Truth and Knowledge*, Cambridge University Press, Cambridge, 1973, part I (especially chap. 1).

6. This comparison should be understood only as an analogy. Thermostats, even properly functioning thermostats, have no beliefs. The reason they do not is not that they lack internal states with an *informational* con-

tent, not that these internal states fail to affect output, but that (as indicated in Chapter 7) these internal states have no appropriate semantic content.

7. After a semantic structure has developed (as a system's selective response to a particular piece of information), it may, of course, be instantiated in response to a signal that *lacks* the relevant piece of information (the information corresponding to the structure's semantic content). In this case, although the structure *means* that *s* is *F*, in the sense that the particular token is a token of a structure type with this semantic content, the token itself does not carry this information. It is only *putative* information—or, as I shall sometimes call it, the *meaning* of the structure token. Hereafter, when speaking of the semantic content of a structure (token), I shall mean the content it inherits from the *type* of structure of which it is a token— i.e., its *meaning*.

8. A view similar to this is presented by Jerry Fodor in *The Language of Thought* (New York, 1975). It is not clear to me, however, whether Fodor wants to describe these preliminary (feature-detection) processes in cognitive terms (as beliefs, judgments, or whatever). He describes the whole perceptual-cognitive process as inferential in character (in terms of the formation and testing of hypotheses), and this certainly suggests that he views the "data" supplied by the feature detectors as occurring in a form (like belief or judgment) from which inferences can be made. Nevertheless, this terminology may be intended as merely a ratiomorphic overlay on an essentially noncognitive process.

9. "Skeletal" because we are still considering the simplest, most primitive kind of belief: a *de re* belief of the form "This is *F*" involving a simple, perceptually acquired concept *F*. I shall, in the following chapter, return to these points and suggest that the analysis is not as restricted as it might now appear.

10. This sort of approach can be found in Wilfrid Sellars' "Empiricism and the Philosophy of Mind," *Minnesota Studies in the Philosophy of Science*, H. Feigl and M. Scriven (eds.), University of Minnesota Press, Minneapolis, 1956, pp. 253-329.

11. I use Dennett as my model for this portrayal of consequentialism. See his *Content and Consciousness*, London, 1969, chap. IV.

12. H. P. Grice, "Meaning," *Philosophical Review*, vol. 66 (1957), pp. 377-388. Also see his "Utterer's Meaning and Intentions," *Philosophical Review*, vol. 78 (1969), pp. 147-177, and "Utterer's Meaning, Sentence-Meaning, and Word Meaning," *Foundations of Language*, vol. 4 (1968), pp. 225-242.

13. *Op. cit.*, p. 77.

14. See the discussion of these experiments, and their implications, in Michael A. Arbib's *The Metaphorical Brain*, Wiley-Interscience, New York, 1972, pp. 153-155. Also see P. Weiss, "Central versus Peripheral Factors in the Development of Coordination" in K. H. Pribram's *Perception and Action*, Penguin Books, Middlesex, England, 1969, pp. 491-514. It is interesting to read Weiss' own interpretation of these experiments: "Coordination

refers to the orderly relation of parts. Such order may or may not be of immediate biological utility. The fact that, in the normal body, coordination usually makes sense when viewed from the standpoint of the biological needs of the organism, naturally suggests that biological utility is a prime factor in determining coordination. This is an illusion, for, as we shall demonstrate below, the basic patterns of coordination develop and persist even in cases in which their effects are utterly contrary to the interests of the individual." (pp. 491–492.)

15. It is important to note in this connection that the animals seemed incapable of learning to compensate for the limb reversal. Some were kept more than a year without any change in behavior (Arbib, *op. cit.*, p. 154). The fact that this inappropriate behavior persists has not the slightest tendency to make us say that the animals have no beliefs about the stimuli they receive, or that they must not believe of the food they see that it is food. Quite the contrary. As long as the inappropriate behavior persists in some consistent, uniform way, it evinces *some* belief. *What* belief the animal has is a matter to be decided by the semantic content of that internal structure producing the inappropriate behavior, and this, as we have argued, is a function of that (type of) structure's information heritage (in this case, perhaps, innate—see Chapter 9 for a discussion of innate concepts).

16. R. W. Sperry, "The Eye and the Brain," *Scientific American*, May 1956; reprinted in *Perception: Mechanisms and Models*, W. H. Freeman and Company, San Francisco, pp. 362–366.

17. I shall, in the next chapter, take up the question of *innate* concepts, a type of semantic structure that is, prior to the relevant kind of experience or learning, selectively sensitive to certain types of information. An innate concept is simply a type of encoding that a system possesses for incoming information that it did not develop or acquire; it was born (prewired, as it were) with this way of digitalizing incoming information.

18. I think this objection captures the spirit of Dan Dennett's account of belief content (see, e.g., *Content and Consciousness*, p. 19). That is, Dennett would be tempted to describe our cat as recognizing the liver, say, *as food*. The cat does not have a belief expressible as "*s* is liver," since there is no response that is appropriate to liver *qua* liver. Rather, the cat has a belief expressible as "*s* is food" (where the *s* refers to what is in fact liver), since there is (according to Dennett) behavior that is appropriate to food.

19. We *need not*, of course, try to explain the animal's behavior in cognitive terms, any more than we *must* describe a computer's operations in such terms as "decision," "believe," "multiplies," and "recognizes." But, by the same token, neither are we *forced* to describe our own operations in these terms. There are neurological explanations that will, or will some day, do as well. The point is, however, that these cognitive explanations *are no less valid* simply because there are alternative causal explanations. The fact that I can describe the operation of a voltmeter in purely causal terms does not mean that an information-theoretic description is false or inapplicable.

20. More of *primitive* concepts in the next chapter. Primitive concepts are

a type of cognitive structure that has no parts that are cognitive structures.

21. Although I have criticized the consequentialist's account of mental content, much of what functionalists say about the reduction of the mental to the physical holds of the present, information-theoretic analysis. For example, Putnam's distinction between *logical* and *structural* states is the same as my own distinction between an informational state (a semantic or cognitive structure) and the physical structure *in which* information (semantic or cognitive content) can be realized. Two quite different physical structures may have the same semantic content. See Putnam's "Minds and Machines" in *Mind, Language and Reality: Philosophical Papers*, vol. II, Cambridge University Press, Cambridge, England, 1975, pp. 362-385.

Chapter 9

1. *Conceptually* identical. Two structures may be conceptually identical (i.e., cognitive structures with the same semantic content) and yet, when they occur in different systems, be *physically different* structures. What makes these physically different structures the same concept is the fact that both structures have the same semantic content. They may, of course, issue in different sorts of behavior, but the difference in behavior (as we argued in Chapter 8) is irrelevant.

2. I think the same remarks can be made about some of Quine's examples (see *Word and Object*, Boston, 1960, chap. 2) –e.g., the difference between believing that s is a rabbit and believing that t (some part of s) is an undetached part of rabbit or the belief that u (some temporal cross section of s) is a rabbit stage. These pieces of information are inseparable. Any structure having the first as its semantic content has the others as its semantic content. Nevertheless, they constitute different concepts (or, when instantiated, different beliefs) because of their compositional differences. I can believe that s is a rabbit without having the concept *part* (or *stage*), but I cannot have the latter beliefs without these concepts. Such conceptual differences are detectable. These examples pose additional problems, however, because of their associated shift in reference.

3. I do not mean to suggest that our knowledge of necessary truths can be identified with our belief in necessary truths. I do not mean to deny it either. The equation is certainly a natural extension of our identification of empirical knowledge with informationally grounded belief, but there are formidable difficulties to extending the account in this "natural" way. Frankly, I do not know what to say about our knowledge of those truths that have an informational measure of zero (i.e., the necessary truths). In some cases (e.g., simple logical and mathematical truths) it seems that mere belief may be enough (for knowledge). In other cases not. Aside from the formal truths, however, there are the laws of nature. Surely belief is not enough here. Yet, if laws are conceived to be necessary truths of some sort (where the necessity in question is supposed to be *nomic*), laws also have an informational measure of zero. They do not generate any information because there are (in the informationally relevant sense of "possible") no possible alternatives to them.

I have nothing particularly enlightening to say about these problems at the present time. The exclusion of logical and mathematical truths (the so-called analytic truths) from the present account of knowledge is not, I believe, a serious omission, since as far as I can tell, every analysis of knowledge seems compelled to make a similar exception. I therefore follow the general practice of restricting the scope of the analysis to *empirical* knowledge. This restriction is already implicit in my restriction (see Chapter 4) to situations in which what is known has a positive informational measure. And my restriction to *perceptual* knowledge (in particular, knowledge of some perceptually given object *that* it is *F*) excludes consideration of how (or whether) the laws of nature can be known.

4. See, for example, Kripke's "Naming and Necessity," in *Semantics of Natural Language*, Donald Davison and Gilbert Harman (eds.), D. Reidel, Dordrecht-Holland, 1972, pp. 253-355; Hilary Putnam's "The Meaning of 'Meaning'" in *Mind, Language and Reality, Philosophical Papers*, vol. 2, Cambridge University Press, Cambridge, 1975, pp. 215-271 [first published in K. Gunderson (ed.) *Language, Mind and Knowledge*, Minnesota Studies in the Philosophy of Science VII, University of Minnesota Press, Minneapolis, 1975]. Also see Dennis Stampe's, "On the Meaning of Nouns," in *Limiting the Domain of Linguistics*, D. Cohen (ed.), Milwaukee, 1972, pp. 54-71.

5. An old empiricist idea in modern (i.e., information-theoretic) dress. "But although our thought seems to possess this unbounded liberty, we shall find upon a nearer examination that it is really confined within very narrow limits, and that all this creative power of the mind amounts to no more than the faculty of compounding, transposing, augmenting, or diminishing the materials afforded us by the senses and experience. When we think of a golden mountain, we only join two consistent ideas, 'gold' and 'mountain,' with which we were formerly acquainted." David Hume, *An Inquiry Concerning Human Understanding*, Section II.

6. For example, P. H. Winston's computer program for recognizing tables, arches, pedestals, and arcades utilizes more primitive concepts (such as *bricks, wedges, supports,* and *marries*) out of which it builds a structural description of the stimulus object; see Margaret Boden's discussion of this program in *Artificial Intelligence and Natural Man*, Basic Books, New York, 1977, pp. 252ff. Without some primitive concepts (even such elementary ones as line, angle, and join) the program would be unable to build up any more complex cognitive structures.

7. It is important that the white objects (that are to appear red) be *selectively* illuminated with red light so that surrounding objects are not also illuminated in the same way. Failure to observe this precaution might trigger a constancy mechanism in the perceptual system of the viewer so that the white objects (although reflecting red light) did not look red.

8. I have adapted Putnam's example to my own purposes. His "Twin 'Earth'" example can be found in "The Meaning of 'Meaning'" *loc. cit.* Putnam uses the example to argue that meanings are not in the head: the intrinsic properties of our internal states do not determine the extensions (hence

meanings) of whatever concepts these internal states may be taken to represent. I reach the same conclusion from a different perspective. Since two physically different structures can have the same semantic contents, the meaning of these structures (what concepts the system has) is not to be found in the intrinsic (physical) properties of the structures themselves. Meanings are not in the head; they are "in" that system of nomic dependencies that define the information-response characteristics of those structures that are in the head.

9. To say that this information was made available to the Earthlings is to assume, of course, that the liquid's being XYZ was *not* a (relevant) possibility for Earthlings (as it was for Tommy on Twin Earth).

10. Putnam notes (p. 241) that if substance XYZ were to be found on Earth, then *it would be water*. The reason it would be water is because what *we* (Earthlings) *meant* when we said that something was water would have been different. This is simply to say (in terms of the way I have adapted Putnam's example) that if XYZ was in *our* lakes and streams (along with H_2O), then we would have developed a concept like Tommy's, one that had both H_2O and XYZ in its extension. If XYZ was as omnipresent on Earth as it is on Twin Earth, then it would *be* water—not what we *now* call water (since this, presumably, includes only H_2O)—but what we *would then* have called water.

11. The subject may, of course, acquire the concept *red* as a complex concept. He might, for instance, develop the concept: *looks red in conditions C*, where *C* stands for those conditions (e.g., sunlight) in which things that look red are red.

12. Technically speaking, these remarks should be restricted to *acquired* (learned) concepts. I shall have more to say about *innate* concepts in the next section.

13. I borrow the "language of thought" metaphor from Jerry Fodor's *The Language of Thought*, Thomas Y. Crowell Company, New York, 1975.

14. The acquisition of language makes possible the development of a richer conceptual system, in part at least, because the language users increasingly rely on language itself for the delivery of information. That is, much of the work of digitalization, fundamental to the process of concept formation, is *already* complete, embodied in that public language which the individual absorbs from his associates. So, for example, it is comparatively easy to get the information that *s* is a tree without getting any more specific information about *s* (e.g., that *x* is a maple, a tall tree, a tree with leaves) when this information arrives in linguistic form (since the language by means of which it arrives already constitutes a digital way of encoding this information), but not so easy when the information arrives in perceptual form (i.e., seeing a tree). Hence, much of an individual's work in developing a network of concepts is already completed for him when he grows up as a part of a community with a shared language. The public language is a repository of the conceptual achievements of our ancestors, and each individual draws upon this deposit when he learns the language.

15. "The Visual Cliff" by Eleanor Gibson and Richard D. Walk, *Scientific American*, April 1960; reprinted in *Perception: Mechanisms and Models*, W. H. Freeman and Company, San Francisco, pp. 341-348.

16. *Ibid.*, p. 341.

17. *Ibid.*, p. 341.

18. *Ibid.*, p. 343.

19. Eckhard H. Hess, "Space Perception in the Chick," in *Perception: Mechanisms and Models*, W. H. Freeman, San Francisco, pp. 367-371.

20. T. G. R. Bower, "The Visual World of Infants," *Perception: Mechanisms and Models*, p. 357.

21. *Op. cit.*, p. 341.

Index

Abstraction, 151-52, 182

Adams, Fred, 254

Ames' Room, 252

Analog, 136-39, (defined) 137. *See* Coding

Analytic, 71, 173-74, 215, 259-60, 265

Anderson, John, 255

Arbib, Michael, 262, 263

Armstrong, D. M., 197, 249, 250, 254, 261

Attneave, Fred, 237, 238

Austin, John, 252

Averbach, E., 257

Bar-Hillel, Yehoshua, 11, 237, 238, 241, 242

Beauchamp, Tom, 240

Behavior, 202-209, 233, 263

Belief: required for knowledge, 85, 229; as carrying information, 90-91, 244-45; of cognitive systems, 171-72; intentionality of, 173-74, 217; false, 190, 208-9, 260; as map, 197; determining response, 197, 201-202; of animals, 209-211; de re and de dicto, 212. *See also* Content; Intentionality; Concepts

Bever, T. G., 259

Bit (amount of information), 5

Black, Max, 241

Boden, Margaret, 265

Bohm, David, 239

Boltzman, 237

Bower, Gordon, 255

Bower, T. G. R., 255, 259, 267

Brunswik, Egon, 251

Burge, Tyler, 246

Calibration, 117, 119, 252

Carnap, Rudolph, 241

Categorization, 139-41, 182

Cause: distinguished from information, 26-30, 35, 38-39, 157; explained, 32-33, 240; causal theory of knowledge, 33, 39-40; sustaining cause, 88-90; information as cause, 87, 198-201, 248-49; causal theory of perception, 156; causal chains, 157-59

Chance, 28-29, 36-37, 74, 75, 191, 246

Channel: physical realization, 38; ghost, 38; capacity, 51, 148, 242; conditions, 115-116, 118, 122, 253; auxiliary, 120-23, 124

Cherry, E. C., 41, 237, 241

Chisholm, Roderick, 248

Classification, 139-141, 182

Code: for transmitting information, 8, 49-50, 244; decoding a signal, 57, 144, 219; analog vs. digital, 135-39, 220, 260; perceptual (sensory), 147, 162-63; changes in, 166-7, 208-9. *See also* Analog; Digital; Experience, information in; Sensory

Cognitive: attitudes, 135, 154, 211; processes (as distinct from sensory), 141-3, 148, 150, 167-8, 257; systems, 175-182; structures, 142, 193, 198, 200, 211, 217, 261; representation, 147,

Garret, M., 259
Gettier, Edmund, 96, 97, 249
Gibson, Eleanor, 151, 232, 234, 257, 267
Gibson, James, 145, 165, 166, 252, 255, 259
Goldman, Alvin, 39, 129, 241, 249, 254
Gombrich, E. H. 241
Gregory, R. L., 253
Grice, Paul, 205, 242, 257, 262

Haber, R. N., 254, 257
Hake, Harold, 243
Hamlyn, David, 255, 256
Hanson, Norwood, 239
Harman, Gilbert, 253, 265
Hartley, R. V. L., 237
Hebb, D. O., 256
Heidelberger, Herbert, 250
Held, Richard, 240
Hershenson, Maurice, 257
Hess, Eckhard, 267
Hiller, Lejaren, 241, 242
Hintikka, J., 241
Hochberg, Julian, 241
Hume, David, 56, 240, 265

Identification, 144, 150, 152
Inference, 91, 200, 256, 262
Information: distinguished from meaning, vii, 22, 41-44, 72-3, 174-5, 247-8; amount generated (average), 7, 10 (*See* Entropy); amount generated by particular signal, 10, 52 (*See* Surprisal); amount transmitted (average), 19; amount transmitted by particular signal, 49, 52; amount generated distinguished from amount transmitted, 15-16, 242-3; distinguished from causality, 26-30, 35, 38-9, 157; content, 41, 47-8, 55, 60, 62, 173 (*See* Content); semantic aspects of, 41, 64, 247-8; ordinary concept of, 44-5; false, 45;

misinformation, 45; semantic theory of, 63-82, 241; applications of (mathematical theory of), 50, 52, 53, 242-3, 246-7; flow of, 58, 149, 191; as cause, 87, 98-9, 198-201, 248-9; absolute character of, 108; social and pragmatic aspects of, 132-34; loss of (digital conversion), 141, 183; extraction of, 144, 147, 148, 150, 152, 153, 181, 249. *See also* Content; Communication, theory; Meaning; Semantic
Intensional, 75-76
Intentionality: explained, 75; of information, 73-6, 172-3; source of, 76, 202-9, 246-7; orders of, 172-4; of verbal behavior, 202-5; of beliefs, 173-74, 217. *See also* Content; Semantic
Interpretation, 57, 181
Inverted Spectrum, 244
Isaacson, Leonard, 241, 242
Ittleson, W. H., 252

Jammer, Max, 240
Johansson, Gunnar, 255
Justification, 85, 96-7, 108, 248

Kilpatrick, Franklin, 253
Klatzky, Roberta, 254
Klüver, H., 151
Knowledge: in definition of informational content, 65, 78-81, 86-7, 243; analysis of (perceptual), 86; of facts, 107; of things, 107; absolute character of, 108-11; social and pragmatic aspects of, 132-4; intentionality of, 173; of necessary truths, 218-19, 264-5
Koch, Sigmund, 240, 251
Kripke, Saul, 221, 222, 265
Kyberg, H. H., 250

Land, Edwin, 259
Language, 143, 167, 202, 209, 230, 266

Library of Congress Cataloging in Publication Data

Dretske, Fred I.
   Knowledge and the flow of information.

      Includes index.
   1. Knowledge, Theory of. 2. Mind and body.
3. Interdisciplinary approach to knowledge. 4. Information theory. 5. Perception. 6. Concepts. I. Title.
BD161.D7   121   81-21633
MIT ISBN 0-262-04063-8